Ethics in Mental Health
and Deafness

Ethics in
Mental Health
and Deafness

———

Virginia Gutman,

Editor

Gallaudet University Press

Washington, D.C.

Gallaudet University Press
Washington, DC 20002

Library of Congress Cataloging-in-Publication Data

Ethics in mental health and deafness / edited by Virginia Gutman.
    p. cm.
  Includes bibliographical references and index.
  ISBN 1-56368-120-X (cloth : alk. paper)
    1. Deaf—Mental health services—Moral and ethical aspects. 2. Deaf services—
Moral and ethical aspects. 3. Deaf—Services for. 4. Psychiatric ethics. I. Gutman,
Virginia.

  RC451.4.D4 E86 2002
  362'.087'2—dc21
                                            2001056900

In memory of
Paul and Martha Gutman
Walter Chmielewski

.

Contents

Preface

This book is designed to fill some of the gaps in the professional literature on ethical practice in relation to Deafness, and to address issues important for those who provide mental health services for deaf people. The authors of the various chapters have extensive experience in both training and service delivery. They were asked to write about their areas of specialization and were given only three limitations in how they approached this: to focus on ethical topics that are particularly relevant or troublesome in working with deaf clients; to include discussion of cases; and to show the reader how they go about thinking through an ethical problem rather than simply giving their conclusions about ethical practice.[1]

Because each author was free to choose topics for discussion as he or she wished, there is considerable variation among chapters, showing a number of different approaches to ethical reasoning and decision making. Several topics are so ubiquitous and multifaceted that they come up in virtually every chapter. Among these are confidentiality, managing multiple relationships, and clinicians' competence to provide services (including competency in communication, understanding of Deafness and deaf people, and knowledge and technical skill in working with the client's specific needs).

This book is designed not only as a resource for students and teachers in graduate and professional programs, but also for clinicians seeking ideas and methods for solving dilemmas encountered in their practice. We assume that the reader already knows or can get access to the code of ethics

---

1. Names and other identifying information of the persons described in the case studies throughout this book have been changed to protect the individuals' privacy.

in his or her own professional field. In this book, we address ways to transcend some of the limitations and inherent contradictions in the codes of ethics by developing methods of thinking through ethical problems in a sound manner. This volume does not provide, however, instruction in these codes. Readers unfamiliar with professional codes of ethics can find them in the references cited at the end of this preface. The primary codes referenced in this volume include those of the American Psychological Association (APA) (1992), the National Association of Social Workers (1996), the American Counseling Association (Herlihy & Corey, 1996), and the Canadian Psychological Association (1991). Also discussed are the codes of the Registry of Interpreters for the Deaf and the National Society of Genetic Counselors, and the APA's guidelines for ethnic, linguistic, and culturally diverse populations (APA, 1993).

REFERENCES

American Psychological Association. (1992). Ethical principles of psychologists and code of conduct. *American Psychologist, 47,* 1597–1611.

American Psychological Association. (1993). Guidelines for providers of psychological services to ethnic, linguistic, and culturally diverse populations. *American Psychologist, 48,* 45–48.

Canadian Psychological Association. (1991). *Canadian code of ethics for psychologists* (Rev. ed.). Old Chelsea, Quebec: Author.

Herlihy, B., & Corey, G. (Eds.). (1996). *ACA ethical standards casebook* (5th ed.). Alexandria, VA: American Counseling Association.

National Association of Social Workers. (1996). *Code of ethics.* Washington, DC: Author.

National Society of Genetic Counselors. (n.d.). *Code of ethics.* Retrieved November 5, 2001, from http://www.nsgc.org

Registry of Interpreters for the Deaf. (1997). *Code of ethics.* Silver Spring, MD: RID Publications.

Acknowledgments

This book developed with help, guidance, and encouragement from many sources. First, the Gallaudet Department of Psychology provided a home base in which I could develop a course that introduced clinical psychology students to issues in professional ethics. Preparing for that course led to a search for published references on ethical issues with deaf clients that made me aware of the need for this book. Various members of the department were generous in talking with me about how they deal with ethical issues that apply to teaching, training, and clinical services. Over many years, Neil Reynolds consistently provided guidance, encouragement, and a model for careful ethical reasoning as a department chair. The late Larry Stewart discussed his extensive experience with characteristic forthrightness. Several members of the psychology department contributed chapters for this book, and others brought me case examples and shared their reactions to scenarios I discussed with them.

Nothing conveys a full understanding of the ethical issues that arise in the immediacy of the consulting room, however, without clinical experience. During my years at the Gallaudet Counseling Center, I was fortunate to work closely with Allen Sussman, at that time the dean of student affairs, who was always willing to provide a sounding board for new issues or ideas. Barbara Brauer provided individual supervision as I was first working with deaf clients, and ongoing collegial consultation. The very astute and talented staff of the Gallaudet Counseling Center (now the Mental Health Center at Gallaudet) helped me become sensitive to ethical issues in deafness, and to understand how experienced clinicians may deal with ethical challenges in a culturally sensitive way. The members of two on-going peer supervision groups provided a supportive forum for identifying and addressing ethical problems I encountered in my private practice.

When I wanted to begin writing on ethics, the Department of Psychology gave me a sabbatical that allowed me to develop the framework for this book. Michael Karchmer, then dean of the graduate school at Gallaudet, provided grant support, and subsequently urged me to publish the results of my work. The individual chapter authors responded enthusiastically to my request for their participation, and also provided excellent ideas and feedback as the outline of the book developed.

Many of the ideas and vignettes used in this book were developed through interactions with students in my Professional Seminar on Ethics and Practice, supervision groups and seminars, and individual supervision. As my ideas on ethical reasoning developed, I presented them to students and learned from their responses. My students improved my thinking by raising critical issues, describing problems they encountered, tactfully challenging any fuzzy thinking on my part, and asking all the right questions.

Ivey Pittle Wallace and Deirdre Mullervy at Gallaudet University Press provided suggestions, encouragement, technical expertise, and patient guidance during the development of the book, helping me and the individual chapter authors to clarify our thinking and our language.

Ethics in Mental Health
and Deafness

1

Ethical Problems in Deaf Mental Health Services

A PRACTITIONER'S EXPERIENCE

Irene W. Leigh

I am a deaf person. This characteristic of mine permeates the diverse identities I have developed over the course of my life to varying degrees, as do my other physical and personality characteristics. Within the context of this chapter, it needs to be noted that I am also a psychologist, a woman, a mother, and a social being, not necessarily in order of importance. I live and work in large part within the deaf community, thereby minimizing the possibility of anonymity in daily activities. By virtue of my work as a psychologist, my deafness, and my various identities, the boundaries between professional and personal roles repeatedly blur, thereby giving rise continuously to ethical dilemmas. Specifically, in the course of providing mental health services to clients within the deaf community, the permeability of these boundaries requires perpetual negotiation and consideration of implications for these clients and for deaf clinicians like myself (Falberg, 1985; Leigh & Lewis, 1999; Patterson & Stewart, 1971; Rich, 1990; Thoreson & Tully, 1971). The ongoing ethical dilemmas profoundly influence how I define my professional and social behaviors, and as such, are an ever-present fact of life for me.

While ethical considerations can never be divorced from professional relationships in the mental health setting, a clinician's deafness may have an impact on his or her deaf clients. Its influence needs to be scrutinized. The small world aspects of the deaf community are an additional complicating factor. The examples I will present are essentially composites of experiences, altered to maintain confidentiality, which deaf clinicians might be exposed to as a consequence of their relationship to the deaf community. These examples, which range from the mundane to the critical, illustrate the need to be ever alert to ethical nuances.

THE GROUP SETTING

When a deaf clinician organized a group of deaf mothers within a clinical setting to discuss parenting and adjustment issues, she emphasized the cardinal confidentiality rule from the outset, as any well-trained mental health clinician would do. Because of the nature of the deaf community, it was critical that each participant feel safe about revealing personal information to elicit advice and support from the group. On the basis of standard procedures for establishing rules governing chance encounters outside the clinical situation at the beginning of treatment (Lytle, 1995), the clinician and the group agreed that outside of sessions they could acknowledge each other during unexpected encounters if the mothers initiated greetings, but membership within the group as well as issues brought up by individual mothers were not to be divulged. Over time, this deaf mothers' group evolved into a tight-knit entity, regarded as a "safe haven" by its members.

One evening, the clinician attended a deaf community function with her husband and happened to notice that some group members were chatting animatedly together. In the course of their conversation, their eyes caught hers and en masse they ran over to hug her delightedly, as long lost friends might do. While this is a standard form of greeting from a Deaf culture perspective, it was not the way the group members and the clinician typically greeted each other when the group was in session. At that moment, the clinician experienced a sinking feeling, a sense of déjà vu. Her sense of relaxation was gone.

In this vignette, the clinician, who was theoretically "off duty" and presenting her deaf social self, has been confronted by an ethical quandary even though she already had established rules for external contact outside the group. The varied levels of meaning attached to this encounter required attention. She had to ask herself how permeable was the boundary between her sense of self as a social being and her sense of self as a professional. At the critical moment in time, she had to decide what approach to take in responding to these women, using tactics that both validated their joy at seeing her and simultaneously protected their confidentiality within the context of a crowd of deaf people. She had to consider how to preserve the feelings of safety these mothers were entitled to when they saw her talking to her husband or to individuals who were in fact her friends. Would they wonder if she was talking about them and subsequently feel threatened? As Gutman (this volume) indicates, the potential for harm, whether real or imagined, to these clients, individually and as a group, is ever present. Their perception of the deaf clinician as a professional is also at stake.

While all these considerations were going through the clinician's mind, she greeted the deaf mothers, taking care to respond to their positive tone with appropriate greetings, and moved on. On the surface, it was an innocuous interaction, but her awareness of their presence put her on guard and colored the rest of her interactions at that event.

POTENTIALLY DAMAGING DISCLOSURE

The American Psychological Association's "Ethical Principles of Psychologists and Code of Conduct" (American Psychological Association, 1992) are more applicable to those who can easily distance themselves from their clients within the anonymity of large urban settings than for small community psychologists who confront, among other realities, overlapping social relationships (Schank & Skovholt, 1997). There are no easy answers, and each ethical dilemma requires renewed attempts to achieve a viable resolution, particularly when chance encounters may have the potential for adverse consequences. Much depends on how clients internalize and interpret the rules for dealing with therapists, particularly in the passion of the moment. The following scenario illustrates a situation that requires extremely delicate handling.

A deaf counselor was participating in an animated conversation with a group of acquaintances in attendance at a Deaf culture festival. Suddenly a former client ran up to him and interrupted the conversation with enthusiastic greetings. The counselor made every effort to remain noncommittal. Finally, the client became exasperated and blurted out in American Sign Language (ASL), "Don't you remember me? It was a long time ago. I was in _____ Prison, and you helped me there with my problems. Because you are deaf, that's really special! You understood me!" This was said in the midst of a group setting. Consequently, all eyes were on the two individuals involved in this interchange.

What is the counselor to do within the constraints of confidentiality? The implicit message is that, despite the sensitive information being conveyed among strangers, the client has given permission to acknowledge this relationship in public. However, we must pause to consider damage control, considering that the client may have overlooked or forgotten the possibility that such a disclosure within a deaf social setting may have potential repercussions for his reputation as well as his future interactions within the deaf community. Therefore, the counselor has to be very careful in terms of evaluating the client's level of disclosure and not volunteer any additional information beyond validating what the client is asking for, namely recognition and "connection." The counselor needs to take into account the sensibilities of the client and decide whether to match the client's enthusiasm or mute the emotional level of the encounter. How the counselor conveys to the client the fact that they are in a public place will factor into the eventual resolution of this encounter in ways that can be affirmative instead of destructive for the client's well-being. The counselor does not want to do anything that might embarrass the client. An additional factor to consider is the public perception of how the counselor handles the situation and whether the counselor is, in fact, trustworthy. In other words, the counselor's public reputation as an ethical professional is at stake here, as well.

SEPARATE, YET CONNECTED

Ethically, it is generally not advisable for a clinician to provide individual therapeutic treatment or counseling to individuals who are connected with each other by virtue of family relationships, friendships, or intimate liaisons outside the context of treatment provided specifically to families or couples. Such situations have the potential to threaten the viability of treatment through, for example, inadvertent disclosure of sensitive information that could negatively affect the clinician's ability to take neutral, affirmative stances for all those involved in the treatment process. The small nature of the deaf community maximizes the chance that deaf clinicians will inadvertently treat several deaf individuals who know each other. Consequently, if the clinician interacts with the deaf community, the possibility that the clinician will have chance encounters with many of these individuals outside the clinical setting is extremely plausible. All of these potential scenarios have implications for ethical concerns related to confidentiality, practitioner competency, and dual relationships.

———

A deaf man was assigned to a deaf social worker for treatment of depressive symptomatology. While medication was of some help, it became apparent after a year that the depression was exacerbated by marital difficulties. Subsequently, he and his wife entered into marriage counseling with the social worker, insisting that they preferred to work with him because he was deaf and understood them "fully" rather than deal with other therapists not well versed in ASL. The man continued in individual therapy. In the process, he began to assert himself as an individual apart from his wife, and his depressive symptomatology diminished. Shortly afterwards, he reported entering into an extramarital affair with a woman whom he perceived as giving him a renewed lease on life. Several months later, a deaf female client who was working on job-related issues with the social worker told him that she was being distracted by an affair with a married man that she wanted to break off. To his dismay, the social worker deduced from the details this client provided that the married man was the first client mentioned above. Additionally, both the client and the couple knew the social worker from past chance encounters in the deaf community outside the clinical setting, heightening the possibility that all could meet at the same time by accident.

———

This type of ethical situation is not easy to resolve, particularly after relationships with clients have been firmly established before the disclosure. The social worker is in a virtually untenable position because of the current situation. His deaf clients desired that rare commodity, a deaf clinician whom they perceived to be the only one who could provide direct, accessible communication within a therapeutic context. However, if he does not intervene to change the situation, the social worker runs the risk that one of the clients will discover the true state of affairs, perhaps by talking with the other clients or via friends, and consequently all the clients involved would be exposed to emotional harm due to loss of privacy and trust. The effort to maintain boundaries and ensure that information provided by one client does not unduly impact the therapeutic relationship with the other client will create a very stressful situation for the clinician. His stress level will also be exacerbated by the need to maintain trustworthiness and demonstrate professional competency. Dual relationships could become an issue if, for example, the clinician found himself attending deaf organization meetings in which one or more of the clients or their family members were also participating. Relative to this scenario, the most viable solution would be to transfer one of the clients, preferably the client that is less dependent on the social worker, to a colleague. This transfer would have to be handled with great care to minimize client feelings of rejection, taking into account the fact that the "real" reason for this transfer cannot be divulged. This transfer would be fraught with even more difficulty if there were no other deaf or ASL-competent hearing therapists available to take the case.

PUSHING BOUNDARIES

The perceived commonality of deafness between client and clinician—who more often than not have been brought together because of resources within the deaf community—can be positive in terms of facilitating the course of therapeutic treatment when used appropriately (Leigh & Lewis, 1999; Lytle & Lewis, 1996). However, deaf clinicians would do well to be aware that there are negative aspects as well. For example, some deaf clients from hearing families where communication has been minimal because family members do not sign and the client utilizes ASL may hunger for the deaf clinician as a friend or as an idealized deaf parent substitute (Langholtz & Heller, 1986; Leigh & Lewis, 1999). While there are ways to effectively address this dynamic within the therapeutic context, such a situation can lead to some unintended consequences for the treating clinician, including confronting ethical aspects related to boundary issues, as the following example indicates.

———

A deaf adult male with a diagnosis of borderline personality disorder and a poor history of social relationships entered treatment with a deaf psychologist stationed in a clinic that served deaf clientele. The client lived with his mother, with whom he fought incessantly. He had not heard from his father since he was a young child, and even then only rare meetings were scheduled. His sibling had moved out to minimize conflict with both him and his mother. Jobs were sporadic and life was often empty for this client. The psychotherapeutic relationship evolved into one in which the client depended almost completely on the clinician for emotional connection despite every effort on the clinician's part to encourage additional support systems. The client felt that the clinician was his best support because he was also deaf, and consequently, the only one who fully understood him. For this reason, the client wanted the clinician's home TTY number. The clinician repeatedly explained clinic policy, which specifically stated that when the clinic was closed the client could phone and be directed to whoever was on call. The clinician also explained that others besides him might answer the home phone, and confidentiality was not guaranteed. The client ignored this aspect and kept maintaining that he could be trusted with the phone number and would use it only in case of dire need. One evening when the clinician was at home, he unexpectedly received a call. The client had obtained a copy of the local TTY directory, which listed the clinician's home number since he was active in the deaf community. The clinician tried to limit the call to absolute essentials only to be confronted with the client's feelings of rejection. This of course had to be handled during the next therapy session. Thereafter, the client would call the clinician's home at regular intervals and threaten suicide, thus forcing the clinician to attend to his needs. The clinician's children picked up the majority of these calls. Even though confidentiality was an issue, the client persisted, and the family was aware that this situation demanded a lot of their father's time. There was no way to protect the children from these calls because of their unpredictability, despite the clinician's efforts to set limits on them. They always knew about this particular client because he identified himself to them and used the clinician's professional name. At times, they were frustrated because their father had to be circumspect about the calls and could not be diverted from them.

———

In addition to the myriad therapeutic issues generated by the client in this vignette, the clinician's deafness became an idealized aspect for the client who was hungry for emotional connection. As a result, the client searched for ways to gain access to the clinician outside of the clinic. The ethical issues brought into play include the loss of boundaries between the client and the clinician's family, which happened because of the client's dynamics and the clinician's participation in the deaf community via his home TTY listing. The clinician had to develop ways to deal with his client without appearing to reject him, thereby minimizing emotional harm. He had to deal with professional issues at home and impose constraints on his children to prioritize the client. To prevent recurrences, the clinician was forced to unlist his TTY number, which he had been reluctant to do as an active member of the deaf community.

IDEOLOGY AND BIAS

Ideological issues related to communication, education, and the medical model versus the sociocultural model of deafness are inescapable facts of life in the deaf community, as Gutman indicates in chapter 2. Clinicians have to analyze their ideological value systems and evaluate how these may facilitate or hamper their work with clients. This process is critical because ethics dictate that mental health professionals need to refer clients elsewhere if ideology conflicts with treatment (Corey, Corey, & Callanan, 1993; Swenson, 1993). Even though the bond of deafness between clinician and client can be a strong one, it does not always override ideology.

The appropriateness of cochlear implants for deaf persons is one example of a potential ideological divide. It is important to understand that, in the recent past, the issue of cochlear implantation has been controversial for a substantial number of culturally Deaf persons, particularly with reference to young deaf children (Christiansen & Leigh, 2002; Tucker, 1998). It elicits intense emotions from these Deaf individuals, in part, because the process has philosophically been equated with the ongoing medicalization of deafness and cultural genocide (Lane, 1992; Lane & Bahan, 1998; Lane, Hoffmeister, & Bahan, 1996; Wrigley, 1996). Consequently, deaf adults who elected to go through the procedure experienced rejection due to the perception that they were betraying Deaf cultural values (Leigh, Sullivan,

Graham-Kelly, & Aiello, 1998). In other words, by going through the process of implantation, these adults were supposedly broadcasting the message that they wanted to distance themselves from the deaf community and stop using ASL, which was not necessarily the case. The deaf community is becoming more accepting of culturally Deaf adults who have been implanted to enhance their experience of sound and still continue to live their lives within the deaf community as they always have (Aiello & Aiello, 2000). Deaf children who have been implanted are also increasingly welcomed into the deaf community (Christiansen & Leigh, 2002).

Suppose a deaf adult, who has been deemed audiologically and medically eligible for a cochlear implant, recognizes the need for in-depth consultation regarding the psychological and social ramifications of the procedure. She therefore requests consultation with a deaf psychologist. The implant candidate might be unaware that this deaf psychologist is closely aligned with Deaf culture perspectives and is also fundamentally opposed to cochlear implants. What is the ethical course of action for the psychologist when approached by this deaf adult? Does the psychologist try to "save" the deaf person from the "horrors" of the cochlear implant procedure by stating his position unequivocally, potentially either resolving or exacerbating the conflict situation for the client; provide consultation as impartially as possible despite the existence of bias; or refer the client elsewhere?

On the other side of the coin, what about the possible scenario of a deaf psychologist, well integrated within the deaf community, who becomes part of a cochlear implant evaluation team with the goal of ensuring that informed consent is actually informed consent. In other words, informed consent is not only a presentation of the potential for sound awareness, improved speech, spoken language acquisition, and integration into the hearing community or the risk of gaining no benefit. Informed consent also incorporates all potential ramifications related to deaf community and Deaf culture participation as enriching life choices (see Pollard, 1996 for a discussion of informed consent as part of the preoperative procedure for cochlear implants). The nature of the medical setting where the evaluation is taking place can encourage the implicit assumption that the cochlear implant is appropriate for more deaf adults and children than may be acceptable to a number of culturally Deaf people. Consequently, participation in such a team may, at some level, convey the message that the deaf psychologist supports the procedure for every candidate, which may not necessarily be the case. Therefore, the integrity and impartiality of the psychologist on the cochlear implant issue may be called into question, even though he or she may be attempting to adhere to fundamental ethical principles related to informed consent.[1]

---

1. In "Does God Have a Cochlear Implant?" Michael Harvey (2001) provides a compelling illustration of critical issues in the cochlear implant debate within the structure of psychotherapy.

CONCLUSION

The examples here illustrate the need to recognize when ethical issues emerge for the deaf clinician. The added dimension of being deaf and connected with the deaf community brings with it a host of treatment considerations and lifestyle issues that deaf clinicians would do well to consider carefully in the interest of developing competent professionalism. These aspects need to be considered during the process of making ethical decisions that will maximize the "helping profession" nature of mental health in the interest of enhancing the positive quality of life for both deaf clinician and deaf client.

REFERENCES

Aiello, P., & Aiello, M. (2000, July). *Misconceptions of cochlear implants in the deaf community*. Workshop conducted at the National Association of the Deaf 45th Biennial Conference, Norfolk, VA.

American Psychological Association. (1992). Ethical principles of psychologists and code of conduct. *American Psychologist, 47,* 1597–1611.

Christiansen, J., & Leigh, I. W. (2002). *Cochlear implants in children: Ethics and choices.* Washington, DC: Gallaudet University Press.

Corey, G., Corey, M., & Callanan, P. (1993). *Issues and ethics in the helping professions.* Pacific Grove, CA: Brooks/Cole.

Falberg, R. M. (1985). Maintaining confidentiality when counseling deaf adults in rehabilitation facilities. In G. B. Anderson & D. Watson (Eds.), *Counseling deaf people: Research and practice* (pp. 105–120). Little Rock: Arkansas Rehabilitation Research & Training Center on Deafness and Hearing Impairment, University of Arkansas.

Harvey, M. (2001). Does god have a cochlear implant? *Journal of Deaf Studies and Deaf Education, 6,* 70–81.

Lane, H. (1992). *The mask of benevolence: Disabling the Deaf community.* New York: Knopf.

Lane, H., & Bahan, B. (1998). Ethics of cochlear implantation in young children: A review and reply from a Deaf-World perspective. *Otolaryngology: Head and Neck Surgery, 119,* 297–313.

Lane, H., Hoffmeister, R., & Bahan, B. (1996). *A journey into the Deaf World.* San Diego: DawnSign Press.

Langholtz, D., & Heller, B. (1986). Deaf and hearing psychotherapists: Differences in their delivery of clinical services to deaf clients. In D. Watson, G. B. Anderson, & M. Taff-Watson (Eds.), *Integrating human resources, technology and systems in deafness,* (Monograph No. 13, pp. 34–45). Silver Spring, MD: American Deafness and Rehabilitation Association.

Leigh, I. W., & Lewis, J. W. (1999). Deaf therapists and the deaf community: How the twain meet. In I. W. Leigh (Ed.), *Psychotherapy with deaf clients from diverse groups* (pp. 45–65). Washington, DC: Gallaudet University Press.

Leigh, I. W., Sullivan, V. J., Graham-Kelly, M., & Aiello, P. (1998, July). *Cochlear implants and Deaf adults: Implications for the Deaf community from within.* Panel conducted at the National Association of the Deaf Conference, San Antonio, TX.

Lytle, L. R. (1995, September). *Ethical dilemmas in the delivery of psychological services to deaf/hard of hearing adults and children.* Workshop discussion at the Department of Psychology Seminar, Gallaudet University, Washington, DC.

Lytle, L. R., & Lewis, J. W. (1996). Deaf therapists, deaf clients, and the therapeutic relationship. In N. S. Glickman & M. Harvey (Eds.), *Culturally affirmative psychotherapy with Deaf persons* (pp. 261–276). Mahwah, NJ: Erlbaum.

Patterson, C. H., & Stewart, L. G. (1971). Principles of counseling with deaf people. In A. E. Sussman & L. G. Stewart (Eds.), *Counseling with deaf people* (pp. 43-86). New York: Deafness Research & Training Center, New York University School of Education.

Pollard, R. (1996). Conceptualizing and conducting preoperative psychological assessments of cochlear implant candidates. *Journal of Deaf Studies and Deaf Education, 1,* 16–28.

Rich, R. O. (1990). The American rural metaphor: Myths and realities in rural practice. *Human Services in the Rural Environment, 14,* 31–34.

Schank, J., & Skovholt, T. (1997). Dual relationship dilemmas of rural and small-community psychologists. *Professional Psychology: Research and Practice, 28,* 44–49.

Swenson, L. (1993). *Psychology and law for the helping professions.* Pacific Grove, CA: Brooks/Cole.

Thoreson, R. W., & Tully, N. L. (1971). Role and function of the counselor. In A. E. Sussman & L. G. Stewart (Eds.), *Counseling with deaf people* (pp. 87–107). New York: Deafness Research & Training Center, New York University School of Education.

Tucker, B. (1998). *Cochlear implants: A handbook.* Jefferson, NC: McFarland & Co.

Wrigley, O. (1996). *The politics of deafness.* Washington, DC: Gallaudet University Press.

2

Ethics in Mental Health and Deafness

IMPLICATIONS FOR PRACTITIONERS
IN THE "SMALL WORLD"

Virginia Gutman

When mental health professionals working in Deafness get together to discuss professional issues, our conversation inevitably turns to topics in the realm of ethics. Managing encounters with clients outside the therapy hour; maintaining confidentiality; working with other professionals and the institutions that employ them; battling rumor and stigma; dealing with the economic, educational, and vocational disadvantages deaf clients face; trying to provide high-quality services when the mental health professional is already stretched too thin; serving clients the service provider was never trained to work with; and maintaining a nourishing personal life while still giving clients what they need are issues that professionals in Deafness wrestle with in communities in every part of the country and every professional setting. All of these topics have implications in the realm of ethics, and all can be challenging to professionals in Deafness, whether they are just beginning their professional lives or have many years of experience as service providers.

In spite of the ubiquity of these concerns, the clinical literature in mental health and Deafness provides little guidance or support. Even major clinical practice issues in mental health and Deafness are only beginning to be defined and articulated (Pollard, 1996; Leigh, Corbett, Gutman, & Morere,

1996; Glickman & Harvey, 1996, Leigh, 1999). Many basic clinical issues, such as selecting appropriate treatments, correctly assessing and diagnosing clinical problems, and providing access to services, are still problematic. Equally important but less visible concerns get even less attention, such as issues of culture, community, language, and competence in clinical areas. No formally established set of practice guidelines is available for working with deaf and hard of hearing populations. Therefore it is not surprising that specific ethical issues in Deafness have not been systematically addressed to date.

To build a conceptual framework for examining ethics in working with deaf and hard of hearing people, this chapter draws on four lines of analysis: one related to ethics in rehabilitation contexts; a second related to ethical practice with minorities (including ethical issues for ethnic, racial, and linguistic minorities; ethics in feminist perspectives; and ethics in work with sexual minorities); a third pertaining to ethics in rural practice; and a fourth exploring ethical reasoning processes for dealing with novel or ethically ambiguous situations. Each of these approaches contains certain important features that are found also in work with deaf people and can pose particularly challenging ethical dilemmas. The suggestions that have been offered for maintaining an ethical stance when working with a minority population, or in a small rural community, or in a rehabilitation context can be adapted to assist those wishing to apply the highest ethical principles to working with deaf populations. As each perspective is discussed, applications in the context of Deafness will be suggested. Along the way, I will also consider two issues that can be difficult in working with deaf clients: the ethical implications of ideology in clinical practice and the role of collegial consultation in supporting ethical behavior.

Because the goal of this book is to provide information to assist clinicians with their decision making, my focus will not be on providing the "right answers" but on helping readers to ask the right questions, which leads to ethically sound clinical decisions.

DEAFNESS AND REHABILITATION ETHICS

To a large extent, deaf services have their roots in the field of rehabilitation, which has provided funding, training, service programs, theory, and standards of practice. With its emphasis on attaining the highest possible level of functioning, rather than on cure, it is part of the bedrock upon which stand today's deaf services professions. Yet the "rehabilitation perspective" has also been criticized for presuming that deaf people are disabled and for creating legions of professionals who have been influential in determining deaf people's fate, individually and collectively. When considering ethical perspectives from rehabilitation, clinicians should remember that this field currently includes a variety of approaches to service delivery and attendant ethical issues.

The traditional and probably best-known ethical perspectives in rehabilitation have grown from medical settings, practices, and models, and they have been labeled "paternalistic," referring to the benevolent parentlike role that the service provider takes vis-à-vis the client or patient, who is regarded as childlike. Recently, however, newer models are competing and coexisting with or are superseding the old paternalistic ones that previously dominated many rehabilitation practice settings, although the older models are still widespread (Deaton, 1996; Wegener, 1996).

In rehabilitation settings, ethical issues constantly arise in selecting treatments, deciding upon goals for a patient, assessing suitability for treatment, deciding when to change treatments, assessing treatment outcomes, and rationing scarce or expensive treatments. Traditional professional–client relationships in Deafness have been described as reflecting the paternalistic rehabilitation model (Pollard, 1996; Lane, 1992), in which the (hearing) professional establishes the agenda, procedure, goal, and desired outcomes of any service, and the (deaf) client or student is considered too immature or ignorant of his or her own best interests to determine what treatments or services are to be provided, when, at what pace, in what form, or by whom.

More recent thinking in rehabilitation differentiates several models of ethical decision making, in which the professional and the patient/client/consumer share varying degrees of empowerment to make treatment decisions and set or reject treatment goals. In additional to the paternalistic model (with treatment decisions largely professionally determined), other models, such as *contractual* (with treatment decisions negotiated), *educational* (in which the professional teaches the client/patient to be knowledgeable enough to participate actively in treatment decisions), and *deliberative* (codetermined by a professional and a client who understand each other's feelings, beliefs, and views) are increasingly important (Wegener, 1996). Similar thinking is found in the area of developmental disabilities, in which ethical thinking is moving from paternalistic decision making to one significantly influenced by client choice, even with clients unable to express their preferences clearly because they lack verbal or cognitive skills (Hayes, Adams, & Rydeen, 1994).

The issue of medical paternalism is very significant to many deaf people because this view suggests that deafness is a disability or handicap (to be prevented or rehabilitated) rather than a cultural, linguistic, or social identity to be developed and promoted as a positive aspect of self (Padden & Humphries, 1988; Leigh et al., 1996; Pollard, 1992; Glickman, 1986; Lane, 1992; Sacks, 1989). For many years, the literature on mental health interventions with deaf populations recommended "directive" treatment methods, reflecting a view that deaf persons were psychologically and socially unsophisticated, inarticulate, and unable to engage in introspection or to benefit from therapies requiring reflection or insight. Thus treatment often consisted of either hospitalization or attempts to instruct the patient in appropriate behavior. This led to many abuses, including inappropriate institutionalization (such as placing deaf persons of normal intelligence in programs for the mentally retarded or long-term hospitalization of deaf adults in programs with no means of communication available) and intrusive involvement of service providers into deaf adults' decision making (such as insisting that adult clients capable of independent functioning live in a particular place, hold a particular job, or go to a specific school).

Ironically, experience with such treatment may lead to two quite different results. Some clients, after years of paternalistic treatment (such as unnecessary long-term psychiatric hospitalization) have great difficulty living independently, the necessary skills having atrophied or never developed. Other clients, after exposure to such treatments, become extremely concerned with and adept at avoiding and protecting themselves from service providers who show the slightest indication of paternalism.

Wegener (1996) analyzes the available ethical decision-making models in rehabilitation in terms of two major principles: that of autonomy (the patient/client should make his or her own decisions) and that of beneficence (all decisions should be in the best interest of the patient). (See also Bersoff & Koeppl, 1993; Beauchamp & Childress, 2001.) When both principles are valued, patients/clients actively participate in decision making, and their wishes (barring a finding of legal incompetence) determine treatment. If beneficence is neglected in favor of autonomy, patients may be asked to make decisions without sufficient information about unfamiliar, expensive, time-consuming, or uncomfortable treatment. If autonomy is not given sufficient weight, then professionals may become paternalistic, believing that they know what is in the patient's best interests, and proceed on that basis.

When professionals engage in a paternalistic style of treatment, the ethical implications of a "trust me, it's for your own good" approach must be considered in light of the client's individual, family, or community history. For example, does this client come from a family or community in which expressing disagreement with a professional is common? Is this an individual who has been taught from childhood to obey authority without question? Does the individual belong to a group of people who have traditionally not had self-determination? If so, an authoritative or directive position by a professional may amount to coercion, even if the patient technically has the "right" to refuse treatment or demand a different treatment or therapist. When clinicians make decisions for clients, they must consider how this will affect the patient's future ability to make autonomous choices and the patient's future regard for and trust in service providers.

Deaton (1996) suggests that medical paternalism is today most wide-spread in regard to the treatment of children. This has particular implications for deaf persons and the Deaf community, since parents are put in the position of making significant medical and educational decisions about their deaf children, often without adequate information about options or expected outcomes. These decisions have significant impact upon the child's development of language and cultural identity, yet neither the young child (lacking legal standing and cognitive maturity) nor the parents (in distress at their child's deafness and having difficulty getting, understanding, and evaluating information) may be equipped to make these early decisions and follow them through. Beneficence/autonomy issues in these cases apply to both the parents and the children. It has been argued that the Deaf community as a whole also has a stake in such decisions, since its traditional ability to raise deaf children within the Deaf culture is at risk.

In such circumstances, finding the correct balance between fostering the client's autonomous decision making and, at the same time, trying to prevent clients from making decisions that the professional regards as serious mistakes can be tricky. For example, is it appropriate for professionals to pressure "misguided" or "poorly informed" parents into particular kinds of medical or educational treatment or particular communication decisions for their child? What if "best outcome" for the child is not the same as "best outcome" for the parents? When child and parents disagree, whose autonomy takes precedence? What if parents have a strongly held belief (e.g., for or against sign language, or for or against mainstreamed educational programs) that the professional sees as not in the best interest of the deaf child? Does the Deaf community have any valid role in decision making for individual families? These considerations are discussed in regard to decisions about cochlear implants in Christiansen and Leigh (2002) and in Leigh's chapter in this volume.

A final possibility from the rehabilitation perspective that has application to Deafness ethics and may apply to the kind of dilemmas proposed above, is described by Wegener (1996) as a "deliberative" model. This model is based primarily, not on beneficence versus autonomy, but rather on empathy. The deliberative model, he suggests, reflects the emotional and personal as well as the professional relationship between the clinician and the patient/client, who both are members of the same "rehabilitation community" (p. 11) and interact with each other to make treatment decisions. This model recognizes the continually evolving relationship between client and professional, as well as the effects of other settings, clients, or caregivers on them both.

A further development in ethical thinking in relation to disabilities and to rehabilitation in general is the "virtue ethics" described in Kerkhoff, Hanson, Guenther, and Ashkanazi (1997), who suggest that ethics should reinforce personal accountability and not substitute for professional or clinical judgment. They view ethical action as the pursuit of the highest professional standards, rather than a legalistic avoidance of liability. In this light, ethical standards of care can be applied not only to the decisions of individuals, but also to the development of public policy in areas related to health care and rehabilitation. We will return to a discussion of virtue ethics later in this chapter.

For deaf consumers of rehabilitation services and the professionals who treat them, a number of issues can be quite complex in terms of the rehabilitation models. These are more appropriately phrased as questions rather than answers. For example, when a deaf person has limited exposure to or understanding of the concepts and information necessary for informed decision making (e.g., risk, harm, negative outcomes, probability of benefit), how can a truly autonomous, well-informed decision be made? What level of ease of communication is necessary in order for the client to adequately understand the risks and benefits of various treatment options? With clients who are not linguistically skilled in English, American Sign Language (ASL), or any other language, is there any way to present decisions and choices so that the client can understand them? When other people in the deaf consumer's life (professionals, family members, or others) are accustomed to making decisions for him or her, is it possible to introduce a new level of autonomy so the individual can consent to treatment? For a deaf person accustomed (at home, school, or work) to being told what to do in matters large and small, is not some kind of "treatment" necessary in order to develop decision-making and assertion skills before the "decision for treatment" can even be made? Kerkhoff et al. (1997) suggest several ways to detect preference in clients who cannot say what they want because of lack of verbal abilities (such as watching what the client does or watching the client's affect when engaging in various options). However, for those deaf clients whose cognitive skills may be superior to their expressive language, such methods do not detect whether the client is making a well-informed decision or operating on the basis of misinformation, misunderstanding, or habit rather than according to some standard of rational choice based on correct information about alternatives.

Some of these issues are discussed in Zitter (1996) with reference to a client with severe behavioral problems and very limited language. Zitter, the therapist, chose to keep her role focused on assisting the client in decision making rather than on coercing the client to do things. If coercion had to be used to protect the client or others, it was done by police or other professionals, not by the therapist. Zitter (1996) further enhanced the client's decision making through a variety of nonlanguage methods such as mime, role playing, drawings, and rehearsal to dramatize the choices the client had, as well as their probable consequences.

Ethical practice—that is, encouraging a client's autonomous decision making or promoting mutual decision making by client and professional—clearly requires not only sensitivity to ethical issues but clinical skills and "professional virtues" as well (see Beauchamp & Childress, 2001). For example, the clinician must know both how to assess the client's current ability to make decisions and how to present information relevant to a decision in a way that is intelligible for the client. Also necessary is the patience to engage in a deliberative process with a client rather than making a quick decision "in the client's best interest." This requires the clinical acumen to differentiate between an emergency situation in which delay to allow the client time to make a decision could be disastrous and a situation in which delayed decision making may be uncomfortable and time-consuming but will not cause serious harm.

DEAF PEOPLE AS A LINGUISTIC AND
CULTURAL MINORITY

While all deaf people have some degree of audiological hearing loss, they comprise an extremely diverse group in all other respects. Cultural and ethnic identity is an important variable for understanding both individual deaf persons and Deaf communities.

Many (but by no means all) deaf people refer to themselves as "Deaf," value their deafness as an essential element of their identity, identify with "Deaf culture," and affiliate with members of the "Deaf community" (Padden & Humphries, 1988; Pollard, 1996; Leigh et al., 1996). The primary language for deaf people is ASL, and competency in ASL is a defining characteristic of those considered to be in the Deaf community (which can also include the hearing children and spouses of deaf people, sign language interpreters, and others who sign with reasonable fluency).

In common with other cultural and linguistic minority groups, deaf individuals historically have suffered from overt and covert discrimination and educational, social, political, vocational, and economic disadvantages. Furthermore, educational, occupational, and social ghettoization and marginalization of deaf people in relation to the majority hearing community are common (Pollard, 1996). Only in 1990 did the Americans with Disabilities Act (ADA) mandate accessibility in virtually all employment, services, facilities, businesses, health care programs, and educational and training settings (National Center for Law and Deafness, 1994). However, the regulations leave many areas undefined, and the lawsuits that will ultimately specify what access is required in various situations are still working their way through the courts (see McCrone, this volume). Meanwhile, deaf people continue to experience discrimination and disadvantage in education, training, employment, health care, mental health services, and a variety of other areas.

In addition to Deafness as a cultural variable, deaf and Deaf people may have other minority identifications as members of cultural, ethnic, racial, religious, or sexual minority groups. The views of various American cultural groups and immigrant communities toward their deaf (or Deaf) members is a topic only beginning to receive attention (Leigh et al., 1996; Cohen, Fischgrund, & Redding, 1990; Christensen & Delgado, 1993; Anderson & Grace, 1991; Zea, Belgrave, Garcia, & Quezada, 1997). Indeed, ethnic and minority issues have not been well integrated into the field of disabilities in general (Uswatte & Elliott, 1997).

Reports from deaf immigrants suggest that while deaf persons in the United States have legally mandated access to all services (although perhaps more in theory than yet in practice), deaf persons in other countries face significantly more educational, economic, and social deprivation. Societal views of Deafness can have deep-seated cultural and religious roots, and in many immigrant communities in this country, deaf persons may not be regarded as able to become productive citizens or to attain the same educational levels expected of their hearing counterparts.

Looked at from this framework, the exploration of ethical concerns important in working with ethnic, racial, cultural, and linguistic minority communities can aid in ethical decision making with deaf clients. A key resource in this regard is the "Guidelines for Providers of Psychological Services to Ethnic, Linguistic, and Culturally Diverse Populations" (American Psychological Association [APA], 1993), which provides guidelines rather than prescriptive rules. These complement and elaborate the codes of conduct adopted by major professional mental health organizations, including the APA's "Ethical Principles of Psychologists and Code of Conduct" (1992), the American Counseling Association's (ACA) *Code of Ethics and Standards of Practice* (1995), and the National Association of Social Workers' (NASW) *Code of Ethics* (1996).

Two of the guidelines (the first and sixth) deal with language. The first suggests giving clients full written and oral information about the treatment in the client's own language, while the sixth advises psychologists to "interact in the language requested by the client, and, if this is not feasible, make an appropriate referral" (p. 3). With deaf clients, this requires that the clinician first determine the client's preferred or "best" language (whether English, ASL, another spoken or signed language, or no formal language), and second that the clinician be able to provide the client with information in this language. The guidelines permit use of translators or interpreters when a referral to a mental health professional with appropriate language skills is not possible. Interpreters who have a dual role with the client are not to be used, according to the guidelines.

Additional guidelines state that psychologists should be knowledgeable about research and practice with the specific population; furthermore, when a practitioner does not have sufficient competency, appropriate consultation and/or referral is suggested. In this regard, Sue (1996) asserts more strongly that "counselors who are not trained in working with a multicultural population and who work with members of that group may be guilty of unethical practice. . . . Multicultural competence requires more than cognitive introduction to the topic. It dictates long-term and continuing education and life experiences with the specific population" (p. 199). This concern is also explicitly addressed in the *Feminist Therapy Code of Ethics* (Feminist Therapy Institute, 1987), which recommends that a feminist therapist recognize her limitations regarding knowledge of class, cultural, or other differences and acquire knowledge about these areas from sources other than clients.

Each of the ethical codes describes a clinician's responsibility to avoid discriminatory practices, show commitment to diversity, and be sensitive to the needs of groups, which have in the past lacked power and self-determination. All the codes include individuals with disabilities as well as linguistic, cultural, racial, ethnic, and sexual minorities under this rubric.

This line of thinking implies that professionals in the mental health disciplines have an ethical obligation to become familiar with the Deaf community and Deaf culture as with any other minority group they are likely to encounter. If they are not familiar with deafness then they should refer deaf clients to a more knowledgeable colleague. Further, the familiarity should not be primarily gained from one's clients. While therapists continuously learn from their interactions with clients, placing a client in a teaching role in order to increase the competence of the therapist is a questionable practice.

Complicating this issue is the requirement under the ADA that deaf clients (as one category of citizens with disabilities) have access to psychological and other health-related services that is equal to the access afforded hearing persons. (National Center for Law and Deafness, 1994; Bruyere & O'Keefe, 1993; Raifman & Vernon, 1996; see also McCrone, this volume).

The two underlying principles—the requirement to treat only populations the professional has considerable knowledge about and the requirement to provide equal access to service—can put the mental health professional in a quandary when faced with a deaf client. Since few mental health professionals have any training in Deafness, one approach is simply to refer all deaf clients to someone experienced in Deafness. However, since the number of psychologists, psychiatrists, counselors, or social workers with extensive training in Deafness is still very small (Pollard, 1996; Crewe, 1994; Gutman & Gibbins, 1991), a blanket policy of referring all deaf persons would, in practice, lead to deaf clients not having access to services for many specialized needs (such as chemical dependency treatment, treatment of issues having to do with behavioral medicine, health-related issues, or specialty clinics in areas such as depression or anxiety disorders). Automatically referring all deaf clients to specialists in Deafness also removes the client's autonomy to choose treatment from someone with no ties in the Deaf community, a choice that some clients may wish to make for a variety of reasons.

Additional sections of the "Guidelines for Providers of Psychological Services to Ethnic, Linguistic, and Culturally Diverse Populations" (APA, 1993) call for practitioners to recognize and understand ethnic and cultural factors in interactions with clients; respect community and family structures, standards, and beliefs (including religious beliefs and values); and understand the importance of "social, environmental, and political factors," (p. 3) such as oppression, powerlessness, discrimination, racism, and poverty. Finally, practitioners are admonished to "work to eliminate biases, prejudices, and discriminatory practices" (p. 4) at not only the individual but the social, or community levels. The guidelines stop short of encouraging political action, emphasizing instead the importance of sensitivity, cognizance, and acknowledgment of the impact of discrimination. Several professional organizations go further. The NASW ethical code charges social workers with the responsibility to society of "acting to prevent and eliminate discrimination[,] ... ensure ... access to resources[,] ... expand choice and opportunity[,] ... advocate changes in policy and legislation to improve social conditions and to promote social justice. . . [, and] encourage informed participation by the public in shaping social policies and institutions" (NASW, 1993, p. 10). Along similar lines, the interdisciplinary *Feminist Therapy Code of Ethics* states that "[A] feminist therapist seeks multiple avenues for impacting change, including public education and advocacy within professional organizations, lobbying for legislative action, and other appropriate activities" (Feminist Therapy Institute, 1987, p. 4).

Viewing deaf/Deaf people as a cultural, linguistic, or disadvantaged minority allows certain ethical issues to be recognized that may not be evident from the beneficence/autonomy concerns of the rehabilitation model. Among these are the impact on services that arise from the professional's cultural competency (or lack of same), language skill, and identity as either Deaf or hearing. Furthermore, differences within the Deaf community based on whether one identifies as deaf, Deaf, hard of hearing, etc.; ethnicity; level of education; and social class can be more clearly seen and understood, as can the differences in the client's level of cultural competence in Deaf and hearing cultures. The importance of a client's experience with discrimination, devaluation, or limited access to education and other resources becomes evident. For example, questions of informed consent hinge not only on the professional's ability to explain clearly the nature, benefits, and risks of treatment to the client, but also on the power relationship that may exist between the professional and the client. This power relationship must be understood not only in terms of the individuals involved but also as to whether either belongs to relatively powerful or powerless groups in society. Such power/status differentials can increase the client's vulnerability to exploitation.

DEAF PEOPLE AS A SMALL COMMUNITY

The "small world" aspects of the Deaf community are continuously apparent to deaf people, particularly those identifying with Deaf culture, and to hearing people who, through personal relationships or professional activities, associate frequently with Deaf people. Shared educational or training experiences, cultural or recreational activities, and occupational contacts bring Deaf people together frequently in local communities, and the "grapevine" spreads important news about individuals or community events throughout the country. The advent of instantaneous and cheap communication via computers and accessible wireless telecommunication systems promises to make the community even more interactive at the national level.

While a close-knit community of people who are interested in each other and involved together in social, political, or vocational activities is a matchless resource, it also provides an arena for several areas of ethical concern, including confidentiality, practitioner competency, and dual/multiple relationships. Similar concerns are discussed by writers on rural mental health, communities of color, feminist psychotherapy, and gay and lesbian mental health. The literature in these areas suggests some methods of ethical decision making regarding these difficult issues that may be applicable within the Deaf community.

In rural areas, large geographic regions may be served by very few or no professionals trained in mental health. Thus clinicians must be generalists, expected to function more broadly than the role traditionally accorded their discipline (such as psychology, social work, or counseling), and expected to work with clients with all kinds of problems in all kinds of settings (Hargrove, 1982). Similar role pressures can arise in any community that must function fairly self-sufficiently and where there are few trained service providers.

The analogy to the Deaf community, where access to mainstream mental health services is curtailed by communication barriers, is clear. Like a resident of a rural area, a Deaf consumer has relatively few treatment options. Service providers are likely to be known and familiar from other settings, since both may be members of the local Deaf community. Furthermore, in Deafness, as in rural settings, the population is geographically far-flung but psychologically in close contact and interdependent upon each other. A final area of commonality is the fact that in Deafness, as in rural areas, contact networks are defined by factors other than choice (place of residence in the case of rural communities, or having a hearing loss in the case of the Deaf/deaf community) (Sobel, 1992).

The generalist role allows for great scope of functioning. However, it may present ethical concerns regarding competency. The APA states that "psychologists . . . provide only those services and use only those techniques for which they are qualified by education, training, or experience" (APA, 1992, p. 1599). The ACA requires that "counselors practice only within the boundaries of their competence, based on their education, training, supervised experience . . . credentials, and . . . professional experience. . . . Counselors practice in specialty areas new to them only after appropriate education, training, and supervised experience" (Herlihy & Corey, 1996, p. 34). The American Psychiatric Association (1995) states that "A psychiatrist who regularly practices outside his/her area of professional competence should be considered unethical" (p. 4). The expectation is that professionals faced with a client who needs assistance in an area outside the professional's competency will refer the client to a more qualified practitioner, or will obtain specialized training and supervision if the client is accepted by the not-yet-competent professional. These options may not be available in rural communities, since specialists may not be available. Hargrove (1986) succinctly cites "situations in which the choice is either treatment from the person who is available or no treatment at all" (p. 22). Either denying service to a needy person or having a negative outcome because a practitioner lacks skills raises ethical problems and also reflects poorly on the clinician's standing and reputation in the community.

Brown (1991, 1994), Smith (1990), and Hill, Glaser, and Harden (1995) comment on similar issues in providing therapy within feminist or gay and lesbian communities. They highlight the fact that within a small community the therapist is highly visible, so mistakes as well as successes can be readily perceived and may influence the willingness of others to seek services. The smaller the group (as with lesbian feminist communities of color), the greater the pressures that may be placed on the mental health professional (Smith, 1990; Sears, 1990a, 1990b). Within the feminist model, these authors recommend that the therapist provide the prospective client with information about the dilemmas associated with having a therapist who is active and visible in community, political, and cultural activities and consider the client's perspective when deciding whether to participate in these activities. Consultation with other professionals (who may or may not practice within the community under discussion) is also recommended (Hill et al., 1995).

A second issue of ethical difficulty in small communities is confidentiality (Wagenfeld, Murray, Mohatt, & DeBruyn, 1993; Hargrove, 1986; Sobel, 1992; Jeffrey & Reeve, 1978). Standard expectations of confidentiality can be compromised by the fact that in a small community the problems of individuals or of families are often well known. Furthermore, the tendency in small communities for service providers to share space (e.g., a rural psychologist working in a public health agency or a mental health counselor in Deafness working in a multiservice deaf resources agency) makes it likely that recipients of mental health services can be seen and recognized when arriving, leaving, or sitting in the waiting room. Furthermore, in multi-service agencies, keeping mental health information in files completely separate from other information (e.g., from audiological, vocational, educational, or other files) may be difficult. Other service providers may expect or demand exchange of information and be offended and unwilling to cooperate in further referrals if client information is not forthcoming. When the mental health professional or other staff of mental health services are themselves members of the community they serve, managing various encounters with clients without inadvertently breaking confidentiality can be difficult. For example, a client may approach a clinician at a community event and seek to discuss a confidential clinical issue. Sobel (1992) discusses an interesting dilemma in which her daughter became friends with a boy who was a client of Sobel and repeatedly asked why she could not invite him over to play. Finally, mental health professionals may be closely watched in such settings to see what information they do or do not reveal. A clinician who talks too freely about others, even if the information shared does not come from clinical contexts, may be perceived as unable to maintain confidentiality (Stockman, 1990). A further hazard described by Stockman is passing on information gained from clients that the clinician assumes to be common knowledge or widespread gossip, only to find that listeners trace the clinician's knowledge of this information directly back to the client.

To address these difficult issues, Jeffrey and Reeve (1978) and Stockman (1990) recommend discussing confidentiality procedures and restrictions in detail with other service personnel and persons making referrals so that the clinician's refusal to share information will not be taken as arrogance. Collaboratively developed procedures for situations when information-sharing is necessary (e.g., feedback to a primary physician who referred a patient) are preferable to policies determined unilaterally by the clinician. In the small community, the clinician (especially one actively involved in community life) would be unwise to unnecessarily alienate or offend colleagues with whom collaboration may be anticipated for many years. On the other hand, clients have the right (and the clinician the ethical duty) to have confidential information protected.

The third area of ethical conflict especially relevant to small communities is that of dual or multiple relationships, which are strongly discouraged in the codes of ethics for counseling, social work, and psychology. Multiple relationships are among the most troubling areas for clinicians in the Deaf community (see especially the chapters by Leigh and by Corbett in this volume). Multiple relationships that are injurious to or exploitative of clients are prohibited by all codes of ethics. Dual/multiple relationships are always suspect because of the probability that the therapist in the dual relationship may have interests that are not focused on the welfare of the client. Professional judgment may be compromised, and standards for professional behavior may become blurred (Koocher & Keith-Spiegel, 1998). The relatively vulnerable and powerless position of the client vis-à-vis the clinician makes it difficult for client or therapist to evaluate fully the potential for harm when a dual relationship is suggested. Even if the client has reservations, he or she may not feel free to clearly express wishes contrary to those of the therapist. The potential for the therapist obtaining profit or gratification from the client or at the expense of the client is especially clear in sexual or employer/employee relationships, but is always a possibility when more than one relationship exists. Thus codes of ethics assume that dual relationships involve heightened risk of harm to clients and so place the burden of proof of the benign nature of the relationship on the mental health professional.

In small communities, however, people may routinely and unavoidably interact with each other in a variety of roles, constituting what some authors prefer to call "overlapping relationships" (Brown, 1994; Rave & Larsen, 1995; Biaggio & Greene, 1995; Gartrell, 1994; Menzano, 1995; Sobel, 1992; Hargrove, 1986; Jennings, 1992). These overlapping relationships are defined as "unavoidable dual relationships . . . [resulting] from socio-demographic proximity" (Brown, 1991, p. 327).

Distinguishing between benign, unavoidable overlapping relationships and those that are harmful and unethical can be difficult for mental health professionals working and living in the context of a small community. A number of ways to assess the risks of overlapping relationships have been proposed. Biaggio and Greene (1995) suggest that multiple relationships become unethical when they include exploitation of the client or boundary violations. Brown (1994) describes overlapping (versus dual) relationships as based on some common interest or activity outside the therapy (such as a political, religious, or social aim), having a larger social context so that the relationship between the client and therapist is not an important inducement to become involved in the activity, the overlap is unavoidable and not initiated by the therapist, and participation in the activity, even with the overlapping relationship, is potentially beneficial to both parties. She warns, however, that such relationships can also be harmful and require careful and repeated examination and discussion with the client both before and after the overlapping relationship occurs.

Ebert (1997) also recognizes the inevitability of certain dual or multiple relationships. He suggests that the mental health service (e.g., psychotherapy) be considered the "primary relationship," and that the nature of the proposed "secondary relationship" determines whether a dual relationship is harmful and unethical, neutral, or possibly even helpful to the client. He recommends considering how close and frequent is the contact involved in the secondary relationship, how easy the secondary relationship is to avoid, what other options may be available, whether objective consultation has been obtained that verifies the harmlessness of the secondary relationship, and how the secondary relationship will reflect upon the profession.

Jennings (1992) posits that in "entangled" situations (i.e., unavoidable personal relationships with a client, a client's family member, or between a client and a family member of the clinician), the intervention must be restricted in proportion to the intensity of the other relationship. Psychotherapy with someone with whom the clinician has another intense relationship is impossible and, according to Jennings, should not be attempted.

Stockman (1990) recommends avoiding dual relationships that involve incompatible behaviors or responsibilities. This includes considering possible conflicts of interest that may arise before accepting community leadership roles, and also being aware of the potential impact of providing professional services to several people who may have intense and conflicted relationships with each other (e.g., the members of a divorcing couple). One example of this impact is when knowledge of the "other side" of an argument compromises a therapist's neutrality with a client.

Kitchener (1988) argues that dual relationships should be analyzed for their propensity to create harm; more harmful ones should be avoided, while less harmful ones might be considered acceptable. She suggests three criteria: the amount of power differential between client and therapist; the potential for a conflict of interest; and incompatibility of role expectations. As each of these increases, so does the possibility that a client will be wittingly or unwittingly coerced into a relationship, and the probability that harm will result.

Other useful judgment criteria are suggested by Faulkner and Faulkner (1997). They propose that at the outset, a mental health practitioner should consider all citizens of a small rural community to be potential or prospective clients. The clinician can assess his or her involvement with various potential clients and activities to see whether the pretherapy relationship (or extra-therapy relationship in the case of current clients) contains elements that would raise the risk of a serious boundary violation in the therapy relationship. The criteria are drawn from the literature on precursors to client–therapist sexual intimacy. For example, a relationship that involves nonsexual touching (such as the clinician's dentist, optometrist, hairdresser, or friends who are greeted with a hug or kiss) or personal disclosures about the clinician (such as might be expected with one's doctor, lawyer, or banker) might raise the risk of boundary violations and rule out that individual from the list of potential clients. Relationships lacking these elements—for example, the purchase of more impersonal products and services, or casual social encounters without much touching or self-disclosure by the clinician—might have no effect on an individual later becoming a client. This type of analysis could assist the clinician in determining what kinds of business and professional relationships can safely be pursued in the town where he or she practices and which might preferably be conducted in a different community.

Further strategies are suggested by Gates and Speare (1990), who focus on offering consultation and mental health information within their small town rather than ongoing psychotherapy with the many people with whom they have unavoidable overlapping relationships. While they may provide a few limited counseling sessions to people with whom they cannot avoid doing business, they do not engage in in-depth psychotherapy in such circumstances, and certain topics (such as the behavior of mutual friends) have to remain off-limits. Faulkner and Faulkner (1997) suggest office-swapping one day a week so colleagues in different towns can see clients who have a too-close outside relationship with the resident clinician.

Gartrell (1994), Jennings (1992), Stockman (1990), Brown (1994), and Menzano (1995) further recommend detailed and specific discussion with clients at the start of a professional relationship in a small community about the various kinds of minor or major contacts that might occur outside the professional context. This discussion should include consideration of the desirability of limiting such encounters and the necessity for discussing them when they are anticipated or have occurred. Also included should be some behavioral agreements for both clinician and client regarding these outside encounters. For example, will they greet or ignore each other?

Zitter (1996) applies similar reasoning to assessing overlapping relationships in the Deaf community. She distinguishes boundaries (fixed and immutable positions necessary for therapy to work) from parameters (which may change depending upon the particular client's situation) (p. 222–223). The boundaries and parameters may vary somewhat from therapist to therapist. She lists certain common dual roles, such as when therapist and client are both involved in advocacy or volunteer work for deaf services in the community. Like previous authors, she endorses involving the client in a discussion of the implications of the dual role both before and after it occurs, and including both the client's and therapist's views in a joint decision-making effort.

DEAFNESS AND IDEOLOGY

The education and treatment of deaf people can be seen as driven by clashing ideologies, which in the western world since the early 1800s has been most often portrayed as a war between supporters of oral versus sign language communication, or as supporting a pathological (medical) model of Deafness versus a cultural identity model (Padden & Humphries, 1988; Lane, 1992; Van Cleve & Crouch, 1989; Pollard, 1996). These ideological debates are far from resolved, although increasing efforts have been devoted to developing empirical means for choosing which educational or treatment practices will be most successful for specific deaf individuals (Johnson & Liddell, 1990; Moores, 1991). At present, a long list of important questions have no clear answers within the scientific literature, so deaf individuals, their families, and the professionals serving these communities have great difficulty obtaining objective information about topics such as: communication methods in the home and at school; the most effective methods for teaching deaf children to read and write English; the advisability of immersion (mainstreamed) educational settings versus separate deaf schools; how to determine who is qualified to teach, assess, or treat deaf children; the most helpful methods for those who are not deaf but hard of hearing; determining what facilitates good adaptation among those who lose hearing in adulthood or old age; whether it is possible to provide mental health services through an interpreter; how competent in various forms of communication a professional has to be to responsibly treat a deaf client; how outcomes of technologies such as the cochlear implant should be evaluated; and how the suitability for such procedures should be defined. The list could continue indefinitely, and clinicians in Deafness are required to make decisions or provide advice daily in these areas.

On all these questions, a variety of opinions can be strongly defended, and professionals (as well as their clients) are likely to base their beliefs on personal factors, including the training program the professional attended, the dominant philosophy within the professional's own discipline, and individual personal and professional experiences. Because the field is so lacking in unity, professionals with comparable levels of training can disagree about best practice in general or for an individual client. Thus the mental health professional may face ethical dilemmas pertaining to how strongly to advocate those methods that he or she believes to be best (in the absence of proof one way or the other), how to deal with colleagues who take other approaches that the professional may believe to be unacceptable on philosophical grounds, and how to interact with institutions and programs practicing the approaches with which the professional disagrees.

One important distinction is between dealing with practices that are generally agreed to be inappropriate versus those in which trained and experienced professionals may disagree. For example, verbally based tests of intelligence and personality are generally considered invalid for deaf persons, so a clinician calculating IQs or determining a psychiatric diagnosis solely from such testing would probably be practicing unethically. This is not a mistake that a clinician experienced in Deafness would be likely to make. On the other hand, currently there is no unequivocal standard that tells us what communication approaches are most successful for deaf children with hearing families, or which children will benefit most from certain approaches. We also have no empirical information on outcomes of various treatment approaches when adapted for use with deaf clients. In these areas, clinicians must depend upon their experience, common sense, careful evaluation of each case, frequent consultation with colleagues, and constantly updating themselves on the emerging literature in order to make good recommendations.

What is an appropriate ethical stance when a clinician is confronted with an educational, medical, or mental health practice that is commonly used in certain professional circles, but which the clinician believes is misguided? This question has been addressed, in somewhat different forms, in literature unrelated to Deafness, beginning with the "Radical Therapy" literature of the late 1960s and early 1970s, which advocated the depathologizing of mental illness and the closing of mental institutions. More recent thoughtful discussions of such issues are found in the feminist therapy literature and in the gay-affirmative therapy literature.

One issue is the therapist's non-neutrality, which may be inevitable for therapists participating in political movements (Cerbone, 1991; Berman, 1990). Some therapists may feel a responsibility to recognize and work to undermine the pervasive power imbalances in society that systematically oppress and disenfranchise certain groups of clients (Webster, 1995; Liburd & Rothblum, 1995; Smith & Douglas, 1990). This responsibility includes analyzing the empowerment/disenfranchisement implications of clients' real-life predicaments and involving oneself, both as a clinician and as a community activist, to redress injustices and power imbalances (Rosewater, 1990). As Cerbone (1991) points out, however, taking political positions that are insensitive to the experiences and needs of a client is counterproductive.

Of particular concern are medical or mental health practices that are seen as continuing or worsening the oppression of disadvantaged groups. Liburd and Rothblum (1995) discuss this issue in terms of medical approaches that increase eating disorders by promoting "fat-phobia" in women, and the continuing debate over the pathologizing womens' experience by including menstrual-related mood changes in the *Diagnostic and Statistical Manual of Mental Disorders* (*DSM–IV*) (American Psychiatric Association, 1994). Haldeman (1994) analyzes some ethical issues in sexual orientation conversion therapies from a similar point of view, specifically questioning whether a patient really has free choice when offered a "cure" for a condition that subjects him or her to social disapproval, discrimination, and abuse. Analogies to the difficulty of parents making decisions about their deaf childrens' upbringing can be drawn. If a particular communication approach (e.g., oral/aural methods) or a particular medical approach (e.g., cochlear implants) is described as making the child "able to participate in society like a hearing child," can a parent objectively analyze the options available?

ETHICAL DECISION-MAKING PROCESSES

Because so many clinical situations in Deafness challenge or fall outside the ethical principles and guidelines generally available, an alternative approach is to emphasize an ethical decision-making process relying on ethical principles rather than specific rules and codes in making choices (Haas & Malouf, 1989; Canadian Psychological Association [CPA], 1991; Kitchener, 1984; Hill, Glaser, & Harden, 1995; Koocher & Keith-Spiegel, 1998; Beauchamp & Childress, 2001). Eberlein (1987) calls this a "problem-solving" as opposed to a "correct answer" approach to dealing with ethical dilemmas. The discussion of professional virtues in rehabilitation described above (Kerkhoff et al., 1997) falls in this category. Such approaches have several common features, although they differ in terminology and emphasis. All regard an ethical decision as one that uses an appropriate decision-making process, rather than one that reaches the "right" answer.

Hill, Glaser, and Hardin (1995) discuss an often-overlooked aspect of ethical decision making—recognizing when an ethical issue exists. They point out that the ability to recognize these issues is enhanced by training in the ethical codes and clinical practice, and also by feedback from supervisors and colleagues, client reactions, and sometimes an undefined sense of discomfort a therapist may experience in a particular case. Consultation may be helpful when deciding if a clinical situation has ethical implications.

If an ethical issue is present, a number of methods for finding a solution have been proposed (Hill et al., 1995; Haas & Malouf, 1989; Welfel & Kitchener, 1992). Generally the first step is to define the ethical problem. What exactly are the ethical issues in this case? Is there an ethical conflict, such as when there are good but contradictory reasons to take incompatible actions? Do two ethical principles appear to require incompatible behaviors? Are there various ethically sound courses of action to be weighed? Which ethical principles or codes are involved and what does each imply for this situation?

Or is there a different kind of ethical problem, such as when a therapist wishes to take a course of action that appears to violate an ethical rule or code? Perhaps the "ethical" course of action seems impractical, is not relevant to the case, or will cause conflict with or even harm to the client. Maybe following the course of action prescribed in the clinician's professional code of ethics could be harmful to the therapist or others, or simply not in the therapist's best interests in some way. Sometimes ethical precepts conflict with legal requirements (see McCrone's chapter in this volume).

An important early step in defining the ethical issue is to determine whose interests must be considered. Who is the client, and who may be helped or harmed in this situation? Eberlein (1987) suggests that the clinician consider everyone involved (client, family members, the therapist, other professionals, etc.) as having rights and responsibilities.

With the ethical issue defined and the parties involved identified, the clinician can identify possible solutions. Ethical decision making requires considering several possible courses of action and defining the expected or predictable outcomes of each (Eberlein, 1987; Hill et al., 1995). This should allow one or more courses of action to be selected.

A final step is to implement and continue evaluating the decision. Decisions can be examined before or after implementation using a variety of criteria, such as whether it "feels right" (Hill et al., 1995). Since this criterion is heavily influenced by the personality, gender, culture, social status, and religious beliefs of the clinician, it cannot be the only criterion; however, it is an important one since it engages the clinician's ordinary sense of moral rightness about the decision (Kitchener, 1986; Welfel & Kitchener, 1992) and affects the clinician's ability to carry out the decision fully and honestly. Other standards could include the golden rule (Would I want to be treated this way?), the rule of universal application (What if everyone did this?), perspective taking (How would this look to each of the people involved?), and a time consideration (Has adequate time been allowed to reflect? Is the decision appropriate for implementation at this time? Is it too early or too late?).

Other considerations might include whether the therapist is abusing or making responsible use of his or her power and authority (Smith & Douglas, 1990) and whether appropriate care for the therapist is included (Adelman, 1990). An additional criterion is suggested by Haas and Malouf (1989), the "well-lit room" test: Would I be willing to take this action if everyone knew about it?

Few options will satisfy all these "tests," and few will perfectly resolve the initial dilemma. The point of the ethical decision-making process is to make a good decision, ethically speaking, which is feasible and appropriate to the clinical situation as a whole (not necessarily the "right" decision). Sometimes this represents a choice among several acceptable decisions. Sometimes it may involve a choice among several inadequate decisions when no truly satisfactory alternative exists. Thus an important final step, emphasized by Eberlein (1987) and the CPA (1986) is for the clinician to take responsibility for the decision he or she has made and for any actions taken and their consequences. The outcomes and results should be monitored carefully so as to take additional action if necessary to more fully resolve the ethical problem, or to mitigate any negative consequence that may have resulted from the original decision. All deliberations, consultations, actions, and outcomes should be fully documented for future reference.

Zitter (1996) gives several interesting examples of how such decision-making processes can be applied to clinical work with deaf clients. One area of special complexity can be communication and the questions that arise about whether or when a therapist with sign language skills should serve as an interpreter or facilitator of communication between a client and a hearing person. She presents the example of a therapist who is called to the emergency room because a therapy client has been brought there by the police in a suicidal state, but no other interpreter has been found. Because this is an ethically ambiguous situation, it is a good choice for applying an ethical decision-making process rather than attempting to find a "correct" answer by consulting an ethical code.

To elaborate upon Zitter's discussion, the clinician could begin by identifying the parties involved (herself, the deaf client, other professionals who do not sign) and determining the interests of each (such as successful outcome for the client, assuring that the client's wishes are known, obtaining all possible information for the professional who must make a commitment decision, conducting an emergency intervention in a way that will be legally acceptable, and the physical safety of all concerned). The responsibilities and duties of each can also be considered.

Then she can generate possible courses of action. The two possibilities she considers are "[talking] to the client and [reporting] to the emergency worker or police officer . . . but [being] clear I cannot interpret; or . . . [interpreting] with the client's permission and with the caveat that I am not in a legal capacity as an interpreter" (p. 228).

She then can evaluate the ethical implications of each course of action: If she refuses to interpret, she avoids a dual relationship, preserves her ability to ally with the client separately from the other staff of the emergency room, and preserves her ability to participate in her professional role in the discussion and to note for her own records anything that is said. However, without an interpreter, the patient's views may not be well understood, and the patient may be unaware of some of the conversation.

If she chooses to interpret, she adds a dual role, and as an uncertified interpreter, might contribute to a misunderstanding between the client and the medical staff or police. Furthermore, her serving as an interpreter may be confusing for the patient or lead him to mistrust her as a therapist. Moreover, her ability to participate as a clinician may be limited, and she may have questions as to what records she can keep of the encounter—Was she an interpreter and bound not to report any of what transpired, or was she a clinician and obligated to put relevant details in the patient's chart? On the other hand, by opening communication between the staff and the patient by interpreting, she might be able to increase the patient's safety and allow the staff to make a more appropriate decision about the patient's needs. The patient may also have more opportunity to make his wishes known. Also, his stay in the emergency room may be shorter than if the staff had to wait hours for a qualified interpreter.

Zitter comes to the decision that she would interpret only if the client's immediate safety was at stake or for a short time until a qualified interpreter arrived. She would also frequently remind all parties involved that she is not an interpreter and is only acting to facilitate communication for a short time.

To continue to follow the model suggested above, a clinician might continue to monitor whether the decision "feels right" as she attempts to implement it, and she might make adjustments or changes in her decision if untoward results seem to be occurring (e.g., if the client seems to be becoming suspicious of her, or if the staff seem to be consistently misunderstanding the patient). She could also monitor the decision by discussing it with the client, before she makes her decision, during the stint in the emergency room, and later after the crisis is past. She could also discuss the situation and its outcomes with colleagues or supervisors for additional feedback on her decision-making process and its consequences.

CONSULTATION

The importance of consultation in any clinically, legally, or ethically ambiguous situation is well known (Pettifor, 1996; Bennett, Bryant, VandenBos, & Greenwood, 1990; Canter, Bennett, Jones, & Nagy, 1994). Whether a rule-based or a process-based approach to ethical decision making is used, an objective, neutral, yet knowledgeable consultant can facilitate the process and assist the clinician to set aside personal biases and blind spots that may impede decision making. For clinicians in Deafness, such support may be especially needed, since ethical and clinical problems are often unusually complex, and the roles the clinician is expected to play can be stressful and demanding (Zitter, 1996; Harvey, 1996; Leigh, this volume). Many factors impede consultation. One is that the small agencies that serve deaf people often lack budgets for consultation and may have very few staff. Trusted colleagues may themselves be involved in the case or may have other relationships with the client that make it difficult for them to serve as consultants. Outside one's circle of coworkers, it can be difficult to find a professional network of peers or supervisors who understand issues in Deafness sufficiently well to give accurate advice when the client is deaf. While most professional associations are helpful in putting members in touch with experts in various ethical issues, these experts often are not acquainted with the special issues that arise in the Deaf community or the social, educational, and access factors that influence treatment with deaf clients.

A third impediment arises from the intrinsic nature of situations that pose ethical dilemmas. When we have an ethical dilemma, *we don't know what to do*. We are afraid of doing "the wrong thing." In such a situation, it is hard to feel confident in oneself or one's decisions. We may feel the situation has a potential for embarrassing us or exposing some area of ignorance or malfeasance. These feelings commonly arise during situations in which ethical dilemmas occur and make it difficult to ask for help or to expose one's potential errors as a therapist to outside evaluation. The small world of Deafness can magnify this concern, as a colleague may also be a friend, relative, in-law, etc. The vulnerable position of the clinician works against getting consultation when it is most needed. Courage and advance planning are both necessary.

A therapist who has established a network of trusted colleagues (whether local or national) and who has frequent contact with these other professionals (in person, by phone, or by Internet) will find it easier to seek consultation and advice when an ethically troubling situation arises in clinical practice. Establishment of ongoing peer supervision groups, or dyads, can assure that support is available when an ethical dilemma arises. Knowing the specialties of various professionals in the community can also help with finding advice quickly when a difficult ethical problem occurs. The establishment of professional-to-professional "help lines" within local professional organizations can be one way to have a readily available list of experts willing to provide consultation for colleagues regarding an area of special interest.

Finally, the reader is encouraged to use the clinical cases presented in this book as fodder for further discussion with your colleagues. Ongoing discussion of these issues among professionals in the field will contribute to the development of further ethical concepts, sensitivities, and applications in Deafness for the continuing improvement of services to deaf individuals and the Deaf community.

REFERENCES

Adelman, J. (1990). Necessary risks and ethical constraints: Self-monitoring on values and biases. In H. Lerman & N. Porter (Eds.), *Feminist ethics in psychotherapy* (pp. 113–122). New York: Springer.

American Counseling Association. (1995). *ACA code of ethics and standards of practice.* [Brochure]. Alexandria, VA: Author.

American Psychological Association. (1992). Ethical principles of psychologists and code of conduct. *American Psychologist, 47,* 1597–1611.

American Psychological Association. (1993). Guidelines for providers of psychological services to ethnic, linguistic, and culturally diverse populations. *American Psychologist, 48*, 45–48.

American Psychiatric Association. (1994*). Diagnostic and statistical manual of mental health disorders* (4th ed.). Washington, DC: Author.

American Psychiatric Association. (1995). *The principles of medical ethics with annotations especially applicable to psychiatry.* [Brochure]. Washington, DC: Author.

Anderson, G., & Grace, C. (1991). The Black deaf adolescent: A diverse and underserved population. *Volta Review, 93*, 73–86.

Beauchamp, T., & Childress, J. (2001). *Principles of biomedical ethics* (5th ed.). Oxford: Oxford University Press.

Bennett, B., Bryant, B., VandenBos, G., & Greenwood, A. (1990). *Professional liability and risk management.* Washington, DC: American Psychological Association.

Berman, J. (1990). The problems of overlapping relationships in the political community. In H. Lerman & N. Porter (Eds.), *Feminist ethics in psychotherapy* (pp. 106–110). New York: Springer.

Bersoff, D., & Koeppl, P. (1995). The relation between ethical codes and moral principles. In D. Bersoff (Ed.), *Ethical conflicts in psychology* (pp. 132–134). Washington, DC: American Psychological Association.

Biaggio, M., & Greene, B. (1995). Overlapping/dual relationships. In E. Rave & C. Larsen (Eds.), *Ethical decision making in therapy: Feminist perspectives* (pp. 91–123). New York: Guilford Press.

Brown, L. (1991). Ethical issues in feminist therapy: Selected topics. *Psychology of Women Quarterly, 15*, 323–336.

Brown, L. (1994). *Subversive dialogs: Theory in feminist therapy.* New York: Basic Books.

Bruyere, S., & O'Keefe, J. (Eds.). (1993). *Implications of the Americans with Disabilities Act for psychology.* Washington, DC: American Psychological Association.

Canadian Psychological Association. (1991). *Canadian code of ethics for psychologists* (Rev. ed.). Old Chelsea, Quebec: Canadian Psychological Association.

Canadian Psychological Association, Committee on Ethics. (1986). Code of ethics. *Highlights, 8*(1), 6E–12E.

Canter, M., Bennett, B., Jones, S., & Nagy, T. (1994). *Ethics for psychologists: A commentary on the APA Ethics Code.* Washington, DC: American Psychological Association.

Cerbone, A. (1991). The effects of political activism on psychotherapy: A case study. In C. Silverstein (Ed.), *Gays, lesbians, and their therapists* (pp. 40–51). New York: Norton.

Christiansen, J., & Leigh, I. W. (2002). *Cochlear implants in children: Ethics and choices.* Washington, DC: Gallaudet University Press.

Christensen, K., & Delgado, G. (Eds.). (1993). *Multicultural issues in deafness.* White Plains, NY: Longman.

Cohen, O., Fischgrund, J., & Redding, R. (1990). Deaf children from ethnic, linguistic, and racial minority backgrounds: An overview. *American Annals of the Deaf, 135*, 67–73.

Crewe, N. (1994). Implications of the Americans With Disabilities Act for the training of psychologists. In S. Bruyere & J. O'Keefe (Eds.), *Implications of the Americans with Disabilities Act for psychology* (pp. 15–23). Washington, DC: American Psychological Association.

Deaton, A. (1996). Ethical issues in pediatric rehabilitation: Exploring an uneven terrain. *Rehabilitation Psychology, 41,* 33–52.

Eberlein, L. (1987). Introducing ethics to beginning psychologists: A problem-solving approach. *Professional Psychology: Research and Practice, 18,* 353–359.

Ebert, B. (1997). Dual-relationship prohibitions: A concept whose time should never have come. *Applied and Preventive Psychology, 6,* 137–156.

Faulkner, K., & Faulkner, T. (1997). Managing multiple relationships in rural communities: Neutrality and boundary violations. *Clinical Psychology: Science and Practice, 4,* 225–234.

Feminist Therapy Institute. (1987). *Feminist therapy code of ethics.* Denver: Author.

Gartrell, N. (1994). Boundaries in lesbian therapist-client relationships. In B. Greene & B. Herek (Eds.), *Lesbian and gay psychology: Theory, research, and clinical applications* (pp. 98–117). Thousand Oaks, CA: Sage.

Gates, K., & Speare, K. (1990). Overlapping relationships in rural communities. In H. Lerman & N. Porter (Eds.), *Feminist ethics in psychotherapy* (pp. 97–101). New York: Springer.

Glickman, N. (1986). Cultural identity, deafness, and mental health. *Journal of Rehabilitation of the Deaf, 20,* 1–10.

Glickman, N., & Harvey, M. (Eds.). (1996). *Culturally affirmative psychotherapy with deaf persons.* Mahwah, NJ: Erlbaum.

Gutman, V., & Gibbins, S. (1991). Training in psychology and deafness. In D. Watson & M. Taff-Watson (Eds.), *At the crossroads: A celebration of diversity* (pp. 173–182). Proceedings of the 12th Biennial Conference of the American Deafness and Rehabilitation Association, New York. Little Rock, AR: American Deafness and Rehabilitation Association.

Haas, L., & Malouf, J. (1989). *Keeping up the good work: A practitioner's guide to mental health ethics.* Sarasota, FL: Professional Resource Exchange.

Haldeman, D. (1994). The practice and ethics of sexual orientation conversion therapy. *Journal of Consulting and Clinical Psychology, 62*(2), 221–227.

Hargrove, D. (1982). The rural psychologist as generalist: A challenge for professional identity. *Professional Psychology, 13,* 302–308.

Hargrove, D. (1986). Ethical issues in rural mental health practice. *Professional Psychology: Research and Practice, 17,* 20–23.

Harvey, M. (1996). Utilization of traumatic transference by a hearing therapist. In N. Glickman & M. Harvey (Eds.), *Culturally affirmative psychotherapy with deaf persons* (pp. 155–169). Mahwah, NJ: Erlbaum.

Hayes, L., Adams, M. A., & Rydeen, K. (1994). Ethics, choice and value. In L. Hayes, G. Hayes, S. Moore, & P. Ghezzi (Eds.), *Ethical issues in developmental disabilities* (pp. 11–39). Reno, NV: Context Press.

Herlihy, B., & Corey, G. (Eds.). (1996). *ACA ethical standards casebook* (5th ed.). Alexandria, VA: American Counseling Association.

Hill, M., Glaser, K., & Harden, J. (1995). A feminist model for ethical decision making. In E. Rave & C. Larsen (Eds.), *Ethical decision making in therapy: Feminist perspectives* (pp. 18–37). New York: Guilford Press.

Jeffrey, M., & Reeve, R. (1978). Community mental health services in rural areas: Some practical issues. *Community Mental Health Journal, 14,* 54–62.

Jennings, F. (1992). Ethics in rural practice. *Psychotherapy in Private Practice*, *10*, 85–104.

Johnson, R., & Liddell, S. (1990). The value of ASL in the education of deaf children. In M. Garretson (Ed.), *Eyes, hands, and voices: Communication issues among deaf people* (pp. 59–64). A Deaf American Monograph, No. 40. Silver Spring, MD: National Association of the Deaf.

Kerkhoff, T., Hanson, S., Guenther, R., & Ashkanazi, G. (1997). The foundation and application of ethical principles in rehabilitation psychology. *Rehabilitation Psychology*, *42*(1), 17–30.

Kitchener, K. (1984). Intuition, critical evaluation, and ethical principles: The foundations for ethical decisions in counseling psychology. *The Counseling Psychologist*, *12*, 43–55.

Kitchener, K. (1986). Teaching applied ethics in counselor education: An integration of psychological processes and philosophical analysis. *Journal of Counseling and Development*, *64*(5), 306–310.

Kitchener, K. (1988). Dual role relationships: What makes them so problematic? *Journal of Counseling and Development*, *67*, 217–221.

Koocher, G., & Keith-Spiegel, P. (1998). *Ethics in psychology: Professional standards and cases,* (2nd ed.). New York: Oxford University Press.

Lane, H. (1992). *The mask of benevolence: Disabling the Deaf community*. New York: Knopf.

Leigh, I. W. (Ed.). (1999). *Psychotherapy with deaf clients from diverse groups*. Washington DC: Gallaudet University Press.

Leigh, I., Corbett, C., Gutman, V., & Morere, D. (1996). Providing psychological services to deaf individuals: A response to new perceptions of diversity. *Professional Psychology: Research and Practice*, *27*, 364–371.

Liburd, R., & Rothblum, E. (1995). The medical model. In E. Rave & C. Larsen (Eds.), *Ethical decision making in therapy: Feminist perspectives* (pp. 177–201). New York: Guilford Press.

Menzano, S. (1995). *Ethical issues in conducting therapy with deaf lesbians, gay men, and other sexual minorities*. Unpublished manuscript.

Moores, D. (1991). The great debates: When, how, and what to teach deaf children. *American Annals of the Deaf*, *136*(1), 35–37.

National Association of Social Workers. (1996). *Code of ethics*. Washington, DC: Author.

National Center for Law and Deafness. (1994). *ADA questions and answers for health care providers*. Washington, DC: Gallaudet University.

Padden, C., & Humphries, T. (1988). *Deaf in America: Voices from a culture*. Cambridge: Harvard University Press.

Pettifor, J. (1996). Maintaining professional conduct in daily practice. In L. Bass, S. DeMers, J. Ogloff, C. Peterson, J. Pettifor, R. Reaves, T. Retfalvi, N. Simon, C. Sinclair, & R. Tipton (Eds.), *Professional conduct and discipline in psychology* (pp. 91–100). Washington, DC: American Psychological Association.

Pollard, R. (1992). Cross-cultural ethics in the conduct of deafness research. *Rehabilitation Psychology*, *37*, 87–101.

Pollard, R. (1996). Professional psychology and deaf people: The emergence of a discipline. *American Psychologist*, *51*, 389–396.

Raifman, L., & Vernon, M. (1996). Important implications for psychologists of the Americans with Disabilities Act: Case in point, the patient who is deaf. *Professional Psychology: Research and Practice*, *27*, 372–377.

Rave, E., & Larsen, C. (1995). Context of feminist therapy ethics. In E. Rave & C. Larsen (Eds.), *Ethical decision making in therapy: Feminist perspectives* (pp. 1–17). New York: Guilford Press.

Rosewater, L. (1990). Public advocacy. In H. Lerman & N. Porter (Eds.), *Feminist ethics in psychotherapy* (pp. 229–238). New York: Springer.

Sacks, O. (1989). *Seeing voices: A journey into the world of the Deaf.* Berkeley: University of California Press.

Sears, V. (1990a). Ethics in small minority communities. In H. Lerman & N. Porter (Eds.) *Feminist ethics in psychotherapy* (pp. 204–213). New York: Springer.

Sears, V. (1990b). On being an "only" one. In H. Lerman & N. Porter (Eds.), *Feminist ethics in psychotherapy* (pp. 102–105). New York: Springer.

Smith, A. (1990). Working within the Lesbian community: The dilemma of overlapping relationships. In H. Lerman & N. Porter (Eds.), *Feminist ethics in psychotherapy* (pp. 92–101). New York: Springer.

Smith, A., & Douglas, M. (1990). Empowerment as an ethical imperative. In H. Lerman & N. Porter (Eds.), *Feminist ethics in psychotherapy* (pp. 43–50). New York: Springer.

Sobel, S. (1992). Small town practice of psychotherapy: Ethical and personal dilemmas. *Psychotherapy in Private Practice, 10*, 61–69.

Stockman, A. (1990). Dual relationships in rural mental health practice: An ethical dilemma. *Journal of Rural Community Psychology, 2*, 31–45.

Sue, S. (1996). Ethical issues in multicultural counseling. In B. Herlihy & G. Corey (Eds.), *ACA ethical standards casebook* (5th ed., pp. 193–204), Alexandria, VA: American Counseling Association.

Uswatte, G., & Elliott, T. (1997). Ethnic and minority issues in rehabilitation psychology. *Rehabilitation Psychology, 42*(1), 61–71.

Van Cleve, J., & Crouch, B. (1989). *A place of their own.* Washington, DC: Gallaudet University Press.

Wagenfeld, M., Murray, J., Mohatt, D., & DeBruyn, J. (1993). *Mental health and rural America: 1980–1993: An overview and annotated bibliography.* Office of Rural Health Policy, Health Resources and Services Administration; Office of Rural Mental Health Research, National Institute of Mental Health; U.S. Department of Health and Human Services, Public Health Service.

Webster, D. (1995). Reproduction/health issues. In E. Rave & C. Larsen (Eds.), *Ethical decision making in therapy: Feminist perspectives* (pp. 153–176). New York: Guilford Press.

Wegener, S. (1996). The rehabilitation ethic and ethics. *Rehabilitation Psychology, 41*, 5–17.

Welfel, E., & Kitchener, K. (1992). Introduction to the special section: Ethics education—An agenda for the '90s. *Professional Psychology: Research and Practice, 23*, 179–181.

Zea, M., Belgrave, F., Garcia, J., & Quezada, T. (1997). Socioeconomic and cultural factors in rehabilitation of Latinos with disabilities. In J. Garcia & M. C. Zea (Eds.), *Psychological interventions and research with Latino populations* (pp. 217–234). Boston: Allyn and Bacon.

Zitter, S. (1996). Report from the front lines: Balancing multiple roles of a deafness therapist. In N. Glickman & M. Harvey (Eds.), *Culturally affirmative psychotherapy with deaf persons* (pp. 169–246). Mahwah, NJ: Erlbaum.

3

Law and Ethics in Mental Health and Deafness

William P. McCrone

Therapists working with deaf clients can and should achieve a basic level of legal literacy in dealing with the unique intersections of ethics and law in therapy with deaf people (McCrone, 1988). The most likely future negligence/malpractice suits by deaf clients against therapists, their supervisors, and human service agencies will be based on alleged ethical violations in areas such as communication and clinical competence, dual relationships, failure to obtain meaningful informed consent, the negligent hiring of unqualified interpreters in therapy, as well as testing and diagnostic errors that cause client harm. The irony is that these suits may be propelled by naive efforts by some hearing therapists who think they are complying with or advancing the goals of the Americans With Disabilities Act (ADA) (Bruyere & O'Keefe, 1994).

This chapter explores a number of issues surrounding the intersection of ethics and law, including the special legal significance of the therapist's code of ethics and its underlying principles; the four essential elements of a "prima facie" (i.e., essential, basic) negligence/malpractice case against a therapist; deafness-related code of ethics case studies to illustrate the elements of potential negligence/malpractice suits against therapists; ethical code clarifications and addenda in serving deaf people; what it means to be a qualified interpreter in mental health settings when that is the only alternative; and ethical teletherapy technology and the training of specialists and subspecialists (e.g., addictions, pastoral counseling, gerontology, child abuse/neglect, cochlear implant adjustments, psychopharmacology) in therapy with deaf people (Miller, 1998). It also offers a basic reference list and several websites on law and ethics for mental health professionals serving deaf people.

KNOW YOUR CODE OF ETHICS AND ITS FUNDAMENTAL ETHICAL PRINCIPLES

Too often, our relationship as therapists to our code of ethics is mechanical and superficial. We are attracted to the notion of an ethical cookbook or checklist. Students often say, "Just tell us the rule and we'll follow it." However, students must learn what seasoned therapists know, which is that all codes of ethics in mental health professions are wonderful, incomplete, evolving documents written by committees.

Codes of ethics can be maddeningly vague in one section and all too specific in other sections. Some codes are brief; others are encyclopedic. Codes of ethics used by therapists are notoriously ineffective in solving conflicts between code sections and setting priorities among code principles. Because they reflect surveys of practitioners' ethical dilemmas, related state statutes, and lawsuits, the codes often tell us more about the past than the present or the future. For example, the "duty to warn" rule regarding specific client threats and identifiable potential victims established by *Tarasoff v. Regents of the University of California* (1976) has been codified in ethical codes and state laws, but those ethical rules and state laws were not in place when the University of California psychologist needed them. Current therapist codes of ethics still do not adequately guide the therapist dealing with clients who claim to be purposely infecting unnamed victims and their sexual partners with deadly diseases.

Codes of ethics are always catching up with practice. For this reason, most experienced therapists know that a commitment to ethics begins with a grounding in the fundamental principles that are the "roots" of all human services codes of ethics. Those principles are nonmaleficence, beneficence, client autonomy, fidelity, and justice (Thompson, 1990). Ethical code language evolves and branches in every direction from these five "roots."

Since the word *deaf* does not appear in any therapist code of ethics, negligence/malpractice suits brought by deaf clients are likely to be resolved at the code principles level rather than in the code itself.

Nonmaleficence

Nonmaleficence, or "do no harm," is appropriately the first ethical principle. Nonmaleficence is not a platitude, particularly with deaf clients. Well-intentioned and not so well-intentioned therapists have harmed deaf clients through pseudoscientific assumptions ("deafness is a pathology," "deaf mothers are unfit," "deaf parents are unfit to raise or adopt hearing children"), invalid psychodiagnostics ("deaf people are innately paranoid"), inappropriate therapeutic interventions (e.g., an inappropriate assignment to a hearing Gestalt encounter group), and through early terminations. Some not so well-intentioned therapists are sexual predators (Chesler, 1997).

Beneficence

Beneficence means we work to promote the welfare of the client. But the welfare of the client is not always easy to determine. In the service of deaf clients there are no greater assaults on beneficence than paternalism, the encouragement of dependency, and ignorance about the existential phenomenology of deafness and the Deaf community experience. It means fostering the competency of the client. Beneficence means a strong commitment to clinical supervision and our own professional continuing education.

Client Autonomy

Client autonomy, the ultimate expression of respect for the client as well as his or her personal and cultural differences, means the therapist aspires to neutrality in facilitating client adjustment goals, insights, choices, and problem solving. Our respect for clients includes our respect for client choices and strategies we think are likely to fail. We leave our baggage at the door. Hearing, deaf, hard of hearing, and children of deaf adults (CODA) therapists, particularly those working without supervision, can have different but equally harmful baggage in working with deaf clients. Meaningful informed consent, including an effective explanation of the limits of confidentiality and treatment options is the central expression of client autonomy.

Fidelity

Fidelity simply means therapists keep their promises. We accurately represent our skills and ourselves. The credibility of our profession rests on keeping client information confidential, particularly in the Deaf community.

Let me divert your attention for a moment. One of the stepping-stones of legal literacy for therapists is knowing that *confidentiality* is a therapeutic term, not a legal term. *Privilege* is a legal term. They are not the same.

Privilege, which belongs to and can be waived by the client, varies from state to state. It is a begrudging judicial waiver of the requirement for the therapist to testify or produce records in court proceedings because it is thought to be in the interests of society to protect certain key relationships. The courts reason that preserving confidentiality in certain key relationships (spouses, attorney–client, doctor–patient, news reporter–source, clergy–

confessor, therapist–client) serves a greater problem-solving good in society than does subpoenaing therapist testimony and records in a particular case.

But there have been significant recent judicial assaults on the therapist–client privilege. One such close call was the U.S. Supreme Court decision *Jaffee v. Redmond et al* (1996). The case involved a white policewoman who sought counseling from a licensed social worker after the policewoman killed a fleeing African American suspect. The family of the deceased suspect challenged the psychotherapist–patient privilege, demanding the social worker's case notes about her work with the policewoman after the shooting. The family hoped to find case note evidence of the policewoman's racist motives. The social worker refused to turn over her case notes.

Like all cases that get to the U.S. Supreme Court, this case involved the relative merit of two legitimate views. Here the question was whether the psychotherapist–patient privilege outweighed a family's right to know if their son was killed by a racist. The psychotherapist–patient privilege won out in this case, but a strongly worded dissent by Justices Scalia and Rehnquist may prevail in future therapist–client privilege cases. Privilege aside, this case shows that the law and professional ethics can collide. Would you have refused to turn over therapy notes, even incriminating notes about a racist police officer/client, risking jail for contempt of court?

Justice

Returning to fundamental ethical principles, the principle of justice means that our professions are committed to the fair distribution of therapeutic services, to deaf children, their parents and families, deaf senior citizens, straight and gay deaf people, deaf prisoners, people who are deaf and blind, deaf people with cochlear implants, rich and poor deaf people, signing and non-signing deaf people, and deaf people of every color and culture. Few communities in the United States have had less justice in the fair distribution of therapeutic services than deaf people (McCrone, 1994).

The emergence of specialists in counseling and therapy with deaf people was the product of (a) Deaf community frustration with harm caused by unqualified, generic therapists working with deaf people; and (b) the neglect of the therapeutic professions regarding the principle of justice (McCrone & Beach, 1994).

UNDERSTANDING THE ETHICAL PRINCIPLES AND THE CODE OF ETHICS IN NEGLIGENCE/MALPRACTICE LAWSUITS

It is essential that therapists working with deaf people know that the ethical code and its foundational principles are the single most important reference points in civil action negligence/malpractice lawsuits alleging that the therapist's act or omission caused client harm. Conversely, the key to prudent legal risk management in therapy with deaf people is mastering the code of ethics and its fundamental principles, and understanding the elements that must be proven in a negligence/malpractice lawsuit (Bennett, Bryant, VandenBos, & Greenwood, 1990).

There are four elements that must be proven for the client to win a negligence/malpractice lawsuit against a therapist. If only three of the four elements are proven, the lawsuit is over. It is thrown out. We must clarify two terms before going on to the elements. Negligence and malpractice suits require evidence of the same four prima facie elements, but these suits differ in two ways (Bednar, Bednar, Lambert, & Waite, 1991).

First, anyone can be sued for negligence. You risk a negligence suit if you drive a car carelessly and harm a pedestrian. But you can only be sued for malpractice if you are a professional. Markers for a profession include licensure, certification, and a code of ethics. The second thing to remember about the distinction between negligence and malpractice is the decision question to the jury. The questions are different in important ways.

In a negligence lawsuit (e.g., careless driver hits child), the question to the jury is "Was this act or omission [failure to act] the behavior of a reasonable person under the circumstances?" "Reasonable person" means what the jury thinks it means. "Under the circumstances," is an essential part of the question to the jury because the expectations of the "reasonable person" differ according to the circumstances. Was the road icy? Was there fog? Was the child a suicidal, intoxicated teenager who threw himself in front of the car?

In a malpractice lawsuit we move to a "reasonable professional" standard that is framed by that professional's code of ethics. The jury question in a malpractice lawsuit is "Did this practitioner's act or omission fall within the boundaries of acceptable practice in this community?"

A careful comparison of the two jury questions again should (a) illustrate the centrality of your code of ethics in a malpractice lawsuit; and (b) show you why it can be easier to lose a negligence lawsuit than it is to lose a malpractice lawsuit. What are "the boundaries of acceptable practice" in your profession? There is much more leeway for an adverse jury decision against the defendant with the negligence jury question than a malpractice jury question. Unless the deaf plaintiff can show a clear ethical violation ("boundaries of acceptable practice"), the malpractice jury question is much narrower, and therefore frequently more difficult to prove because of the "in this community" language.

There is an important link between the malpractice jury question and professional liability insurance. Therapist liability insurance covers only unintentional client harm caused by the therapist within the boundaries of acceptable practice as framed by the therapist's ethical code, relevant law, and published agency policies.

Does the "in this community" part of the malpractice jury question help or hurt the deaf client allegedly harmed by the therapist if all the community therapists are incompetent with deaf clients?

Two final clarifications before moving on to the prima facie elements in negligence and malpractice suits. The burden of proof in every element is on the person who initiates the lawsuit, the plaintiff, the person who contends he or she was harmed by the defendant psychotherapist. In most jurisdictions, it is also the plaintiff's strategic decision whether to have his or her case decided by a judge or a jury. In cases involving complex legal and factual issues, some plaintiffs and their attorneys will prefer that a judge decide the case. On the other hand, some plaintiffs/clients and their attorneys will feel that a jury will be more understanding and/or sympathetic in deciding their case.

The plaintiff has the burden of showing all four of the following prima facie elements in a negligence or malpractice case.

Duty of Reasonable Care

The attorney for the deaf client alleging harm caused by the therapist has the burden of proving that, through an explicit or implicit exchange of expectations, there was a therapist–client relationship. Then the attorney for the client must show that the therapist had a "duty of reasonable care" in working with the client. The parameters of that "duty of reasonable care" are found in the therapist's code of ethics.

I emphasized the principles underlying the code of ethics earlier because many of the negligence/malpractice suits brought against therapists do not hinge on a specific rule or standard in the ethical code. If the alleged harm to the client involved a specific rule or standard of the code of ethics, a lawsuit would have been far less likely. Specific Tarasoff "duty to warn" language was not part of therapist ethical codes until after the Tarasoff lawsuit. My point is that it is more likely than not that a negligence/malpractice lawsuit against a therapist alleged to have harmed a deaf client will be decided on the principles level.

Breach of the Duty of Reasonable Care

The attorney for the deaf client alleging harm caused by the therapist has the burden of showing that the therapist "breached" his or her duty of reasonable care in working with the client. That is most effectively done when the client's attorney shows that the therapist violated an ethical code rule or principle (e.g., dual relationship, competency, the negligent communication error regarding informed consent, working without clinical supervision).

The attorney for the deaf client alleging harm caused by the therapist will generally try to prove this breach of duty of reasonable care to the judge or jury by using an "expert witness," to make the complicated ethical code or ethical principle violation clear to the judge or jury. The expert witness for the deaf client could be a professor who teaches ethics from a respected training program in mental health counseling, clinical social work, or clinical psychology with deaf people. Juries are often very responsive to professors who have everyday experience explaining complicated concepts in the classroom. Along the same lines, the deaf client alleging harm by the therapist may have a strategic credibility advantage using an experienced deaf expert witness.

Who qualifies as an expert witness? In short, an expert witness can be anyone the judge allows to be an expert witness. But most often, the judge will consider the academic background and work experience of the proffered expert, as well as his or her familiarity with the scholarly literature on ethics and therapy with deaf people.

Keep in mind that expert witnesses can be offered on both sides of the ethical question. You may recall that the criminal trial of Ronald Reagan's would-be assassin, John Hinckley, involved several expert witnesses on each side of the question of Hinckley's sanity and criminal culpability. You may wonder if one or more expert witnesses on both sides of an ethical/malpractice/civil case or a sanity/criminal case are confusing for the jury. The courts have great confidence in the jury's ability to sort out credible and noncredible expert witness testimony.

Causation

If the attorney for the deaf client alleging harm caused by the therapist can show a duty of reasonable care, and a breach of that duty, he or she must still show that the therapist's act or omission was the "cause" of the harm to the deaf client. The central question in this evidence category is "Was it foreseeable that the therapist's act (e.g., taking on a deaf client he/she cannot communicate with effectively) or failure to act (e.g., duty to warn a potential victim of your client's violence) would cause the harm or injury to the client (and/or a third party)?" "But for" the therapist's negligence, would the client have been harmed?

The insightful reader is already compiling a list of risk management rules for avoiding ethics-related and other kinds of negligence/malpractice suits against therapists. For example, you should have a detailed, thoughtful understanding of your code of ethics and its principles. Second, always have clinical supervision. Third, always consider the foreseeability that your acts or omissions might cause harm to your client or a third party. Use client process notes to document these rules.

A determination of causation by the jury is very tricky. There is no formula beyond the causation question given above. The circumstances of every case differ enormously, as I will illustrate in the case studies. How will the jury interpret the word *foreseeability*?

Let me illustrate the foreseeability problem in two ways.

Imagine 10 people standing near the tracks waiting for a train. Person 1 playfully pushes person 2, who falls on person 3, who trips on person 4, et cetera, until person 10 falls in front of a moving train. Was it foreseeable that person 1's playful push would have killed or injured person 10? What if all 10 people were children? What if there were 50 people rather than 10? What if it was raining? What if? What if? Even if person 1 technically acknowledges that his playful action set the tragedy in motion, he could say, "It wasn't foreseeable to me that my playful act would hurt or kill person 10." What will the jury make of this regarding causation?

Still considering the topic of jury interpretation of causation and foreseeability, what if a skilled hearing therapist with a strong commitment to the ADA, very basic sign skills, and several deaf distant cousins, takes on a deaf client who uses only home signs? Because of significant communication problems all around, the game but struggling hearing therapist misses the extent of the client's drug abuse and depression. The client attempts suicide between the second and third appointments. What would you make of this situation on the foreseeability issue? Was it foreseeable that the therapist would cause a potential suicide in this case because he violated his own ethical rules regarding his competence to work with deaf people and his obligation to refer the deaf client to a competent therapist?

Would it make any difference to you as a jury member if this was the only therapist with any sign skills within five hundred miles? A thousand miles? Does it make any difference to you that the client used homesigns rather than American Sign Language? Would it make any difference to you as a juror if the therapist agreed to take on the deaf client because a judge offered the client a therapy option as an alternative to jail? Would it have made a difference if the hearing therapist retained a qualified interpreter? An unqualified interpreter? What if the hearing therapist relied on the deaf client's hearing mother to interpret? Given the history of drug abuse and depression, might the client have attempted suicide had he never met the hearing therapists? I could go on and on offering details or nuances that might influence a jury about causation and foreseeability.

Damages

The plaintiff has the final burden of showing that the alleged harm caused by the defendant resulted in damages. If the first three required prima facie elements are proven, but there are no damages, the case is thrown out.

Did the deaf plaintiff lose a job and income because of the therapist's invalid, incompetent projective and IQ testing? Did a sexual relationship with the predatory therapist cause the deaf plaintiff a divorce and significant emotional damage? Did the deaf client kill him- or herself because the therapist hired an incompetent, unethical interpreter who revealed private client information to the community? Might the addicted deaf client have not incurred the cost of hospitalization if the unqualified therapist had referred him to a qualified therapist in a timely manner? Might the depressed deaf plaintiff with minimal English skills have not overdosed on the Zoloft prescribed by a psychiatrist who communicated by written notes?

CASE STUDIES

For each of the following case studies, consider how the prima facie elements can be applied to

1. assess the legal-ethical status of the therapist in each of the four elements of the malpractice suit.
2. find the specific ethical code or ethical principle issue(s) likely to be raised by the deaf client's attorney and expert witnesses.
3. consider how you might have advised the therapist about reconciling practice, supervision, ethics, and law so the malpractice suit might have been avoided.

Case 1

Brad is a 51-year-old, recently divorced, deaf, licensed psychologist. He is a strong advocate for the rights of deaf people. Brad is a charismatic and controversial leader in great demand as a consultant and lecturer. Most recently, he has led the fight against cochlear implants for deaf children. While Brad enjoys all of this adulation, his extensive lecture travels leave him exhausted and leave his deaf clients with no one to contact in an emergency. It is sometimes difficult for Brad, some of Brad's colleagues, and his clients to separate out their perceptions of his political advocacy and his therapeutic work.

After Brad's divorce, he moved to a mid-sized town for a fresh start. He knew very few people in town, hearing or deaf. But the town had a school for the deaf and enough potential deaf adult clients to supplement his lecture/consulting income.

Brad's accomplishments stand in stark contrast to his background. He was the only deaf child in a very religious hearing family that could not communicate with him. Brad was a bright child who was enrolled in eight different K–12 public schools because of his father's frequent military transfers. He never had sign training or interpreters in school. Brad only blossomed and focused when a hometown vocational rehabilitation counselor who picked up on Brad's potential referred him to Gallaudet College.

Brad has essentially worked without clinical supervision since earning his PhD. He is among a handful of highly qualified deaf therapists in the United States. Brad's experience with hearing supervisors who use interpreters and know little about Deaf culture has been negative. Similarly, Brad struggles to keep up with his licensure maintenance continuing education requirements. He still experiences endless hassles arranging for interpreters for these continuing education workshops. Because of the low-level reading skills of most of his deaf clients, Brad does not use a written informed consent form.

Perhaps because of Brad's postdivorce vulnerability and loneliness, he became very close to a 24-year-old, cocaine-addicted, deaf female client named Eileen. He often ran into Eileen at social events in the local Deaf community. Through their dream analysis and projective testing work during therapy, Eileen discovered what she thought to be repressed memories of sexual abuse by her hearing, widowed, non-signing, alcoholic father. Perhaps as a result of his own difficult childhood with non-signing hearing parents, Brad's face flushed with anger at the thought of Eileen's abuse experience.

Because he had not explained his legal and ethical duties to report child abuse at the beginning of the counseling relationship, Brad had to backtrack quickly to help his naive client understand his responsibilities.

Eileen begged Brad not to report the memories of sexual abuse. She said she never would have brought up her repressed memories had she known it would cause problems for her elderly, frail father recently diagnosed with Alzheimer's disease.

Concerned that Eileen would terminate therapy in a community where there were no other signing therapists, Brad agreed not to report Eileen's abuse memories. He thought the hearing police might not understand. Perhaps his dream analysis and projective testing work with Eileen evoked false memories of abuse. What was the impact of Eileen's long-term addiction and depression on her dreams and her memories? Were Brad's sympathy for, affection for, and personal identification with Eileen clouding his ability to spot organic or psychotic markers?

As Eileen left her meeting with Brad one evening, they hugged and kissed. Brad made nothing of this, thinking that physical affection was part of Deaf culture. But Brad also recognized that he was very attracted to Eileen, her vulnerability, and her adoration for him. Since it was the end of his day, Brad decided to postpone writing his case notes until the next day.

He never got to it.

That same night, Eileen committed the details of her session with Brad to her diary. In rough notes, she worried that she was wrong about her repressed memories of abuse. Was she simply trying to please Brad, a therapist who had a special commitment to projective techniques? She was found dead of a drug overdose the next morning.

After the police handed over Eileen's diary to her family members, the family retained a skilled attorney to sue Brad for malpractice. They alleged that Brad's ethical violations were the cause of Eileen's death.

Let's go through the elements of a negligence/malpractice suit and the malpractice jury question to determine where Brad stands. How might you have advised Brad if you were his supervisor?

Duty of Reasonable Care

A lawyer representing Eileen's family would have little difficulty showing that Brad and Eileen had an implicit therapist-client relationship. An exchange of expectations occurred. The lawyer for Eileen's family would also have little trouble finding ethical code language, starting with the preamble of the American Psychological Association's (APA) "Ethical Principles of Psychologists and Code of Conduct" (1992).

Breach of the Duty of Reasonable Care

Brad may argue each point, but the attorney for Eileen's family will have no trouble using the APA code to argue that Brad breached his duty of reasonable care with Eileen regarding multiple relationships [Sec. 1.17], exploitative relationships [Sec. 1.19], record-keeping [Sec. 1.24], informed consent [Sec. 4.02], as well as possibly boundaries of competence [Sec. 1.04] and test interpretation [Sec. 2.02] if there is any hint that Brad's projective training was deficient, or his projective test interpretations were without scientific basis. The attorney for Eileen's family will argue that these acts, these ethical violations, caused Eileen's death. The attorney for the family will argue that it was foreseeable. The APA ethical code and expert witnesses will be used to show that Brad was practicing outside the boundaries of acceptable practice in the community.

Damages

The attorney for Eileen's family has no problem showing that a young life was lost. The family will seek actual damages (i.e., hospital costs, funeral costs, lost income) and punitive damages for pain and suffering, arguing the outrageousness of Brad's professional conduct.

Case 2

Don is a 30-year-old deaf man who has been chronically unemployed for six years. He has just learned that he was rejected for a good paying Internet mail order clerk job two years ago because a hearing consulting psychologist had labeled him as mentally retarded during the pre-employment testing required of all applicants. Because of its small number of employees, this mail order company is not required to comply with Title I of the ADA.

Don is a healthy, highly motivated individual who indicated on his job application that he had earned a high school certificate of attendance. He also documented completion of a noncredit remedial reading course at the local community college.

Working without an interpreter, the psychologist administered the verbal and performance sections of a popular IQ test. When these scores were combined, Don was labeled as a person with mild mental retardation. Based on this assessment of Don's thinking ability, and perhaps some corporate discrimination against deaf job applicants, Don was turned down for the clerk job. In a phone conversation, the employer told Don's hearing parents that Don would have been hired if his IQ score had been higher.

Don was informed by a local attorney that he had no cause of action under the ADA; however, the attorney encouraged Don to sue the consulting psychologist for the malpractice that caused him to lose a substantial income for two years.

Again, go through the elements of a negligence/malpractice suit and the malpractice jury question. Where does the counselor stand? How might you have advised the counselor if you were his supervisor?

Case 3

A large rural state has retained a skilled, hearing, CODA, feminist social worker who is employed at a nonprofit advocacy center for deaf people to provide direct therapy for clients via "teletherapy." Teletherapy is an innovative, cost-effective way to link broadly distributed deaf clients with a qualified therapist by secure computer-connected video cameras and phone lines.

This technique permits more deaf clients to be served by a therapist who now spends very few hours driving from one counseling site to another. After some initial concerns among deaf leaders about privacy and confidentiality were alleviated, the new teletherapy program began.

The social worker provided telecounseling for a 48-year-old deaf woman, Jodi, for about eight weeks, excluding several missed appointments. After a slow start, the teletherapy progressed to include discussions of the client's sexuality and her reports of an emotionally abusive ex-husband who now had custody of their three hearing children.

What could not be seen on the therapist's monitor were the severely bitten fingernails, the dilated pupils, the body odor and poor hygiene, the slight hand tremors, the slash scars on the wrists, the demonic tattoos, the needle tracks on the deaf woman's arms, and her restless leg rocking. The client also made what the therapist thought to be a joke about God and heaven in the television box.

Because the client had been so expressive about her sexuality, ex-husband, and children, the therapist felt the teletherapy was succeeding. Three weeks after the last teletherapy session, the client stabbed her ex-husband with an ice pick, and she was hospitalized for a drug/alcohol overdose.

The client and family members sued the therapist for malpractice alleging that the stabbing and overdose were caused by an unethical therapist who, using the experimental teletherapy to cut costs, missed several key indicators of severe psychopathology. The family also alleged in this malpractice suit that a tape of the teletherapy sessions with Jodi was seen by the therapist's office staff and her graduate feminist therapy class without Jodi's permission.

Once again review the elements of a negligence/malpractice suit and the malpractice jury question. Where does the social worker stand? How might you have advised her if you were her supervisor?

FUTURE DIRECTIONS IN LAW AND ETHICS IN MENTAL HEALTH SERVICES WITH DEAF PEOPLE

Beyond a fundamental understanding of the centrality of professional codes of ethics in deaf client malpractice lawsuits against therapists, it is time to start generating proactive strategies to ensure that deaf mental health clients are served ethically and effectively.

1. The time has come for social workers, psychologists, mental health counselors, and psychiatrists and their graduate training programs to generate and publish addenda to their standard professional ethical codes regarding essential communication and cultural competencies in serving deaf clients.
2. Future amendments to the ADA should clarify that reasonable accommodation in mental health services with deaf clients means direct communication with culturally competent therapists (Harkin, 1991).
3. When direct communication is not currently feasible, we must count on our colleagues in the Registry of Interpreters for the Deaf to require extensive specialist training for interpreters in mental health settings.
4. Deaf community leaders must take the lead in making sure that public and private community mental health service providers know how to use qualified interpreters and know how to refer deaf clients to qualified therapists.

5. The academic community and front-line practitioners must build on this book to develop and publish guidance regarding the ethical-legal nuances of subspecialization in therapy with deaf people.

In closing, 90% of successful therapist liability risk management depends on ethical behavior and good supervision. Therapists working with deaf clients who wish to stay in the mainstream of discussion and case law about law and ethics can use the following web sites:

- Mental & Physical Law Reporter www.abanet.org/disability
- American Psychiatric Association www.psych.org
- American Psychological Association www.apa.org

REFERENCES

Americans With Disabilities Act of 1990, 42 U.S.C.A. §12101 *et seq.* (West, 1993).

Bednar, R. L., Bednar, S. C., Lambert, M. J., & Waite, D. R. (1991). *Psychotherapy with high risk clients.* Pacific Grove, CA: Brooks/Cole.

Bennett, B. W., Bryant, B. K., VandenBos, G. R., & Greenwood, A. (1990). *Professional liability and risk management.* Washington, DC: American Psychological Association.

Bruyere, S. M., & O'Keefe, J. (1994). *Implications of the Americans With Disabilities Act for psychology.* New York: Springer.

Chesler, P. (1997). *Women and madness.* New York: Four Walls Eight Windows.

Harkin, T. (1991). Drug abuse and prevention: Equal access for deaf children. In F. White, W. P. McCrone, C. L. Trotter (Eds.), *Drug and alcohol abuse prevention with deaf and hard of hearing students.* (Vol. 1, p. 36). Washington, DC: Gallaudet University, Department of Counseling.

Jaffee v. Redmond et al., 518 U.S. 1 (1996).

McCrone, W. P. (1988). *Legal literacy for rehabilitation counselors.* Buffalo, NY: University of Buffalo.

McCrone, W. P. (1994). A two-year report card on Title I of the Americans With Disabilities Act: Implications for rehabilitation counseling with deaf people. *Journal of the American Deafness & Rehabilitation Association, 28*(2), 1–20.

McCrone, W. P., & Beach, R. L. (1994). A score of success: Gallaudet's Department of Counseling reflects on its first two decades. *Gallaudet Today, 24*(3), 18–23.

Miller, B. G. (1998). *Deaf and sober.* Silver Spring, MD: National Association of the Deaf.

Tarasoff v. Regents of the University of California, 551 p. 2nd 334 (Cal. 1976).

Thompson, A. (1990). *Guide to ethical practice in psychotherapy.* New York: John Wiley & Sons.

4

Ethical Issues in Working With Deaf Children, Adolescents, and Their Families

Patrick J. Brice

Working with deaf children and their families is both challenging and very rewarding. To have the opportunity to share the struggles and triumphs of deaf children in school, within their families, and in their social lives is a privilege. It is not, however, without its ethical pitfalls and dilemmas.

COMPETENCE

A major ethical issue for those working with deaf children and their families is *clinical competence*. Consider the following situation:

Dr. Newgrad has just finished her training, obtained her license, and now has a job in a mental health agency. During her training, Dr. Newgrad took two courses on child development, assessed four child cases, and carried one family and child case in treatment during an externship. She took sign language classes while in graduate school, and worked with several deaf adults during her training. Her role at the mental health agency is to provide treatment and psychological evaluations.

The director approaches her one day to discuss the possibility of the agency obtaining a contract with the local public school system to provide assessments of special needs children, including deaf and hard of hearing students. The director understands that very few people can work with deaf and hard of hearing children, and that the school system pays reasonably well for outside evaluations. This could be an asset to the agency, which, like all agencies, is searching for additional sources of funding.

———

Dr. Newgrad faces an interesting situation here. She has some training in work with children and some training in deafness. Does she have enough? There presently are no formal guidelines or certification requirements that must be met before a psychologist or other mental health professional can accept children or families into his or her practice. Once general state licensure requirements have been satisfied, a practitioner is free to conduct his or her practice as that practitioner sees fit. The American Psychological Association's (as well as those of other professional associations) code of ethics requires training and competence in a particular area before providing services. But, how much training is necessary? How much supervised experience with particular populations should be obtained prior to working independently? How much coursework should be completed prior to this? These questions are not yet answered, and in the real world of clinical practice, practitioners often find themselves accepting clients with whom they have less than adequate training to treat, and then looking for consultation or supervision.

While this is true of general child and family work, it takes on great significance when working with deaf people and their families. There is no certifying or regulating body that has spelled out the minimum competencies that clinicians should have before working with deaf children and their families. There have been standards of care proposed for deaf clients (Myers, 1995). However, these standards have yet to be officially adopted and lack any method of enforcement. And, many clinicians still believe that their deaf clients can read lips and do not need much in the way of special consideration. A result of this situation is that it is unclear what sorts of training and competencies clinicians and psychologists who work in the Deaf community should have. What clients are individual psychologists qualified to accept and treat, and under what circumstances?

A dilemma that many who work with deaf children and their families are likely to encounter relates both to psychological and cultural expertise. For example, a psychologist who works in the Deaf community and understands Deaf culture and American Sign Language (ASL) could be asked to see a wide range of children with a wide range of problems, ranging from adjustment disorder to pervasive developmental disorder. He or she may be asked to perform custody evaluations, assess whether a child has been abused, or evaluate dangerousness or the need for institutionalization. Few psychologists in the hearing world have the range of skills necessary to see all these kinds of clients; it is much harder with deaf children. Similarly, psychologists who specialize in particular clinical areas, such as Attention Deficit Hyperactivity Disorder (ADHD), may be asked to evaluate or treat deaf children, perhaps conducting the work with the assistance of an interpreter. Without, however, appropriate knowledge of the psychological issues associated with the development of deaf children and an appreciation for Deaf cultural issues, valid assessment and treatment could not be conducted. The challenges here will grow when the child is a native user of ASL or has any sort of very limited language skills.

Thus, there are two different, though related, bodies of knowledge and skills clinicians need to master in order to have the necessary competencies to work with deaf children. They must first become competent through their professional training program in working with children and families (no easy task). Second, they must become intimately familiar with the growing body of knowledge regarding the Deaf community and its culture, the psychological development of deaf children, and the educational and socio-emotional concerns of deaf children and adolescents, as well as (in many situations) master some level of sign language proficiency. As anyone who has attempted to learn a second language as an adult knows, becoming fluent can be a formidable task. Furthermore, with deaf children in today's society, one may be asked to communicate in ASL, Signed English, or more recently, Cued Speech. Each of these presents unique challenges. Thus, Dr. Newgrad is in a difficult situation, with little to guide her in her discussions with the agency director.

A complicating factor in considering individual clinical competence is the "small world" phenomenon. Mental health professionals capable of working with this low-incidence population are not plentiful. As with hearing populations, there are more therapists focusing on adult rather than child work. Thus, once identified as someone in the community with a particular specialization, practitioners are likely to receive many inquiries and requests for their services. Making a referral of a case that is outside of one's area of expertise may simply not be possible, as no other person in the locale may be able to provide services. The dilemma is whether to provide services that may not be quite appropriate or effective because they are outside the realm of training and competence, or refuse to become involved knowing that no services or treatment may then be provided. Psychologists who work in rural settings with general hearing populations are probably quite familiar with this dilemma.

The small world concern naturally leads to dual role issues. As a clinician works in a particular community and in some ways becomes a member of that community, it is likely that he or she will be confronted with the possibility of working professionally with a person or family where there is another kind of relationship, professional or personal. The dilemma here is deciding how to make referrals when services are lacking and there may not be another qualified person in the area.

PSYCHOLOGICAL ASSESSMENT

Psychologists are frequently involved with deaf children and their families through the process of conducting psychological and psychoeducational evaluations. Almost every deaf child in any given school system will receive special education, meaning that they will go through a psychoeducational assessment every three years, with psychological reviews happening more frequently. This suggests significant psychologist involvement with deaf children. And, not only will school psychologists become involved, but independent practitioners as well, since many children find themselves the subjects of special education hearings to determine the most appropriate classroom placement and services.

There is a relatively low incidence of hearing loss in school-aged children and adolescents (Moores, 2001). And, to complicate matters further, the children that are considered to be "deaf" may vary widely in any number of characteristics, ranging from degree of residual hearing, ability to use residual hearing, degree of sign language used and fluency in sign language, intelligibility of speech, etiology of hearing loss, additional special education considerations, and so forth. The educational setting may vary as well, from total inclusion in classrooms for hearing children with no supportive services, to use of an amplification system, to use of an interpreter of sorts (e.g., oral, Cued Speech, sign language), to partial integration with hearing children and partial enrollment in self-contained classes, to complete education in self-contained classes, to day schools for the deaf, to residential schools. Each of these educational settings may have "deaf" students that have very different characteristics, identifications, and abilities.

A result of this extreme heterogeneity is that there is no single way of approaching or evaluating a deaf child, and no single set of tests or battery of measures that is always appropriate. In fact, there are no widely used measures of intelligence that have deaf norms, though some measures such as the Wechsler scales (Wechsler, 1991; 1997) may have included some deaf or "hearing-impaired" children in their normative sample under the "other disabilities" group. The Hiskey-Nebraska Test of Learning Aptitude (Hiskey, 1955) did have deaf norms and was developed for use with deaf children, but it is quite old and has never been updated. There were deaf norms for the performance scales of the Wechsler Intelligence Scale for Children (WISC) Revised, but none yet developed for the WISC-III. Spragins, Blennerhassett, and Mullen (1998) have compiled and reviewed a list of measures frequently used with deaf and hard of hearing children.

However, few of these included deaf children in the standardization sample or developed standardized procedures for use with deaf children.

Our ethical obligation to evaluate our clients in their native language and with instruments that are fair can lead to a certain degree of creativity and consultation in the evaluation process. It is imperative to remember that psychological tests are only tools that a psychologist uses when conducting an assessment. The need for additional, confirming tests and procedures, as well as the employment of various other nontest procedures such as observations, interviews, and record reviews is greater when working with deaf children and adolescents.

The issue is even more complicated than simply a lack of appropriately normed measures for deaf children. As Braden (1994) points out, the question of test bias is highly complex. In his evaluation of the bias involved in intelligence testing with deaf individuals, he concluded that,

> the majority of the evidence points toward no evidence of bias. The psychometric indices of bias extracted from studies of deaf people, such as reliability, consistency, and factor structure, are generally similar to values found for normal hearing peers. Likewise, there is no evidence of differential validity for intelligence tests to predict IQ over time or external criteria, such as academic achievement. Provided one retains the distinction between clinical versus statistical bias, and nonverbal versus verbal tests, it appears that test bias is not a major influence on the IQs obtained by deaf people. (Braden, 1994, p. 129)

The result is that a clinician's competence is once again paramount. While IQ measures may or may not indicate something about a deaf child's inherent "ability," they may predict something about his or her performance in certain situations, though not necessarily in the same ways as they do for normal hearing children. Hence, the practitioner who is not experienced (or not receiving supervision from someone experienced) with deaf and hard of hearing children is likely to be in over his or her head. This will even be true when using nonverbal measures, as they often overestimate academic achievement (Braden, 1994).

Hard of hearing children are especially vulnerable to inaccurate assessments when done by evaluators not trained with this particular population. It is common for people to assume that the hard of hearing child either reads lips or hears well enough to be given all of the verbally oriented measures with little accommodation. Again, while the information gleaned from this activity may prove valuable in some respects, it may not be an accurate assessment of their verbal reasoning abilities. Even though many hard of hearing children can function quite well within classrooms of hearing children, it is a mistake to conclude that they have similar access to the information presented as do their hearing peers.

While the discussion thus far has focused on IQ or academic testing, the situation is the same when assessing social/emotional behavior. Once again, only a few social/behavioral rating scales have included deaf children in their standardization samples. And when they have, they often are limited. The Vineland Adaptive Behavior Scales (Sparrow, Balla, & Cicchetti, 1984), for example, use a group of deaf children for comparison purposes. However, the age only goes up to 12 years. Other research (Sporn & Brice, 1998; Kelly, Forney, Parker-Fisher, & Jones, 1993) suggests that deaf children may be overdiagnosed with ADHD when conventional rating scales are used. The range of acceptable and culturally significant behaviors in groups of deaf children may be different from those of hearing children. Thus, when relying upon observations made by adults, such as parents or teachers, care must be taken in the interpretation.

Gaining a degree of competence in the assessment of deaf children is not a simple process. When combined with the small world dilemma, psychologists can find themselves in a true bind. Do I conduct an evaluation for which I am not properly trained, or allow someone else to do it who also may not be trained, or see the evaluation put off? The lack of proper services may also place an evaluator in the position of suggesting interventions, such as individual or family therapy, and then being the most likely person to conduct the treatment. This sort of conflict of interest must always be closely monitored.

TREATMENT AND PSYCHOTHERAPY

Koocher and Keith-Spiegel (1990) point out that in working therapeutically with children and their families, there will be a certain amount of role conflict and differences in the "power relationships" among the identified patient, which is usually the child, and others involved, such as parents and teachers. They further suggest that in this work, therapists are very likely to confront their own value systems as they attempt to work with children and their parents. Both of these points are sharpened in working with families that have deaf children or adolescents. Additionally, the stress that families with deaf children experience is substantial and usually ongoing, meaning that parents and siblings may be clients as well, even when the format is not necessarily a traditional family therapy model.

Psychologists are bound by their code of ethics to serve the best interests of the child. However, determining those interests and how to serve them is highly complex, with correct answers seldom being obvious. The line between values and scientific knowledge is fine. While there is a fair amount of research on development in deaf children, we are far from concluding what general approaches to education, communication, or development work best. Yet, we all have our own world views regarding sign language, oral methods of communication, integrated versus self-contained classrooms, the Deaf community, Cued Speech, cochlear implants, and other topics of extreme importance to deaf people. These world views influence how we counsel clients and even how we design and interpret research. Navigating the therapeutic environment in such a way that children and families are empowered to make their own decisions and feel supported— even when their decisions conflict with the values of the therapist—is critical.

Methods of communication or choice regarding education are not the only areas where value conflicts between therapists and families can occur when working with deaf children. Disciplinary approaches, often a heated issue, can be equally challenging with families with deaf members. Most therapists and psychologists have their own personal views on child rearing and child discipline, informed partially by research and partially by experience and culture. When the issue is not clearly one of abuse or neglect, but of a disagreement in the choice of disciplinary strategies, a potential ethical dilemma exists. This is common in work with children in general, but is exacerbated when the child is deaf.

There is literature suggesting that in-depth communication is more limited between deaf children and their hearing parents (Schlesinger & Meadow, 1972; Greenberg, 1980; Meadow, Greenberg, Erting, & Carmichael, 1981). Explanations for the rationale underlying rules for the consequences of behavior, for separations between parents and children, and myriad other everyday occurrences are terse and often simplified. One byproduct of this situation is that disciplinary approaches may be more problematic. Parents might either be overly lax in establishing limits on behavior (excusing many inappropriate behaviors), or may enforce rules without explanations, relying on physical discipline in the absence of adequate communication. These explanations, however, aid children in learning about the world. Teasing out cultural influences, family values, and parental skill is important when working with families with deaf members in order to guide interventions in respectful and efficient ways.

Working therapeutically with adolescents, who are in the midst of developing a sense of self and a separate unique identity, often leads to role conflict. Those who work in the field are accustomed to hearing stories of teenagers who refuse to wear hearing aids, even though the family has purchased them and expects them to be worn; teenagers who stop voicing in conversations at home; and young people who argue with their parents over which school they should attend. Koocher and Keith-Spiegel (1990) advocate for including the child patient, even young children, in the goal-setting process for psychotherapy. When working with young deaf people and their families, the goals of the parents can be diametrically opposed to those of their children when identity as a deaf person or choice of communication is at the heart of the matter.

Another issue that bears mentioning is functioning as an interpreter for the family. This pertains mostly to therapists who are fluent enough in sign language to be able to interpret if necessary. There are times when the therapist will be asked to interpret or will feel the need to act as an interpreter in meetings with families. Some therapists believe in bringing trained and certified interpreters into the therapeutic situation, while others will argue that the therapy can be more dramatic and perhaps more effective when families are confronted in front of the therapist with their communication limitations. Neither situation is easy to resolve, and simply stating that therapists should never interpret because of a role conflict is probably too pat and simplistic. There are parts of the country where there is no hope of getting a qualified interpreter to work with families, and when there is, the interpreter may have already been interpreting for the child all day in school. Transference and countertransference reactions abound at such times. Clarifying ahead of time what can be done, when or how the therapist can interpret, and toward what goal probably are more reasonable than simply deciding that interpreting by the therapist can never be done (see Harvey, 1989, for an in-depth discussion of communication logistics in family therapy; Harvey, 1996, for a discussion of transference/countertransference issues; as well as Roe & Roe, 1991).

CONFIDENTIALITY

No chapter on ethics and children would be complete without touching on the issue of confidentiality. Parents legally hold the privilege to confidentiality and have the right to know what issues their children are facing and how the treatment is progressing. There are also limits to confidentiality that are sometimes difficult to articulate ahead of time. Therapists are obligated to report abusive situations or suspected abuse, and are obligated to break confidence when they learn of information that puts the client or someone else in danger. Yet, what constitutes danger and how imminent should this be? What are the risks to the youngster in terms of dangerousness, and to the therapeutic process if confidence is broken? And most important, how do we go about making such decisions?

Koocher (1976) has argued that it makes more sense to be straightforward with child and adolescent clients, treating them truthfully and with respect, than it does to make blanket statements regarding confidentiality. He points out that explaining the limits of confidentiality is influenced by the developmental level of the child. Therefore, it is often difficult for young children to believe that other adults do not talk about them with their parents.

When working with deaf children, explaining limits of confidentiality can be doubly difficult. First of all, depending on the language level of the child, simply finding a way to describe confidentiality can be a challenge (one school counselor used two stacking cups, with private matters written on the inner cup, and public ones written on the second outer cup as a way to explain confidentiality). Second, overcoming the belief that all adults talk with each other about the children can be equally challenging. In small schools, such as residential schools for the deaf, as well as unique school programs, such as self-contained programs in mainstream or integrated educational environments, adults do talk about children. Information is shared on a regular basis both in and outside of school. The author has actually witnessed personal issues regarding students being discussed openly at a staff party. Convincing children that the relationship with the therapist will be different from these other experiences generally is not easy.

Therapeutic or professional confidentiality takes on greater significance in the Deaf community because privacy is a major issue. Managing confidentiality has different nuances, depending on the specific group within the Deaf community. There even may be a hierarchy in terms of difficulty levels. When working with deaf parents and their deaf children, the therapist will be immersed in the Deaf community. It is likely that his or her name will be checked out, credentials assessed, and skills referenced—all within the community. Discussion of cases considered normal in many training centers or clinics may often be interrupted with people excusing themselves because they are too familiar with the clients, or have some involvement with them. Or, in contrast, the therapist may be given information about his or her client's behavior outside of therapy by colleagues who know or associate with that person. The therapist then finds him or herself in the awkward position of having personal information about the client that was not shared by the client, nor even with the client's permission. Even recognizing people that one knows in waiting rooms of professional offices or clinics is an issue. For example, a child and her teacher may both be clients at the same deaf service agency. Maintaining confidentiality in these situations will require heightened sensitivity, awareness, and precautions. Scheduling the sessions to be sure that acquaintances are not coming to sessions back-to-back, extra discussion around releasing notes or reports related to assessments or therapy, discussions with parents regarding specific information to be discussed with or released to teachers, and other precautions must become routine.

It is easier, in terms of confidentiality, to work with deaf children of hearing parents, who form roughly 90% of the deaf population, particularly if they come from integrated or mainstream educational programs. Hearing parents are less likely to be immersed in the Deaf community, so it may be less likely that they will recognize other clients in the waiting room. However, it is still likely that when working with deaf children, therapists will hear them talk about other deaf children who may have been seen as clients, and may even share that they see the same therapist. This issue often arises in other special education settings, where students know which counselors or psychologists see which students. This in itself can present a whole new dilemma, and is different from what most professionals in independent practice face. What does one do with information regarding a client that is learned inadvertently?

Another point regarding confidentiality with deaf children is that parents may not have access to important information about their child. Communication problems between deaf children and adolescents and their parents are common in therapy referrals. When the child is an ASL or even Signed English user, it may be the case that parents simply do not understand what their child is thinking, wishes for, or feels. Frequently, when families are seen together, it becomes clear that either the child changes what and how he or she says things so that parents can understand, or does not say important things at all. This can be an area where it is important to find ways to enhance the sharing that goes on or can go on between parents and their deaf children. The decision about what to share, how to share it, and how to communicate with the child regarding sharing is extremely important and may be more critical when working with deaf children and their hearing parents. This is not to say that hearing parents are not able to communicate with their deaf children. But, clinicians who work in the area will be familiar with a fair number of cases where parents talked to the therapist while the child had no idea what was being said, asked the therapist to tell the child something for them, or signed a few words while speaking many. The result is that many aspects of the communication are unclear and left ambiguous.

RESEARCH

Koocher and Keith-Spiegel (1990) recommend strongly that researchers learn as much as possible about children in general before proceeding with their specific research projects. This normally would mean more than simply taking some college or graduate courses on child development. It would include spending time with children in settings where it is possible to interact and become comfortable with them, and to learn what they are like at different ages.

Similarly, Pollard (1992, 1996b) argues that hearing people who choose to work in the Deaf community need both sign language fluency and a level of cultural competence, and need to involve the community itself in the research. As with learning what children are like, this will not come from sitting in classes or taking coursework, or from watching movies about sign language. It comes from "consistent and culturally appropriate interaction with persons who are deaf" (Pollard, 1996b, p. 393). Deaf adults and children have served as subjects for research projects for many years. For the most part, these were situations where hearing professionals entered the Deaf community, involving deaf people in research projects, and then published the results. Statements were made that implied deaf children had no formal language (Furth, 1971) (ASL was not recognized as a language), or that their behavior was immature or impulsive (Baroff, 1963; Vernon, 1967; Harris, 1978; Bachara, Raphael, & Phelan, 1980; Chess & Fernandez, 1980).

The sad fact was that much of the empirical work had been carried out by people who were not necessarily familiar with deaf children, their schools, their language, or their culture. Behavior was judged using a different framework than the one used by Deaf culture. As a result, many of the early studies described deaf children in fairly pejorative terms, such as impulsive, immature, cognitively delayed, and "concrete" (Myklebust, 1953, 1964; Levine, 1974).

Beyond the possibility of obtaining research results that are damaging to a culture or community, having limited knowledge of deaf language and culture involves other ethical conflicts. Children are not deemed competent to consent to participation. Parental permission is required for that. However, children are to be given the right to decline to participate. Researchers have an obligation to obtain a child participant's *assent* before continuing with a research project. Yet, explaining to a deaf child that they can decline to participate is jeopardized when language and cultural understanding are limited.

At least in part because of the nature of early research and the researchers themselves, there is greater need to protect deaf children from harm as a result of participating in psychological or educational research projects. The Deaf community, as mentioned earlier, is highly heterogeneous, with various subgroups holding strongly to particular values and/or beliefs (e.g., advantages of ASL over Signed English, preference for oral communication over signed, etc.). Researchers usually come to study a particular population with a bias toward the issue. It is important that steps be taken both to be clear that people understand the researcher's bias ahead of time, and to ensure that the bias has not compromised the welfare of any of the participants. While this is always true in psychological research, the intensities with which values and beliefs are held in the Deaf community make it even more critical and more of an ethical issue in work with deaf children. Pollard (1992) has argued strongly and persuasively for involving the Deaf community in all phases of research and maintaining an open dialogue to ensure appropriate and ethical research.

Privacy and the protection of privacy are an enormously sensitive issue in the Deaf community. This was touched upon earlier, but bears mentioning again. Melton (1992) emphasizes the fact that, "The privacy interests of both children and their families are serious matters deserving great weight in decisions about whether and how to conduct research involving them" (p. 75). And, the more sensitive the issue, the more private. Here, there is additional duty to take extra steps in the care and handling of the participants and the data. It is unlikely that hearing researchers viewing tapes of research participants from a project conducted far away and in a large city will recognize the participants. It is different in the Deaf community. In fact, the opposite is more likely the case—that at least some deaf participants may be recognized by someone even when there is great distance between the people. For children, the issue is greater since a child appearing on a videotape may be recognized long after he or she is grown. Again, this points to the exceptional need for care, respect, and effort to evaluate risks, take steps to minimize them, and treat the data with uncommon caution. An in-depth assessment of the risks involved must be weighed against the potential benefits very carefully. Research that is trivial in nature, or is being conducted simply because the students are a "captive audience" (e.g., you work in the school where the deaf children are enrolled) should not be allowed or encouraged.

EMERGING ISSUES

The Deaf community is a dynamic, changing entity encountering myriad new issues and conflicts as we move into the new millennium. None may be more challenging than those brought by advancing technology, especially in the form of the cochlear implant. This procedure, which is moving along rapidly in development and becoming more and more sophisticated, leads to tremendous emotional and scientific debate, including the ethical question of whether children should be implanted before an age at which they can decide for themselves. For some groups, there is no doubt about this, and it sounds like a ridiculous question. Early intervention is critical for successful use of an implant, so the earlier the better. Yet, for other communities, the idea of implanting a child is tantamount to genocide or the destruction of a culture.

The arguments as put forward by Balkany, Hodges, and Goodman (1996) center on two questions: Who should make decisions for the child, and based on what standards should those decisions be made? They argue that on both ethical and legal grounds, parents have always made decisions about their own children. Parents have the right to raise their children according to their own standards, values, and beliefs (Buchanan & Brock, 1989). Further, Balkany et al. argue that, "Parents will usually do a better job of deciding what is best for their child than anyone else for a number of reasons. Parents care more deeply for their children than do strangers. Parents know their children best and are more concerned with their welfare" (Balkany et al., 1996, p. 749). The central argument Balkany and his colleagues make relates to the welfare of the child. The child's needs must be met first, and the needs of any other group second. Balkany et al. state unequivocally that being deaf is a disability, and any medical interventions that can limit the degree of disability are in the best interests of the child.

In direct contrast, the arguments of Lane and Bahan (1998) assert that prelingually deafened children are not disabled, but are a cultural and linguistic minority. The analogy they draw is between deaf people and Native American or African American peoples. Here they point to the protection that has been sought in the courts by these groups when children who are Native American or African American are adopted by European American families. The fear is that these cultures are being put in danger by the adoption of children into a different, majority culture. Lane and Bahan contend that the Deaf world feels the same way about deaf children, believing that Deaf culture is being endangered by non-deaf peoples making uninformed decisions.

A second major argument involves the "experimental" nature of cochlear implants. Based on their review of the literature, Lane and Bahan conclude that the evidence demonstrating that cochlear implants lead to improved speech and hearing in prelingually deafened children is scant at best, leaving cochlear implantation as an innovative but unproven procedure, with concomitant ethical dangers. Interestingly, Balkany, Hodges, and Goodman (1998), in a commentary on Lane and Bahan's paper, use the same references to argue their own point regarding the effectiveness of cochlear implants. The truth of the matter is far from clear.

Professionals are facing a conundrum. Clearly the research on cochlear implantation can be interpreted in different ways. Research on the psychosocial ramifications of implants is sorely lacking, as is good knowledge regarding how to assess readiness and appropriateness for implantation (Pollard, 1996a). And, as implantation is performed at younger and younger ages, assessment becomes less a question of individual psychological readiness, and more a question of family functioning.

Pollard (1996a) points out that one of the most significant issues, and one where psychologists will continue to play a major role, relates to informed consent. Parents receive a wide variety of information, some in the form of a marketing "pitch," as well as some in a factual manner. Assessing what parents and their children understand accurately, or where they have misinformation or distorted perceptions, is critical in the preoperative assessment process. Psychologists will have a role here, as well as in defining research programs that help sort out and evaluate not only the cognitive and linguistic advantages that an implant may or may not provide, but the psychosocial and emotional effects as well.

CONCLUSION

Helping parents make decisions about the future of their deaf children will continue to be a task for psychologists and mental health professionals. Providing assessments and treatment that are appropriate and effective while being culturally respectful is our duty, yet can involve ethical dilemmas. While working in the Deaf community presents numerous ethical challenges, they are challenges that need to be taken up, and are being taken up by increasing numbers of deaf and hearing professionals. Furthermore, it is the collaboration of deaf and hearing professionals, working side by side, that will lead to strategies for providing the highest quality services, including research, to deaf and hard of hearing children.

REFERENCES

Bachara, G. H., Raphael, J., & Phelan, W. J. (1980). Empathy development in pre-adolescents. *American Annals of the Deaf, 121,* 331–345.

Balkany, T., Hodges, A., & Goodman, K. (1996). Ethics of cochlear implantation in young children. *Otolaryngology: Head and Neck Surgery, 114,* 748–755.

Balkany, T., Hodges, A., & Goodman, K. (1998). Additional comments on ethics of cochlear implantation in young children: A review and reply from a Deaf-World perspective. *Otolaryngology: Head and Neck Surgery, 119,* 297–313.

Baroff, G. S. (1963). Rorschach data and clinical observations. In J. D. Rainer, K. Z. Altshuler, F. J. Kallman, & W. E. Deming (Eds.), *Family and mental health problems in a deaf population.* New York: Columbia University Press.

Braden, J. P. (1994). *Deafness, deprivation, and IQ.* New York: Plenum Press.

Buchanan, A. E., & Brock, D. W. (1989). *Deciding for others: The ethics of surrogate decision making.* Cambridge: Cambridge University Press.

Chess, S., & Fernandez, P. (1980). Impulsivity in rubella deaf children: A longitudinal study. *American Annals of the Deaf, 125,* 505–509.

Furth, H. G. (1971). Linguistic deficiency and thinking: Research with deaf subjects 1964–1969. *Psychological Bulletin, 76,* 58–72.

Greenberg, M. T. (1980). Hearing families with deaf children: Stress and functioning as related to communication method. *American Annals of the Deaf, 125,* 1063–1071.

Harris, R. I. (1978). The relationship of impulse control to parent hearing status, manual communication, and academic achievement in deaf children. *American Annals of the Deaf, 123,* 52–67.

Harvey, M. A. (1989). *Psychotherapy with deaf and hard-of-hearing persons: A systemic model.* Hillsdale, NJ: Erlbaum.

Harvey, M. A. (1996). Utilization of a traumatic transference by a hearing therapist. In N. S. Glickman and M. A. Harvey (Eds.), *Culturally affirmative psychotherapy with deaf persons* (pp. 155–167). Mahwah, NJ: Erlbaum.

Hiskey, M. S. (1955). *Nebraska test of learning aptitude for young deaf children.* Lincoln: University of Nebraska Press.

Kelly, D. P., Forney, J., Parker-Fisher, S., & Jones, M. (1993). Evaluating and managing Attention Deficit Disorder in children who are deaf or hard of hearing. *American Annals of the Deaf, 4,* 345–357.

Koocher, G. P. (1976). A bill of rights for children in psychotherapy. In G. P. Koocher (Ed.), *Children's rights and the mental health professions.* New York: Wiley-Interscience.

Koocher, G. P., & Keith-Spiegel, P. C. (1990). *Children, ethics and the law.* Lincoln: University of Nebraska Press.

Lane, H., & Bahan, B. (1998). Ethics of cochlear implantation in young children: A review and reply from a Deaf-World perspective. *Otolaryngology: Head and Neck Surgery, 119,* 297–313.

Levine, E. S. (1974). Psychological tests and practices with the deaf: A survey of the state of the art. *Volta Review, 76,* 298–319.

Meadow, K. P., Greenberg, M. T., Erting, C., & Carmichael, H. S. (1981). Interactions of deaf mothers and deaf preschool children: Comparisons with three other groups of deaf and hearing dyads. *American Annals of the Deaf, 126,* 454–468.

Melton, G. B. (1992). Respecting boundaries: Minors, privacy, and behavioral research. In B. Stanley & J. E. Sieber (Eds.), *Social research on children and adolescents: Ethical issues.* Newbury Park, CA: Sage.

Moores, D. F. (2001). *Educating the deaf: Psychology, principles, and practices* (5th ed.). Boston: Houghton-Mifflin.

Myers, R. R. (Ed.). (1995). *Standards of care for the delivery of mental health services to deaf and hard of hearing persons.* Silver Spring, MD: National Association of the Deaf.

Myklebust, H. (1953). Toward a new understanding of the deaf child. *American Annals of the Deaf, 98,* 345–357.

Myklebust, H. (1964). *The psychology of deafness.* New York: Grune & Stratton.

Pollard, R. Q. (1992). Cross-cultural ethics in the conduct of deafness research. *Rehabilitation Psychology, 37,* 87–101.

Pollard, R. Q. (1996a). Conceptualizing and conducting preoperative psychological assessments of cochlear implant candidates. *Journal of Deaf Studies and Deaf Education, 1,* 17–28.

Pollard, R. Q. (1996b). Professional psychology and deaf people: The emergence of a discipline. *American Psychologist, 51,* 397–406.

Roe, D. L., & Roe, C. E. (1991). The third party: Using interpreters for the deaf in counseling situations. *Journal of Mental Health Counseling, 13,* 91–105.

Schlesinger, H., & Meadow, K. P. (1972). *Sound and sign.* Berkeley: University of California Press.

Sparrow, S. S., Balla, D. A., & Cicchetti, D. V. (1984). *Vineland Adaptive Behavior Scales.* Circle Pines, MN: American Guidance Service.

Sporn, M., & Brice, P. (1998). *Use of the test of variables of attention in assessing deaf children.* Unpublished manuscript.

Spragins, A. B., Blennerhassett, L., & Mullen, Y. (1998, October). *1997–1998 Update: Cognitive assessment instruments used with deaf students.* Retrieved October 20, 1999, from Gallaudet Research Institute web site: http://gri.gallaudet.edu/~catraxle/INTELLEC.html

Vernon, M. (1967). Characteristics associated with post-rubella deaf children: Psychological, educational, and physical. *Volta Review, 69,* 176–185.

Wechsler, D. (1991). *Manual for the Wechsler Intelligence Scale for Children* (3rd ed.). San Antonio, TX: Psychological Corporation.

Wechsler, D. (1997). *Manual for the Wechsler Adult Intelligence Scale* (3rd ed.). San Antonio, TX: Psychological Corporation.

5

Ethical Considerations for Counseling Deaf and Hard of Hearing Older Adults

Janet L. Pray

When mental health professionals discuss issues specific to counseling and psychotherapy with deaf and hard of hearing people, older clients or patients are not typically a major focus (Pray, 1989, 1992). This is not surprising since the mental health field does not focus as much attention on older persons as it does on other age groups. This reality is of concern since the aging population has been increasing steadily (Butler, Lewis, & Sunderland, 1998), and between 2020 and 2030, approximately one in five U.S. citizens is expected to be over age 65 (U.S. Bureau of the Census, 1996). Older persons are also more likely to have hearing loss than any other age group (Schein & Delk, 1974; Hotchkiss, 1987), and among older adults, hearing loss is the third most commonly reported chronic condition (National Center for Health Statistics, 1986).

It is likely that in the course of professional practice, a mental health professional whose clientele includes those who are deaf and hard of hearing will be involved either directly or indirectly with older people. It is almost inevitable that those providing services to an older clientele will find themselves working with people who have hearing loss, including those who seek counseling or therapy because of adjustment problems stemming from hearing loss associated with aging.

There are many conditions commonly found in the aging population (which includes deaf and hard of hearing older persons, of course) for which mental health services can be beneficial. The incidence of depression among older adults is high, and disability has been found to increase the risk of depression (Steffens, Hays, & Krishnan, 1999). Because people are living longer, Alzheimer's disease is a growing mental health concern, and there is a need at times to determine whether an older person has Alzheimer's, depression, hearing loss, or some combination of two or more of these conditions. Medical conditions such as stroke and Parkinson's disease frequently produce psychological changes in addition to the physical changes, adding to the challenge of successful adaptation.

This chapter identifies a number of issues in the area of values and ethics about which mental health practitioners working with older deaf and hard of hearing clients should be aware and examines approaches to dealing with these issues.

CONTEXT FOR IDENTIFYING THE ETHICAL ISSUES

Ethical issues, dilemmas, and conflicts in practice with older deaf and hard of hearing people arise within the context of societal attitudes, the personal values and attitudes of the professional, and professional values and ethics articulated in the codes of ethics of professions such as counseling, medicine, nursing, psychology, and social work. Professionals are not immune to attitudes in the social context in which they were reared and in which they practice; thus, the personal values of the professional will often reflect attitudes predominant in society. For instance, in the United States, we live in a society characterized by "ageism," a concept first described by Butler (1969). Ageism is characterized by prejudices, stereotypes, and devalued status based on age, which are akin to attitudes rooted in racism and sexism. Butler et al. (1998) note that "Mental health personnel not only have to deal with leftover feelings from their personal pasts, which may interfere with their perceptions of older persons, but they must also be aware of a multitude of negative cultural attitudes toward older persons, which pervade social institutions as well as individual psyches" (p. 208). In a similar vein, Orr (1982) earlier notes parallels between children, youth, and older adults as having in common being treated with paternalism and having limited participation in decisions affecting their lives. Orr notes that, "To be identified with an age community is to become a member of a peculiar minority group, whose precarious social status is made even more problematic by the fact that it is not one that historically has been identified as disenfranchised" (p. 256).

We live in a society that also stigmatizes deaf and hard of hearing people and makes assumptions about people with hearing loss. Wax (1982), writing about aging and hearing loss, suggests the concept of "double and multiple jeopardy" for people who have more than one kind of devalued status or stigma. Other writers have minimized the effects of hearing loss among older persons. Erikson, Erikson, and Kivnick (1986) interviewed 29 octogenarians who were followed since 1928 in a study by the Institute of Human Development at the University of California at Berkeley to ascertain how this cohort was dealing with the issue of "integrity versus despair" in their later years. They note that most participants in their study reported hearing and vision loss, yet characterize these sensory losses as "simple impairments."

Becker (1980) and Tidball (1986) suggest that, for people who are deaf all or most of their lives, adaptations developed through life in response to stigma, discrimination, and social isolation, as well as their perception that they are members of a minority group, may promote successful aging. This perspective challenges stereotypes practitioners may hold and has implications for providers of mental health services to older deaf persons.

Because of the diversity of perspectives and beliefs about aging and about deaf and hard of hearing people, a practitioner is likely to have to deal with ethical as well as diagnostic issues involving societal, personal, and professional values when working with an older deaf or hard of hearing client. The literature on values and ethics is clear about the importance for the individual practitioner to develop self-awareness regarding personal biases, needs, and values and to take whatever steps necessary to ensure that they do not intrude upon the professional relationship with clients nor preclude practicing within the code of ethics of the profession (Congress, 1999; Corey, Corey, & Callanan, 1998; Corker, 1995; Linzer, 1999; Welfel, 1998).

To illustrate some of the ethical issues a practitioner may encounter, two cases are discussed in this chapter. The first involves a hard of hearing older adult and the second, a deaf older adult. In each case summary, the discussion includes the ethical issues involved, the choices facing the clinician, and the rationale for the approach taken.

HARD OF HEARING OLDER ADULT

The following case scenario has elements common to those found among older persons and their families when hearing loss develops later in life (Burnside & Schmidt, 1994; Cox, 1993; Kaplan, 1985, 1988; Pray, 1992). In the process of conducting an assessment and developing an appropriate intervention plan in response to the daughter's request for help with her father, the clinician had to confront a number of issues related to values and ethics.

The History of the Presenting Problem

EM is a 79-year-old man with Parkinson's disease and hearing loss that has become progressively more severe since it became noticeable at about age

60. He has mobility problems and difficulty communicating with his family. He is a widower and has been living with his 42-year-old daughter, her 45-year-old husband, and their two children—a 15-year-old son and a 10-year-old daughter. EM often complains that people do not speak clearly, lack patience with him, and attempt to talk to him when he cannot hear over the sound of the television, other conversations, etc. He has withdrawn increasingly from his friends, his church, and the numerous social activities in which he formerly participated. EM insists that he wants to be left alone to read the newspapers and books. Since he cannot understand his grandchildren who make brief remarks to him while they are "on the run," he sees no point in trying to have a conversation with them. His daughter is distressed by the loss of the previously close relationship between her children and their grandfather and has tried unsuccessfully to get him to see an audiologist for a hearing aid evaluation. EM expresses the view that hearing aids are too expensive, won't do any good, and are too much trouble to learn to use. EM retired at age 62 after 35 years as a high school teacher, in part, because he had increasing difficulty understanding his students when they spoke to him. He and his wife, also a retired schoolteacher, were active in church, traveled extensively, and had many friends. EM was devastated when his wife died suddenly after a stroke two years ago. Because of his own increasing mobility problems, he accepted an offer to move in with his daughter and her family. His current attitude is that he has little to live for since his wife died, and he wants to be left alone. He becomes angry when his daughter suggests that he get his hearing evaluated, become more involved with the family, or engage in the activities he once enjoyed.

Recently, EM and the family came to the agreement that EM will enter a rehabilitation center/nursing home because his mobility problems have progressed to the point that he experienced frequent falls. The family home is on three levels, and both EM and his daughter fear he is at risk for serious injury, including the possibility of a hip fracture. Although her husband and her father have both assured her that the move to a residential facility is "for the best," she suspects her father has mixed feelings and she feels enormous guilt. She is concerned that her father, who is already withdrawn and isolated, will experience even greater isolation in an institutional environment, particularly because of his hearing loss, and she fears that the move, though necessary, could even hasten his death.

Clinician's Intervention

Soon after submitting the application for admission to the nursing home, EM's daughter made an appointment with the clinical social worker on the staff of the nursing home. She wanted the nursing home to arrange for an evaluation by an audiologist because she believed that if he got hearing aids, he would be more likely to interact with the residents and staff and less likely to be as withdrawn as he had become at home. She told the social worker that even though her father had declined such an evaluation in the past, she felt the nursing home could offer—even require—this evaluation as part of the medical evaluation needed for admission.

The social worker's initial assessment of EM, based on the history provided by the daughter, was that he was still grieving the loss of his wife and was likely to be grieving two other losses as well:

- loss of function and independence related to the Parkinson's disease;
- diminished communication and quality of relationship with his family because of communication barriers created by his progressive hearing loss.

Since several weeks would transpire before EM's medical appointment for admission to the rehabilitation center/nursing home, the social worker recommended that the daughter encourage EM to be evaluated for depression before attempting to address any of his other issues. The social worker suggested that EM might agree to such an evaluation if it were presented as offering the possibility of helping him cope with the many losses he has experienced. The social worker arranged to meet with his daughter again to discuss her feelings about her father's condition and the consequences of his impending move to the nursing home.

Just as EM had earlier declined an audiological evaluation, he also declined his daughter's efforts to get him to see "a shrink." He asserted his right as an adult—"and as your father, I might add!"—to make his own decisions and stood firm in his refusal to do anything more than submit to the medical evaluation required for EM's admission to the rehabilitation center/nursing home. Several weeks later, based on admission examination and the history provided by the daughter, the admitting physician who evaluated EM prescribed an antidepressant, which EM reluctantly agreed to take. The admitting physician did not recommend an audiological evaluation and responded to the daughter's objections by noting that most of the residents "can't hear;" older people don't find hearing aids useful; and of the residents who do come into their facility with hearing aids, most leave them in the dresser drawer.

EM's daughter returned to see the social worker, expressing frustration that the nursing home physician refused to have her father evaluated by an audiologist. She hoped the antidepressant would help him feel less despondent, but she considered hearing aids to be the "key" to reducing her father's withdrawal and social isolation. The social worker acknowledged the concerns she had for her father, the commitment of time and energy she had invested, her frustration about the failure to have her father's hearing evaluated, and supported her efforts to secure the best care for him. The social worker also suggested that her father should be involved in deciding what would be done about his hearing loss. Although doubting that it would "do any good," EM's daughter agreed to the social worker's plan to meet with her father upon his admission to the nursing home. It was understood that the purpose would be to offer assistance with his early adjustment process to the rehabilitation center/nursing home and to discuss factors that could influence that process, including EM's hearing loss.

During the meeting with EM, the social worker ascertained that he was ambivalent about moving into the rehabilitation center/nursing home and saw it as "the end of the line." In the weeks since he had begun taking the antidepressant, he had begun to feel less "gloomy," but he also felt that there was little that was hopeful in his situation. He expressed awareness of the inevitable decline he would experience because of his physical condition and the aging process itself, which could bring other health problems. He also felt that he could neither initiate nor sustain relationships with people because he was experiencing increasing difficulty understanding what people were saying to him, noting problems in communication even with his own family. He became easily fatigued when straining to understand conversations and was frustrated by constantly having to ask people to repeat themselves. His daughter had been "nagging" him about getting hearing aids, but most of the people he knew who tried hearing aids either couldn't get used to them or didn't find them helpful. Furthermore, he already had plenty of ailments that made him look and feel old, and he didn't want hearing aids as yet another reminder that he was aging.

The social worker and EM met several times to discuss EM's concerns about loss of independence and adjustment to the rehabilitation center/ nursing home. They discussed the problems created by his hearing loss— communication difficulties, the reactions of others, isolation from family and friends, and the effects on EM's self-esteem. The social worker affirmed EM's right to decide whether he would have his hearing evaluated, and if he did, what action would be taken as a result of the evaluation. EM increasingly understood the effects his hearing loss was having on major areas of his life and on his feelings of self-worth. Since it became clear to him that the social worker did not intend to pressure him into getting hearing aids, EM decided that it "wouldn't hurt" to be tested and find out "how bad" his hearing really was and what, if anything, might be done.

The evaluation by the audiologist identified a bilateral, moderately severe hearing loss, and hearing aids were recommended for both ears. True to his word, EM rejected the hearing aids. In response to his request for an alternative, a personal assistive listening device was suggested. Using a small microphone and a headset that reminded EM of the sort used by joggers to listen to music, EM was able to have successful one-on-one conversations with family members and staff and residents of the rehabilitation center/nursing home. As advised by the audiologist, he was also able to attach the microphone to the television and, using the headset, was once again able to enjoy television.

In the course of the ongoing work with the social worker and while continuing to take antidepressant medication, EM worked on his unresolved feelings about his wife's death, as well as his feelings about the decline in his physical capabilities and his relocation to an institutional environment. The work also focused on the relationship of his hearing loss to the grieving process and his withdrawal from people.

The Ethical Issues

In this case, as with most older people with hearing loss who are seen by mental health professionals, there is a complex mix of medical, psychosocial, and ethical issues, none of which should be addressed in isolation (Pray, 1989; 1996). EM's daughter was seeking the best care for her father but reflected ageist and paternalistic attitudes in deciding that an assessment of her father's hearing, and perhaps the use of hearing aids, should be imposed over his objections. Would such an action even be considered if EM were 39 rather than 79?

For the social worker or any clinician in this situation, the ethical considerations in deciding how to respond to the daughter's request and in the approach taken with EM need to be both personal and professional. What are the clinician's own attitudes toward aging and personal views about the relative importance of coping with the progressive loss of function associated with a progressive disease and the effects of hearing loss? From the perspective of professional ethics, the clinician must decide whether to support the daughter's concern for what she believes to be in the best interest of her father (beneficence) or support the father's right to make his own decision (autonomy, self-determination), irrespective of whether the clinician considers EM's choice to be in his best interests, or whether to maintain a stance of professional neutrality. The concepts of beneficence, autonomy, and self-determination are explored by numerous authors on values and ethics, such as Beauchamp and Childress (2001), Congress (1999); Corey et al. (1998); Linzer (1999), and Welfel (1998).

In the initial contact with EM's daughter, the social worker does not have to confront this issue directly because the initial assessment suggests that evaluation for depression should be the first priority. Furthermore, such an evaluation could lead to treatment that would offer the potential for altering EM's feelings of hopelessness and refusal to address his hearing loss. At the same time, the social worker models inclusion of EM in decision making when suggesting the daughter discuss securing an evaluation for depression with her father. Nevertheless, EM declines the evaluation and asserts in strong terms his intention to make his own decisions. For a man who has experienced many losses and who is likely to feel that there is little in his life over which he has control, it is understandable and also a strength that he endeavors to preserve his right to autonomy when possible. His subsequent acceptance of medication from the rehabilitation center/nursing home physician may have been perceived as less threatening since it did not require him to see a "shrink," which may have implied to him that his mind as well as his body was deteriorating.

The social worker had other options available to him. He could instead have supported the daughter's position and attempted to arrange for an audiological evaluation despite EM's objections. Had he chosen such an approach, however, the social worker would have denied EM the right to participate in decisions about his own health care, and in so doing, would have reflected society's paternalistic attitude toward older adults discussed earlier in this chapter. In view of EM's negative response to his daughter's efforts to persuade him to have his hearing evaluated, it is likely that ignoring his objections would have jeopardized the potential for the social worker to establish rapport with him. Had EM felt that the social worker was in collusion with his daughter, it is unlikely that he would have been open to discussing the losses he felt related to his physical condition, aging, and moving into a residential facility. It is also probable that he would not have undergone the audiological evaluation.

The social worker also had the option of more aggressively asserting the rights of EM when his daughter objected to the physician's refusal to have her father's hearing evaluated. Instead, when meeting with EM's daughter after the physician's evaluation, the social worker was careful to acknowledge her efforts on her father's behalf, at the same time reaffirming the importance of including him in the decision making. This balanced approach made it possible for him to avoid alienating the daughter who was obviously interested in her father's well-being, at the same time making clear his stance with respect to her father's rights. It is precisely this balanced perspective that made it possible to keep both EM and his daughter engaged in the process of dealing with the major changes that were occurring in their lives.

When EM was offered the opportunity to discuss the issues with which he was dealing as he entered the rehabilitation center/nursing home, and was not pressured by the social worker for any particular action, he spoke freely. It is reasonable to conclude that there were three key factors in EM arriving at his decision to secure an audiological evaluation and his subsequent decision to use an assistive listening device to help him communicate with his family and the people at the rehabilitation center/nursing home:

- the social worker's respect for EM's autonomy by assuring him that undergoing a hearing evaluation was his decision; and if he did receive an evaluation, the decision about what action to take next would also be his;
- the therapeutic process the social worker used during which EM addressed his many losses and adjustment to the institutional environment (Burack-Weiss, 1992);
- the antidepressant medication (Butler et al., 1998).

The admitting physician's decision to neither require an evaluation of EM's hearing nor even discuss it with him presents a complex ethical issue. She does not address the hearing loss at all because she does not expect a person of EM's age and condition to be interested in nor benefit from a hearing aid. Like Erikson et al. (1986), she appears to view hearing loss as simply one of the inevitable effects of aging—another manifestation of ageism. There is a body of research and clinical observations that support the physician's views about the dissatisfaction with hearing aids and inclination not to use them among large numbers of older persons (Franks & Beckman, 1985; Humphrey, Gilhome-Herbst, & Faurqi, 1981; Trychin, 1990). In addition, Nerbonne, Smedley, Tannahill, Schow, and Flevaris-Phillips (1989), in a chapter from an aural rehabilitation text, take the position that

> the disengagement process is commonly observed in the elderly—a tendency on the part of many older people to become progressively introverted and interact less with others. For some this will be an important step toward disengagement from the 'world' and can be a healthy process in preparation for dying. Therefore, the aural rehabilitationist should not, in his/her enthusiasm, be too aggressive if the client is clearly not interested. After making a reasonable effort, the audiologist should be generally accepting of this disengagement attitude and channel efforts to other persons whose emotional status is more conducive to remediation activities. (p. 555)

Disengagement theory has been widely criticized in the gerontology literature, and specifically related to hearing loss, Butler et al. (1998) offer a different perspective.

> Hearing loss in older patients in mental hospitals and nursing homes is likely to be neglected. The attitude may be that it hardly matters. Yet institutions should ideally be places where verbal communication is both necessary and rewarding to patients. The results of careful diagnosis and treatment can be favorable even in a large population of institutionalized patients. (p. 180)

This perspective is also consistent with much of the aural rehabilitation literature that promotes the use of hearing aids, assistive technology, teaching speechreading, and other communication strategies with older adults (Bally & Kaplan, 1988; Harless & McConnell, 1982; Kaplan 1985, 1987, 1988). EM's response to the antidepressant medication and therapy with the social worker, his subsequent agreement to have his hearing evaluated, and his use of an assistive listening device to enhance his relationship with family and others are persuasive arguments against making assumptions about disengagement and unwillingness to find ways to cope with hearing loss.

A final concern is that medical management and psychotherapeutic intervention are being handled without any evidence of collaboration between the social worker and physician. The most effective approach to dealing with the complex mix of medical, psychosocial, and ethical issues noted earlier in the chapter is through interdisciplinary assessment and planning. In this situation, medication management and psychotherapy are being handled by two different professionals. The situation is particularly complex because of the many factors that play a part in EM's depression: grief over the death of his wife, loss of physical function because of Parkinson's disease, loss of independence, and loss of hearing. Best practice dictates that the social worker and physician consult with each other concerning treatment and monitoring the treatment outcomes.

Typically, in the type of setting in which EM is residing, if the non-physician does not initiate the contact, it may not occur. There are many issues that should be addressed in such a contact. Consideration should be given to having a geriatric psychiatrist evaluate EM for the most appropriate medication and dosage since older persons may have adverse reactions or be overmedicated when receiving a dose that is appropriate for a younger adult (Hooyman & Kiyak, 1999). Aside from the issue of who should prescribe the medication, the social worker can provide input into understanding EM's response to the medication as well as the numerous other factors that influence the course of the depression, including the psychotherapeutic work that is being done to strengthen EM's ability to cope with the many losses he has experienced and those that are anticipated to occur over time.

DEAF OLDER ADULT

The following case scenario poses a particular challenge because with the current level of awareness of the Americans With Disabilities Act (ADA), it may be difficult to relate to the client's insistence upon using a family member as an interpreter after the therapist suggests providing a certified interpreter.

The History of the Presenting Problem

EF is a 69-year-old deaf woman referred to the mental health clinic by two of her adult children. They are concerned because she has become increasingly nervous and upset about arguments between her and her husband. They have told their parents they should get marriage counseling, but EF's husband refused to consider it. Because EF is so distraught by the problems, they thought the mental health clinic might help her cope better with the situation at home.

EF signs using American Sign Language (ASL), graduated from a residential school, and went to college for one year. When she married and became pregnant with their first child, she withdrew from college. Periodically, throughout the marriage she worked part-time to supplement their income. EF's husband is deaf, attended the same residential school as his wife, and worked in construction until retiring five years ago. Stresses in their relationship have increased since his retirement.

Ethical Dilemma

The mental health clinic had no deaf therapist on the staff and assigned EF to see a hearing therapist who had taken several sign language classes at a community college and had worked with a few deaf clients who were college students during a five-year period at the clinic. The work with those clients had gone well. During the intake interview with EF, the therapist thought she understood most of what EF was expressing, but she had difficulty fully comprehending the ASL. She did feel confident that she had understood that EF and her husband were arguing about finances and whether they should relocate to a warmer climate. When the therapist asked EF if she understood her signing, EF nodded her head affirmatively. The therapist was doubtful that EF fully understood her since she knew her ASL skills were limited, but she proceeded with the interview, seeing no other alternative given EF's statement that she understood her.

When EF arrived for her second appointment, it was apparent that she was very upset. Her face was red and her eyes were filled with tears. She signed very rapidly, and the therapist was only able to understand that there had been a particularly angry quarrel the night before and that there was some discussion about leaving. She was uncertain, however, as to whether EF was thinking of leaving, her husband was thinking of leaving, or if the issue was whether the couple would leave the area. The therapist attempted to have EF sign more slowly and to repeat parts of her story, but she was too upset to do so. The therapist knew that effective therapy could not take place under these circumstances and she suggested to EF that the clinic attempt to secure an interpreter. EF's initial response was an emphatic "no." She told the therapist that the Deaf community was small and that she was afraid that if she discussed her problems in front of an interpreter, everyone in the Deaf community would learn that she and her husband were having problems. She reiterated that she understood the therapist "fine" and that an interpreter was not necessary. The therapist indicated that she was concerned that her ASL skills were not good enough, she was not always sure she understood EF, and that EF had the right to be fully understood. Again, EF assured the therapist that they were "doing fine."

The following week, EF came to the appointment with her hearing daughter, whom she said could "help out" and interpret if the therapist had any trouble understanding her. She indicated that because her daughter had grown up using sign language, she was better than any interpreter, and she already knew about the problems between EF and her husband. She thought having her daughter there to interpret would ease the therapist's concerns about understanding her. EF also informed the therapist that she knew she could trust her daughter not to spread any gossip about their sessions with anyone in the Deaf community.

The therapist attempted to refocus the discussion to how the client's best interests would be served by having a professional interpreter, at the same time respecting the client's expressed comfort level with her daughter, and commending her daughter for her willingness to assist her mother. During this discussion, EF occasionally looked to her daughter for clarification of what the therapist said. It appeared to the therapist that the daughter was uncomfortable, and she attributed this to the obvious reluctance of the therapist to have her in the role of interpreter. She decided to bring the daughter into the discussion, commenting again about her obvious concern for her mother, but also indicating that it is usually awkward for everyone in the family when a member is in the role of interpreter.

The daughter said she was glad to help her mother out, but acknowledged feeling uncomfortable with the idea of sitting in on her mother's therapy sessions. EF quickly responded that her daughter knew about the problems and the fights already, and said some other things in ASL that the therapist wasn't able to understand. Her daughter replied that it was different being a witness to the arguments and sitting in the therapist's office seeing her mother discussing these personal matters. EF looked surprised and seemed not to fully comprehend the distinction her daughter was making.

The therapist took this opportunity to discuss in some detail the role of a professional, certified interpreter and the code of ethics regarding confidentiality that was similar to the code followed by the therapist. EF looked dubious, but her daughter was gently encouraging her mother to "give it a try." EF asked, "So you don't want to come?" Her daughter replied that she really didn't feel right knowing all of her mother's personal "business," feelings, etc. EF said she would have to think about it and would let the therapist know.

The Ethical Issues

At the start of the third interview, the clinician had to decide whether to accept EF's daughter as the interpreter; reopen the discussion of the clinic providing a professional, certified interpreter; or suggest they resume their efforts to communicate without an interpreter. Limiting the choices to these three options was based on the knowledge that there was no clinician proficient in ASL in the community to whom the client could be referred.

Attempting to continue working with EF without an interpreter could be dismissed as an option since it was apparent that the clinician did not have adequate command of ASL to fully understand her client. As noted above, during the early sessions, she was not able to determine whether EF was considering leaving her husband, whether he was considering leaving her, or whether they both were considering leaving the area. It should be clear that continuing without an interpreter posed too great a risk of misunderstanding and resultant errors in assessment and treatment.

From the ethical perspective of privacy and a client's right to confidentiality, using a family member as an interpreter for therapy is never recommended. In addition, family members, by virtue of their personal involvement, cannot be expected to maintain the objective stance that is expected of an interpreter. Using adult children as interpreters creates concerns from another perspective. The current generation of older deaf adults raised their children during a time that professional interpreters were virtually nonexistent. Many were placed in the position of using very young children to interpret their own parent–child conferences at school, medical appointments, business dealings, etc. This created a role reversal and gave children access to information that children would otherwise never have. Thus, even in circumstances where the client expresses the desire to use a family member as an interpreter, the inherent problems greatly outweigh any perceived benefits.

The most desirable of the three options was to use a professional interpreter. EF's concerns about confidentiality were addressed by emphasizing to her that interpreters certified by organizations such as the Registry of Interpreters for the Deaf are governed by a code of ethics that has stringent requirements for confidentiality, just as the code of ethics for the clinician does. In addition, the daughter was uncomfortable in her appointed role as interpreter. The therapist provided emotional support for the daughter by recognizing her interest in being helpful to her mother and also "universalizing" about the awkwardness for family members who act as interpreters. This approach also conveyed to EF that the daughter's encouragement to consider a professional interpreter was not an expression of disinterest in being helpful to her mother.

From the point of view that there should be "linguistic matching" between clinician and client, it could be argued that introduction of an interpreter should have been pursued more aggressively at the outset. For there to be linguistic matching, the therapist should be able to communicate in the client's preferred, most comfortable language/communication method (Corker, 1995; Harvey, 1989). Lacking such matching, a professional interpreter is the most desirable alternative.

If one is inclined to argue that the deaf woman in this case is denied her right to self-determination when her daughter is not accepted as the interpreter, the counter-argument is that to support that choice is to perpetuate role reversal and paternalism. Is it truly freedom of choice when the deaf person raised her children during a time that there often was no choice but to use even very young children as interpreters? Is it not more empowering and ultimately liberating to assert the right of the client to have the same privacy and objectivity that hearing people have when they are consumers of mental health services?

Because of the ADA, greater availability of certified interpreters, TTYs and relay services, pagers, and other technology, it is likely that deaf persons of any age will be increasingly less likely to ask family members to serve as interpreters. Deaf people of all ages are becoming more aware of their legal rights and are more accustomed to having professional interpreters in mental health, medical, educational, business, and other situations covered by the ADA.

CONCLUDING THOUGHTS

It is not possible in a single chapter to address every ethical issue that might face a mental health practitioner who works with older deaf and hard of hearing clients. Because older people and people who are deaf or hard of hearing are members of stigmatized groups, this chapter focused on ethical issues that stem from social attitudes of paternalism and dependency and emphasized values that are consistent with self-determination and autonomy.

REFERENCES

Bally, S. J., & Kaplan, H. (1988). The Gallaudet University aural rehabilitation elderhostels. *Journal of the Academy of Rehabilitative Audiology, 21,* 99–112.

Beauchamp, T. L., & Childress, J. F. (2001). *Principles of biomedical ethics* (5th ed.). New York: Oxford University Press.

Becker, G. (1980). *Growing old in silence.* Berkeley: University of California Press.

Burack-Weiss, A. (1992). The losses of late life: Elder responses and practice models. In F. J. Turner (Ed.), *Mental health and the elderly* (pp. 10–24). New York: Free Press.

Burnside, I., & Schmidt, M. G. (1994). *Working with older adults* (3rd ed.). Boston: Jones and Bartlett.

Butler, R. N. (1969). The effects of medical and health progress on the social and economic aspects of the life cycle. *Industrial Gerontology, 1,* 1–9.

Butler, R. N., Lewis, M. I., & Sunderland, T. (1998). *Aging and mental health: Positive psychosocial and biomedical approaches.* Needham Heights, MA: Allyn and Bacon.

Congress, E. P. (1999). *Social work values and ethics: Identifying and resolving professional dilemmas.* Chicago: Nelson-Hall.

Corey, G., Corey, M. S., & Callanan, P. (1998). *Issues and ethics in the helping professions* (5th ed.). Pacific Grove, CA: Brooks/Cole.

Corker, M. (1995). *Counseling—The Deaf challenge.* London: Jessica Kingsley.

Cox, H. G. (1993). *Later life: The realities of aging* (3rd ed.). Englewood Cliffs, NJ: Prentice-Hall.

Erikson, E. H., Erikson, J. M., & Kivnick, H. Q. (1986). *Vital involvement in old age.* New York: Norton.

Franks, J. R., & Beckman, N. J. (1985). Rejection of hearing aids: Attitudes of a geriatric sample. *Ear and Hearing, 6,* 161–166.

Harless, E. L., & McConnell, F. (1982). Effects of hearing aid use on self-concept in older persons. *Journal of Speech and Hearing Disorders, 47*(3), 305–309.

Harvey, M. A. (1989). *Psychotherapy with Deaf and hard-of-hearing persons: A systemic model.* Hillsdale, NJ: Erlbaum.

Hooyman, N. R., & Kiyak, H. A. (1999). *Social gerontology: A multidisciplinary perspective* (5th ed.). Needham Heights, MA: Allyn and Bacon.

Hotchkiss, D. (1987). *Demographic aspects of hearing impairment: Questions and answers.* Washington, DC: Center for Assessment and Demographic Studies, Gallaudet University.

Humphrey, C., Gilhome-Herbst, K., & Faurqi, S. (1981). Some characteristics of the hearing-impaired elderly who do not present themselves for rehabilitation. *British Journal of Audiology, 15,* 25–30.

Kaplan, H. (1985). Benefits and limitations of amplification and speechreading for the elderly. In H. Orlans (Ed.), *Adjustment to adult hearing loss* (pp. 85–98). San Diego: College-Hill Press.

Kaplan, H. (1987). Assistive communication devices. In H. G. Mueller & V. C. Geoffrey (Eds.), *Communication disorders in aging: Assessment and management* (pp. 464–493). Washington, DC: Gallaudet University Press.

Kaplan, H. (1988). Communication problems of the hearing-impaired elderly: What can be done? *Pride Institute Journal of Long Term Health Care, 7*(1), 10–22.

Linzer, N. (1999). *Resolving ethical dilemmas in social work practice.* Needham Heights, MA: Allen and Bacon.

National Center for Health Statistics, Moss, A. J., & Parsons, V. L. (1986). Current estimates from the National Health Interview Survey, United States, 1985. *Vital and health statistics* (Series 10, No. 160, DHHS Publication No. PHS 86–1588). Washington, DC: Government Printing Office.

Nerbonne, M. A., Smedley, T. C. , Tannahill, J. C., Schow, R. L., & Flevaris-Phillips, C. (1989). Case studies: Adults/elderly adults. In R. Schow & M. Nerbonne (Eds.), *Introduction to aural rehabilitation* (pp. 541–573). Austin, TX: Pro-Ed.

Orr, J. B. (1982). Aging, catastrophe, and moral responsibility. In P. L. McKee (Ed.), *Philosophical foundations of gerontology* (pp. 243–260). New York: Human Sciences Press.

Pray, J. L. (1989). Older persons with hearing loss: A neglected minority. *Disability Studies Quarterly, 9*(3), 15–17.

Pray, J. L. (1992). *Aging and hearing loss: Patterns of coping with the effects of late onset hearing loss among persons age 60 and older and their spouses/significant others.* Unpublished doctoral dissertation, The Union Institute, Cincinnati, OH.

Pray, J. L. (1996). Psychosocial aspects of adult aural rehabilitation. In M. J. Moseley & S. J. Bally (Eds.), *Communication therapy: An integrated approach to aural rehabilitation with deaf and hard of hearing adolescents and adults.* Washington, DC: Gallaudet University Press.

Schein, J. D., & Delk, M. T. (1974). *The deaf population of the United States.* Silver Spring, MD: National Association of the Deaf.

Steffens, D. C., Hays, J. C., & Krishnan, K. R. R. (1999). Disability in geriatric depression. *American Journal of Geriatric Psychiatry, 7,* 34–40.

Tidball, L. K. (1986). *A study of the coping strategies developed by older adults who have been deaf since adolescence and possible application of the strategies to the aging process.* Unpublished doctoral dissertation, University of Nebraska, Lincoln.

Trychin, S. (1990). Why people don't acquire and/or wear hearing aids from a psychologist's point of view. *Shhh, 11*(3), 13–16.

U.S. Bureau of the Census. (February 14, 1996). *U.S. population estimates by age, sex, race, and Hispanic origin: 1990–1995* (PPL-41). Washington, DC: Population Projections Branch, Population Division, U.S. Bureau of the Census.

Wax, T. M. (1982). The hearing impaired aged: Double jeopardy or double challenge? *Gallaudet Today, 12*(2), 3–7.

Welfel, E. R. (1998). *Ethics in counseling and psychotherapy.* Pacific Grove, CA: Brooks/Cole.

6

Ethical Issues When Working With Minority Deaf Populations

Carolyn A. Corbett

Particular issues arise when providing mental health services to deaf persons of color. The author is an African American hearing psychologist who has worked for many years within the Deaf community. From these experiences, the author considers some of the particular dynamics that emerge when race, class, and culture meet in psychotherapy.

ETHICAL ISSUES RELATED TO CULTURAL COMPETENCE

Cultural competence is the primary and essential component for providing ethical mental health services to deaf persons of color. Attaining and maintaining cultural competence is a lifelong process, which requires a personal commitment on the part of the mental health professional (Corbett & Leigh, 1998). Although ethical standards (American Psychological Association, 1992) and accreditation procedures for many graduate programs require training in cultural issues, procedures for actual monitoring of specific competencies in this area are lacking (Sue, Arrendondo, & McDavis, 1995; Pope-Davis & Dings, 1995). In addition, despite inclusion of culturally specific coursework and infusion of culturally relevant materials into graduate training programs, there is an overall attitude within the mental health field that treatment of persons of color should be handled by professionals or laypersons of color (Comas-Diaz & Greene, 1994). Very few professionals go on to receive additional training in minority issues after they complete their graduate training. Mental health professionals who have decided to receive

84

advanced training in cultural issues have often reported a lack of recognition and compensation by administrators in the agencies where they work (Gerner de Garcia & Corbett, 1999; Leigh & Corbett, 1998).

Despite these difficulties, the culturally competent mental health professional who provides services to deaf persons of color must be aware that his or her clients are involved in several cultures at once. For example, in order to understand the cultural experience of an African American deaf person, the professional would be required to know about Deaf culture, hearing culture, African American hearing culture, and African American Deaf culture. The therapist must not underestimate the importance of any of the cultural groups to which the client belongs (Valentine, 1996; Anderson & Grace, 1991; Aramburo, 1992). The therapist also brings into the relationship with the client his or her own racial and cultural identity. Within the therapeutic relationship, there will be places where issues of race and culture converge, diverge, or conflict (Tyler, Brome, & Williams, 1991). Therapists who have done the self-work required for attainment of healthy racial and cultural identities have been hypothesized to provide the best therapeutic environment for minority clients (Carter, 1995).

CULTURAL COMPETENCE: VIEWS FROM THE FIELD

The field of mental health and deafness brings with it additional competence issues, especially where race and culture are concerned. The author has personally examined her roles as "oppressed" versus "oppressor," "member" and "not a member" of the minority Deaf community, as well as the issues of being "on duty" as a psychologist all of the time and the difficulties associated with maintaining professional boundaries and confidentiality.

"Oppressed" Versus "Oppressor"

Unique to the mental health treatment of deaf persons is how the hearing therapist deals with his or her own "hearingness." As an African American hearing psychologist, the author has been required to personally address the issue of being "oppressed" based on racial status, and an "oppressor" based on hearing status. The minority therapist may share the experience of racism or other forms of oppression with deaf clients, who are also members of minority groups, but should not overestimate the importance of this "similarity" to the minority deaf client (Corbett, 1999). Although the minority deaf person may see race or color as a commonality, the client is also significantly aware of the therapist's "hearingness." Hearing therapists who work with deaf persons must personally examine the privileges attached to being members of the hearing majority and how they may knowingly or unknowingly oppress deaf persons. This issue is one that is quite difficult to examine, especially for therapists who are aware of what it feels like to be oppressed based on race or culture.

"Member" Versus "Not a Member"

As a minority hearing psychologist, the author has also been required to examine the issue of being a "member" and "not a member" of the community in which she works. After working through this issue, the author has resolved that "membership" within the minority Deaf community is often extended to hearing persons who work within it for specific activities, such as conferences, social events, or live performances. However, "membership" within the community should not be assumed; it is extended by invitation only, for a specific reason. Please consider the following example:

An African American hearing counselor worked with a deaf ministry at her church. She interpreted the Sunday morning services twice a month. She had provided this service for three years and was well known by the deaf members.

The deaf ministry tended to sit in the four rows of seats designated for them in the church. Generally, two of these rows were used each Sunday for deaf members. One week, when she was not officially interpreting, the counselor came to church with her husband and daughter. They all sat in the last row of the deaf ministry seats. Several deaf members became angry, stating, "Hearing people can sit anywhere in the church. Why is she taking away seats from deaf people? Why are they sitting there?"

As an observer of this interaction, the author believed that the problem was not "space," because there was plenty of room. The true issue at hand was that the hearing counselor had made an assumption about her membership in the community that the deaf people had not made.

Always on Duty

The minority Deaf community is extremely small, and there are a limited number of mental health professionals trained to provide quality services. The number of minority mental health professionals who work within this community is smaller still. Therefore, even though you may not know all of the members of the minority Deaf community, chances are many people unknown to you know who you are and what you do. Members of the community view you as a psychologist, social worker, or counselor, even when you are grocery shopping or at church. Thus, you are always "on duty" and being evaluated.

———

A hearing Cuban psychologist at a college counseling center was in the process of doing an intake evaluation with a deaf Puerto Rican graduate student in the counseling department. The Cuban psychologist was psychodynamically trained, and maintained a very traditional demeanor during the intake interview. The client complained, stating, "I saw you in the snack bar yesterday. You were getting lunch. You were talking with your friends, smiling, and having a good time. You seemed like you had such a fun personality. Now, you just seem so serious. Not what I expected at all."

———

CONFIDENTIALITY AND BOUNDARY MANAGEMENT

Confidentiality and the ability to maintain appropriate professional boundaries are two issues that arise frequently for professionals who work with minority deaf persons. Members of the minority Deaf community who also have serious mental illnesses are a small and readily identifiable group (Anderson, 1992). Since the number of individuals trained to work with these clients is also small, the therapist is often readily identifiable as well.

———

A hearing African American male social worker was walking down the street in a major city and saw an African American deaf man coming in the opposite direction, alone, signing frantically to himself. The social worker recognized the deaf man as the boyfriend of a former client, M, whom he had seen for individual therapy 10 years previously. The social worker had terminated services with the client 10 years previously because he was relocating. The social worker subsequently moved back to the same city, and resumed his practice there again. Although *he had never actually met the boyfriend*, he had seen pictures of him in court-related documents. The boyfriend was known to be psychotic, as well as physically and sexually abusive to his former client and their children. As he was passing by, the social worker said hello to the deaf man, as it was customary for African Americans to speak to each other in this major city. The deaf man then signed, "I know you! You were M's counselor! M is still a bad girl. M still needs help. I'm going to get a new girlfriend, get rid of M. What do you think? Do you think I should get rid of M and get a new girlfriend?"

———

CULTURAL COMPETENCE: A LIFELONG PROCESS

When providing services to minority deaf clients, the mental health professional takes on the responsibility of addressing and, at times, monitoring issues that are of concern to the community to which the client belongs. Common themes that may arise in the counseling session may include racism, economic issues, spirituality, health concerns, and environmental/community issues.

Racism is an unpleasant reality that occurs in the everyday lives of minority individuals in the United States (Takaki, 1993). Minority deaf individuals often report that they experience racism not only in the population at large, but also within the Deaf community (Hairston & Smith, 1983; Corbett, 1991, 1999). Within the process of psychotherapy or counseling, the issue of racism is very likely to arise, and the therapist must be prepared to address it (Tyler, Brome, & Williams, 1991; Carter, 1995). Failure to respond to or directly address the issues of race, racism, and/or cultural differences in treatment may have a negative impact on the therapeutic relationship (Carter, 1995; Atkinson, Casas, & Abreu, 1992).

Minority deaf persons come from a variety of socioeconomic backgrounds. However, each socioeconomic group has faced barriers to furthering their ability to compete within the current economic demands of society. Minority deaf persons who have a history of chronic mental illness often live on government subsidy, which necessitates that they live in low-income areas. Poor neighborhoods tend to have more crime, and the standard of living is much lower than middle-income areas (Anderson, 1996). Lower middle-class individuals may report feelings of frustration over limited job opportunities and limited opportunities for career advancement. College-educated deaf persons have reported similar concerns as well, specifically regarding access to graduate-level educational programs (National Black Deaf Advocates, 1996).

Religious organizations have played a significant role in many minority Deaf communities. For example, in the African American Deaf community, many churches have deaf ministries that have historically served as a place of support, news, leadership, and community involvement. Within minority communities, there has been a long-standing conflict about whether people should go to a religious leader or a counselor for help with problems (Comas-Diaz & Greene, 1994). A culturally competent mental health professional should anticipate that issues related to spirituality will come up in treatment with minority deaf individuals. The theme of spirituality has been known to arise in therapy with persons of color, regardless of whether the person regularly attends religious services.

There are specific health issues that are particularly of concern to minority individuals. When providing mental health services to minority individuals, questions about health history and monitoring chronic health concerns may be an integral part of the treatment. This is especially true for minority deaf individuals, who may not have had the opportunity for detailed explanations about their health problems from their doctors. Minority individuals tend to be at greater risk for hypertension, diabetes, kidney disease, cancer, and Acquired Immune Deficiency Syndrome (AIDS) (Center for Disease Control, 1999). When working with minority deaf individuals, the counselor should assess whether the client has had a recent physical examination, whether he or she has received treatment for any of the above disorders, and whether the person has been compliant with their doctor's orders.

Culturally competent mental health professionals cannot be "commuters" when they are providing services to minority deaf persons. The term *commuter* in this sense, relates to being disconnected from the environmental or community issues that the client lives with on a daily basis. Mental health professionals must stay abreast of what is going on in the communities of the clients that they serve. Essential information may include the names of and signs for community leaders, important places, and issues that may be of importance in upcoming elections. Major news stories that involve persons of color, or court decisions affecting minority individuals are also important to know. For example, the O.J. Simpson trial was a long-term event, which had a rather controversial outcome. It would not have been unusual for a minority client to raise this topic in treatment during that time. Each community also has a culture by which it labels things that are important to it. For example, in Washington, DC, people often describe parts of town based on what high school is located nearby. As a therapist providing services in this community, it has been important for the author, who is not a native Washingtonian, to pay attention to the location of high schools in order to understand what clients are talking about.

The issues covered in this chapter are only a few in a long list of items, which can be included in an ethical treatment plan for minority deaf clients. It is important to note, however, that each area requires the gathering of information over a lifetime, which underscores the nature of cultural competence as a life-long process.

NONTRADITIONAL ROLES

When working in a community that has been traditionally underserved, it is not unusual for a mental health professional to take on some nontraditional roles. When assuming these roles, the professional must constantly weigh the implications of his or her activity as it relates to his or her professional ethics. Nontraditional roles that the author has taken on have included religious interpreting, beauty pageant judge, and sorority advisor.

Each one of these roles has raised unique ethical concerns worthy of examination.

As stated previously, religious organizations have played a central role within the African American Deaf community. The author's church also happened to have a deaf ministry. Many of the author's deaf colleagues and students are active participants in this church. As a new member of the church, it happened that all of the people that the author knew were deaf, so sitting with the deaf ministry seemed logical. However, as a person who knew sign language, it was expected that eventually the author would help out with interpreting. Although the author has worked for many years in the Deaf community, she has never received training as an interpreter. Nevertheless, it was expected that she would take on some interpreting responsibilities, even if it was only a small role. The author had to get used to the idea that she would receive feedback about her interpreting from the deaf members, which consisted of a small piece of notebook paper listing her mistakes. Things became complicated when former clients visited the church and sat with the deaf ministry while the author was interpreting (and were witnesses to their therapist receiving the feedback sheet). In addition, the minister of the church was a very charismatic speaker and very dramatic, characteristics the author was required to relate during the interpreting process. This acting or emoting was quite different from the demeanor the author usually used in therapy. Thus, the author was uncomfortable with being seen "out of role" in this manner. Finally, when church officials found out that the author was a psychologist who also signed, they said, "Great! Now you can work in our counseling ministry and see deaf clients when they come in!" The author was able to successfully decline this suggestion.

The author was also asked by colleagues to serve as a judge for the local Miss National Black Deaf Advocates pageant. It was the author's assumption that the contestants would be undergraduate students from Gallaudet University. At the time, the author did not anticipate any conflicts because she no longer provided counseling services to undergraduate students, and had been out of that role for approximately five years. However, once the pageant began, it was evident that the contestants were high school students, undergraduate students, and professionals working at the university. Although none of the contestants were former clients of the author, the potential for an ethical conflict was there. In addition, the role of a psychologist deciding whether someone was "beautiful" or not was a pretty loaded issue. The author decided that beauty pageant judge was not a role that she would take on in the future.

For four years, the author served as a certified advisor for a chapter of a national sorority. This advisory role was conducted prior to the passage of the Americans With Disabilities Act. Several ethical dilemmas arose during the author's performance of the advisory role. First, the sorority had no experience in working with deaf persons, so communication was an issue. There was no understanding of interpreting needs or the fact that interpreting was a paid profession. Thus, the chapter and the advisor often struggled with the sorority officials over mandatory meetings or activities where no support services were provided. Although the organization promised support services when the deaf members were initiated, these services quickly waned when new national officers were elected. Thus, the author experienced helplessness and oppression, along with the deaf members, when the organization failed to respond appropriately. An additional issue was that the role of advisor and the role of member competed with each other. The duty of the advisor was to make sure that the sorority rules were followed. The goal of the undergraduate sorority members was to find ways to have fun without the advisor knowing about them. This set of conflicting roles led to a tense relationship between the advisor and the membership. The role of advisor as an "enforcer" of the rules conflicted with the role of a psychologist who, as a rule, was supposed to be empathic and caring.

Finally, the sorority proposed that undergraduate chapters should select an advisory team. Two of the advisors on the team for this chapter happened to be mental health professionals. The advisors had to switch to being mental health professionals during a crisis at a chapter retreat, where the following scenario occurred:

———

During the retreat, there were many team-building activities in order for members to get to know each other better. Members decided that they wanted to do a lifeline activity, where they would provide a history of important events in their lives.

One of the members, who had a long history of mental illness, gave a lifeline with many upsetting details in it. Specifically, she described the death of one of her siblings after a long illness, and how none of her family members had told her that the sibling was sick because she was deaf. The member described going home for the funeral and becoming so upset that she attempted to get into the casket with her sibling. This member began to decompensate when she told this story, which upset the other 10 members who were watching. The advisors had to stop the lifeline activity, provide counseling for the member, and debrief the other members.

———

In this situation, the advisors had knowledge of the mental health status of one of the members; however, this information could not be revealed due to confidentiality. The person met all the requirements for membership in the sorority, and therefore, could not be excluded from participation. In the role of sorority advisors, the mental health professionals were supposed to facilitate activities during the retreat, be positive role models for the sorority, and educate the younger members about sorority traditions. However, given the crisis at the retreat, the advisors had to now become mental health professionals again in order to diffuse an emotional situation. They had to make sure that the member in distress was not a danger to herself or other people. They also had to meet with the other members in order to make sure that they had the opportunity to debrief and discuss their concerns about the incident. Thus, for the members of the sorority, there may have been some confusion as to what the advisor's role should be, because they saw their advisors switch to the role of clinicians during the retreat.

ETHICAL ISSUES IN CLINICAL PRACTICE

When minority individuals have a mental health problem, they are more likely to seek help within their communities first. This means that family, friends, or religious leaders may be initially called upon to help resolve the problem. When the individual comes in to see a mental health professional, this more than likely suggests that the person's community resources were not effective, and that they are now seeking a less-preferred alternative (Dana, 1993). The conflict about whether to "air one's laundry" to individuals outside one's community is frequently played out in negotiations about structuring the therapy process. The idea of seeking treatment outside the community, and paying for it, is a new one for many minority clients in general. Minority deaf clients may have received counseling at residential or day programs for deaf people. However, the idea of paying a fee for such services is often met with resistance.

Minority mental health professionals receive additional pressure from the minority community to provide free services or sliding scale rates, even when the client is more than adequately covered by health insurance. Many minority clients can afford to pay for services; however, they may need assistance in understanding the nuances of their health insurance policies. This is especially true now in the time of managed care, authorizations, and time-limited services.

An African American deaf female undergraduate student contacted a psychologist in private practice in order to arrange services. The psychologist agreed to see the client for a free intake appointment to determine whether a working relationship could be established. The client came in to see the therapist, and explained that she was feeling depressed over a past history of abuse. After leaving home and moving to her college dormitory, she now wanted to address these issues in therapy. After essential information gathering, it was determined that the client would begin treatment after she ironed out her insurance information. She was fully covered by health insurance, but needed to change her address so that information about therapy was not sent to her parents' home. The client contacted the therapist and set up her next appointment, but then failed to show up for it. The client did not respond to attempts by the therapist to reschedule. Several weeks later, the client sent the therapist a note stating that she had decided against changing her address for insurance purposes and would not be seeking treatment at this time.

Two months later, the therapist began to receive calls from minority colleagues about a student in crisis. They began to explain details of the case, and the psychologist recognized the client as the one whom she had seen previously for intake. She could not reveal that she knew who this client was, however, and made an appropriate referral to an on-campus counseling agency that was free and open to all students. Several minority colleagues began calling from all over the campus, stating that this student had come to see them. The colleagues began to demand that the psychologist see this client for free, stating, "Don't you have a private practice?"

As a mental health professional who provides services to the minority Deaf community, the therapist must, in an ethical manner, balance his or her own need for personal financial viability and responsibility to the underserved group. Although therapists are not required to take on low-income clients, many mental health professionals reserve some space in their practices for people who cannot pay regular rates. If a therapist finds that he or she cannot take on a new client, it would be important to keep a list of resources for low-income clients, which will facilitate referrals to appropriate agencies.

A second issue in clinical practice is related to confidentiality in the training and supervision process. As stated previously, minority deaf persons who are mentally ill are a relatively small and easily identifiable group. When the individual is chronically mentally ill, chances are that he or she will receive services in a public hospital or community agency from a specific group of people for a very long period of time. As a result, confidentiality and boundaries become blurred and difficult to maintain. In addition, the treatment planning procedures and agency philosophies of many organizations serving deaf persons involve a multidisciplinary team, where every team member knows every client. Finally, chronically mentally ill clients tend to stay within the same geographic area for many years. As a result, there is an additional problem of "grandfathering" during the supervision process, where trainees may eventually get clients that the supervisor used to have when in training.

—

A deaf clinical psychology graduate student brought into supervision a case where she conducted a court-ordered psychological evaluation. The referral question was whether the client, an Asian American deaf female, was fit to be a parent. The client had a history of bipolar disorder and frequently left her children without supervision during manic episodes. The client was also involved in a long-term relationship with an African American deaf man who had a history of schizophrenia. The couple had two children in foster care placement due to a history of neglect and alleged physical and sexual abuse. The student provided information from an intake interview that was quite sketchy, and many details were missing. The student stated that the social worker who referred the case did not provide any background information, and stated that a fresh perspective was desired. As the student read the case, the supervisor recognized the client as a person she worked with in psychotherapy while she was a clinical psychology intern. At that time, 10 years earlier, the client had been referred to the supervisor for court-ordered psychotherapy. The supervisor was puzzled by the history presented, because she distinctly remembered that the couple had two other children as well. The supervisor also knew additional information about the case that had not been provided.

—

Under the current circumstances, the supervisor knows information that was obtained through a previous confidential relationship with the client. The goal of the supervision under these circumstances was to guide the student toward obtaining as much relevant information about the case in order to make the best recommendations for the client.

ETHICAL DIFFICULTIES WHEN WORKING IN COMPLICATED FAMILY SYSTEMS

The following is a case example of the types of ethical dilemmas that may arise when working in the large bureaucracies of a major city. The case involves the Kelly/Rosados family, who were referred for a psychological evaluation by the state department of social services. Informants included the client, Mariel Kelly, the client's guardian, Esteban Cruz, and the client's biological father, Hector Rosado.

—

Mariel Kelly is a 15-year-old biracial deaf female (African American and Dominican) originally from Newark, NJ. Mariel was born into a family in which all of the members were deaf. At the age of 3, Mariel was placed into foster care due to allegations of physical and sexual abuse by her parents. A younger sibling, Amparo (age 1), was also placed at that time. Mariel's biological parents, Hector and Angela Rosado, were both deaf and had long histories of drug and alcohol abuse. Mr. and Mrs. Rosado were frequently incarcerated for illegal activities related to their drug use. From initial placement, Mariel and her sister resided with the Kelly family. The Kellys were in their 50s at the time they became foster parents. The Kellys were hearing, but were teachers of the deaf in the local public school. After several years of continued drug use, incarceration, and failure to follow through on the foster care plan, the Rosados' parental rights were terminated. The Kelly family formally adopted Mariel and her sister Amparo when Mariel was 6 years old.

Mariel Kelly never quite attached to the Kelly family. The Kellys had consistent problems with Mariel from initial placement. Mariel became increasingly distressed after mandated visits with her family, during which she was allegedly told by Mr. and Mrs. Rosado, "Don't listen to the Kellys. We are your parents; remember us." At the time Mariel was adopted, negotiations were made so that she could maintain contact with an older sibling, Marta, who had been placed in foster care several years previously. Mariel maintained telephone/TTY contact with Marta, and the three sisters occasionally visited each other at Christmas for a period of six years.

When Mariel was 12 years old, the Kelly family retired and moved from Newark to Hawaii. Mariel's contact with her sister Marta became less frequent after this 6,000-mile separation. As her contact with the Rosado family decreased, the more Mariel acted out. She stated, "The Kellys are nice people, but the Rosados are my family. Amparo thinks of the Kellys as her parents. I do not." Due to increased acting out behaviors, the Kellys placed Mariel in two exclusive private schools (with interpreters); she was expelled from both of them. By age 15, she had been hospitalized on two occasions for suicide attempts, and she was engaging in runaway behaviors.

Shortly after her 15th birthday, Mariel received a call from Marta informing her that Mrs. Angela Rosado had died from cancer approximately six months previously. Mariel's behavior deteriorated drastically and included drug and alcohol abuse and possible gang involvement. Mariel was also arrested for shoplifting.

Mrs. Kelly's health began to deteriorate, and she sought assistance from social services in Hawaii regarding a placement for Mariel. At their wits' end, the Kellys called Marta (now age 25) and asked her if she would be willing to take Mariel. Marta agreed and social services in Hawaii facilitated Mariel's flight to the Rosado home in Philadelphia, PA.

Marta and her new husband Esteban resided in an apartment complex directly across the street from Mr. Hector Rosado. Although the agreement with social services was that Marta and Esteban would be Mariel's guardians, Mariel's "bad attitude at the airport" upon arrival led Marta to decide to let her sister live with their father instead. As stated previously, Mr. Rosado's parental rights were previously terminated due to allegations of physical and sexual abuse.

Mr. Rosado was on parole and employed as a chef for a major hotel chain. He had a rather unorthodox living arrangement that included his current girlfriend, a former girlfriend, and two female roommates. All of the women were also deaf. There were seven children in the household, four of whom were under the age of five. There were 12 full-time residents of this household prior to Mariel's arrival. There was no room available for Mariel at her father's, and she was assigned to sleep on the living room couch. There was no opportunity for privacy, and due to the chaos of the household, no place to do homework. Mr. Rosado's girlfriends/roommates expected Mariel to take on primary babysitting duties after school. Mariel acted out over this issue, much to everyone's dismay. Mariel has run away overnight, uses drugs and alcohol, has become involved in numerous sexual relationships with men, and is suspected to be involved in a gang. Attempts by Mr. Rosado, his girlfriends, and Marta and Esteban to set limits have yielded no results. At the time of the evaluation, Mariel is 16 years old, and the family wants her "out."

——————

There are several ethical issues that may arise for the mental health professional working with this family. The first is the issue of abuse/neglect. Mariel was placed in foster care 12 years previously because there were findings of physical and sexual abuse perpetrated by her parents. Now, she is again living with one of the alleged abusers. Although the abuse is not a family secret, family members have opted to disregard the past history, and now consider it unimportant. As the mental health professional in this situation, it is an ethical requirement to inform social services directly of the situation, and immediately minimize the risk to the client. The client is in a high-risk situation because she is in a low-privacy, chaotic environment, which is not designed for a teenage girl. Additionally, she is engaging in high-risk sexual behaviors.

The second ethical issue relates to the appropriate supervision of the other minors in the household. The county where Mr. Rosado resides has specific laws about the age of caretakers, and how long one child may be left to care for another. A 16-year-old cannot legally be left to care for seven other children.

Parenting is this case's third ethical issue. Social services in Hawaii made an agreement with Marta and Esteban Cruz to serve as parents to Mariel upon her arrival in Philadelphia. However, they immediately gave up parenting responsibilities to Mr. Rosado. Given their age (25) and inexperience, the Cruz's did not see themselves as able to handle the responsibilities of a teenager with the types of problems Mariel presented. Under Mr. Rosado's supervision, Mariel took on the parenting role for his children. The female members of Mr. Rosado's household additionally placed parenting responsibilities on Mariel. This case presents a situation where no one is available to provide appropriate parenting to a child who has desperately sought a family. Given Mr. Rosado's past history as a perpetrator of sexual abuse, he is not an appropriate candidate for parenting Mariel. Marta and Esteban Cruz might be appropriate candidates for parenting; however, given the history, they cannot be trusted to maintain appropriate boundaries between Mariel and her father. Ethically, the psychologist will need to inform social services of the need for an alternative placement for this client. This is unfortunate, under the circumstances; however, it is the only way to guarantee this client's safety.

A final ethical consideration in this case relates to assessment of dangerousness to self and others. Mariel is currently associating with an unsavory crowd, some of whom are known to be members of a local gang. She is also engaging in alcohol and drug abuse and inappropriate sexual relationships. Mariel has a previous history of suicide attempts and hospitalizations for mental health problems. Given her emotional instability and the prospect of losing another family, she may need a residential treatment facility to help her handle the upcoming transition.

SUMMARY

This chapter has provided an overview of many of the ethical issues that may arise when working with minority deaf persons. The mental health professional must consistently work on defining his or her role, especially given the demands placed on him or her by members of the Deaf and hearing communities. However, after working through these issues, the mental health professional is more competent to provide much-needed services.

REFERENCES

American Psychological Association. (1992). Ethical principles of psychologists and code of conduct. *American Psychologist, 47,* 1597–1611.

Anderson, G. B., & Grace, C. A. (1991). Black Deaf adolescents: A diverse and underserved population. *Volta Review, 93,* 73–86.

Anderson, N. B. (1996, April). *Why African Americans get sick and die faster than other groups.* Paper presented at Gallaudet University, Washington, DC.

Anderson, R. P. (1992). Black, deaf and mentally ill: Triple jeopardy. In College for Continuing Education (Ed.), *Proceedings of the empowerment and Black Deaf persons conference* (pp. 89–103). Washington, DC: Gallaudet University.

Aramburo, A. J. (1992). Sociolinguistic aspects of the Black deaf community. In College for Continuing Education (Ed.), *Proceedings of the empowerment and Black Deaf persons conference* (pp. 67–88). Washington, DC: Gallaudet University.

Atkinson, D. R., Casas, A., & Abreu, J. (1992). Mexican-American acculturation, counselor ethnicity and cultural sensitivity, and perceived counselor competence. *Journal of Counseling Psychology, 39*(4), 515–520.

Carter, R. T. (1995). *The influence of race and racial identity in psychotherapy: Toward a racially inclusive model.* New York: John Wiley & Sons.

Comas-Diaz, L., & Greene, B. (1994). *Women of color: Integrating ethnic and racial identities in psychotherapy.* New York: Guilford Press.

Corbett, C. A. (1991). *Dual minority status and college adjustment: An examination of social and academic adjustment in Black Deaf college students.* Unpublished doctoral dissertation, Pennsylvania State University, University Park.

Corbett, C. A. (1999). Mental health issues for African American Deaf persons. In I. W. Leigh (Ed.), *Psychotherapy with deaf clients from diverse groups.* Washington, DC: Gallaudet University Press.

Corbett, C. A., & Leigh, I. W. (1998, June). *Multiculturalism in the classroom: The hot spot!* Paper presented at the International Convention of the Alexander Graham Bell Association for the Deaf, Little Rock, AR.

Dana, R. H. (1993). *Multicultural assessment perspectives for professional psychology.* Needham Heights, MA: Allyn and Bacon.

Gerner de Garcia, B., & Corbett, C. A. (1999). *Mentoring of minority professionals in deafness: A qualitative analysis.* Unpublished manuscript.

Hairston, E., & Smith, L. (1983). *Black and Deaf in America: Are we that different?* Silver Spring, MD: TJ Publishers.

Leigh, I. W., & Corbett, C. A. (in press). Multicultural competence: Toward a lifetime process of growth for mental health professionals. In M. Bienenstock (Ed.), *Proceedings of the Second Biennial Multicultural Deaf Conference.* Beaumont, TX: Lamar University.

National Black Deaf Advocates. (1996, August). *Program of the 17th annual conference of the National Black Deaf Advocates.* Los Angeles: Author.

Pope-Davis, D. B., & Dings, J. G. (1995). The assessment of multicultural counseling competencies. In J. G. Ponterotto, J. M. Casas, L. A. Suzuki, & C. M. Alexander (Eds.), *Handbook of multicultural counseling* (pp. 287–311). Thousand Oaks, CA: Sage Publications.

Sue, D. W., Arrendondo, P., & McDavis, R. J. (1995). Multicultural counseling competencies and standards: A call to the profession. In J. G. Ponterotto, J. M. Casas, L. A. Suzuki & C. M. Alexander (Eds.), *Handbook of multicultural counseling* (pp. 624–644). Thousand Oaks, CA: Sage Publications.

Takaki, R. (1993). *A different mirror: A history of multicultural America.* Boston: Little, Brown.

Tyler, F. G., Brome, D. R., & Williams, J. E. (1991). *Ethnic validity, ecology, and psychotherapy: A psychosocial competence model.* New York: Plenum.

Valentine, V. (1996, December/January). Being Black and Deaf. *Emerge, 7*(3), 56–69.

7

Ethical Challenges in Training Professionals for Mental Health Services With Deaf People

Kathleen Peoples

The interface between the mental health fields and the Deaf community has undergone momentous transformation. The Deaf community was once a group subjected to procrustean psychological assumptions, a group whose specific needs and unique characteristics were stretched to pathological proportions or trimmed to insignificance. Today, the Deaf community is a recognized cultural entity and service population with corresponding mental health specialists and specialties. The deaf individual was once the passive, dependent recipient of forced, patronizing services or suffered expedient custodial neglect. In the past 30 years, these roles have rapidly disappeared, and the deaf person now interacts with the mental health fields as an active agent, as a consumer, a professor or researcher, and a professional practitioner. Moreover, hearing mental health professionals may now choose Deafness as a legitimate clinical domain.

The current consumer position of the Deaf community and the burgeoning scope of responsibilities and opportunities for deaf, hard of hearing, and hearing professionals who provide mental health services to deaf clients are promising. However, such promise demands that professionals in Deafness be carefully prepared for service to avoid past pitfalls, meet current standards for ethical practice, and develop such standards as may be specific to the field. As roles undertaken by mental health and applied social science practitioners have increased, public awareness and expectation of consistent ethical standards has increased in lockstep, as have litigation, peer review, and censure (Bass et al., 1996). Thus, the field of mental health services provision in Deafness is obligated to carefully prepare the practitioners entering the field, exposing them to the ethical concerns peculiar to it, so that the expertise and ethical structure of the discipline is on solid ground.

The preparation involves several aspects. Tipton (1996) asserts, "Sound education and training is the foundation of competent ethical practice." Hall (in Anderson, Needles, & Hall, 1998) advises, "The professional must have a grounding in the general ethical rules of conduct before she or he can presume true expertise in specialty areas." Further, Bass et al. (1996) point to "a growing awareness of need to understand factors related to culture and ethnicity in order to provide competent psychological services and to . . . a need for sensitivity to multi-cultural diversity to provide appropriate training."

Appropriate training in a focus area will therefore produce practitioners who are (1) competent in the content and application of the mental health disciplines; (2) thoroughly trained in the content and application of the overarching ethical principles and codes established in these fields; and (3) prepared knowledgeably to address the guidelines regarding service delivery to ethnic, minority, and vulnerable populations. This chapter addresses the ethical challenges presented when training professionals in the discipline of mental health and Deafness. Within the field of Deafness, students must be aware of the ways these ethical issues will uniquely impact their professional and personal identities, as well as how they affect the service provision in the Deaf community. The dilemmas covered under these topics should serve to raise the awareness of and prepare those training to professionally provide mental health services to deaf persons.

THE CHALLENGE OF DUAL OR MULTIPLE RELATIONSHIPS

The issue of dual relationships has become one of critical importance in any number of mental health practice areas, as our knowledge of the detrimental effects of poor boundaries has increased (Sonne, 1994; Bennett, Bryant, VandenBos, & Greenwood, 1990; Rutter, 1991). We have seen a progression from the naively casual conventions of the past to an intense awareness of conflict-of-interest concerns, overlapping roles, and therapeutic influence; professionals as well as clients are increasingly aware of the delicacy, specificity, and potential dangers of the therapeutic relationship (Claiborn, Berberoglu, Nerison, & Somberg, 1994; Reaves, 1993; Pope & Vetter, 1991). Moreover, mental health professions have clearly identified numerous circumstances where dual relationships may interfere with therapeutic, academic, or training progress or may corrupt such processes altogether (American Psychological Association [APA], 1992; American Counseling

Association [ACA], 1995; American Association for Marriage and Family Therapy, 1991). The endemic nature of dual relationship issues in the Deaf community has been addressed in chapter 2 of this volume; and as we will see, it permeates the discussion of every training challenge to follow, in one way or another.

Prospective providers to the Deaf community must be informed that the "perils of propinquity" and "small world hazards" can expand to an exasperating frequency (Koocher & Keith-Spiegel, 1985). Dual relationships can arise between supervisor and supervisee, faculty member and student, and trainee and client. Even graduation, termination, or referral do not mean definite breaks in contact; the deaf client, student, teacher, and supervisor remain part of the community and part of the social fabric of the mental health worker's environment. The APA ethical code (1992), Sonne (1994), Bograd (1993), Gottlieb (1993), and Kitchener and Harding (1990) present guidelines for evaluating acceptable multiple relationships and decision-making strategies to make sure that improprieties do not occur. Familiarity with these rules is not sufficient insulation for the provider of services to deaf persons however, as there are dual relationship hurdles unique to this practice population.

As mentioned above, association is often forever in the Deaf community, and the end of therapy does not necessarily mean the end of a relationship. The concern in the field about changing therapy relationships from therapeutic to personal therefore has special relevance here. Pope and Vasquez (1998) caution that pursuing dual relationships even after termination can alter therapeutic benefit. Conflicts of interest and compromised objectivity may result, and may affect the credibility of the therapist if he or she were ever required to send reports or testify about aspects of the completed therapy. For the deaf or CODA provider, preexisting relationships will also influence which services he can offer to whom. His or her family history and the alliances and activities of relatives are in the public domain and will impact decisions to offer services.

In the general literature, the issue of personal or sexual relationships after therapy terminations is often addressed (Herlihy & Corey, 1997; Schoener, 1996; ACA, 1995; Lamb, 1992). Outside of this volume, however, post-therapy relationships are discussed remarkably little in the published literature on Deafness (Zitter, 1996), although the issue is very likely to arise in the career of the provider of mental health services to deaf clients as a function of the small size of the community. As in other populations, the instances in which a post-therapy romantic or sexual relationship might be ethically permissible (i.e., where both the mutual interest exists AND the ethical criteria outlined by APA [1992] and elaborated by Schoener [1996] are met) will be quite rare indeed. Nevertheless, the probability of other types of post-termination relationships will be much greater in the Deaf community.

Therefore, the ethical practitioner in Deafness is obligated to devote special care to evaluate dual relationships and make decisions that not only protect the welfare of current clients, but also safeguard the reputation of the field in the eyes of future mental health consumers in the community. The wise provider will recognize that dual relationships, even though blameless at the outset, still present the danger of a "slippery slope," which can lead to harmful or exploitative behavior (Gutheil & Gabbard, 1993). Familiarity with ethical principles and community standards, as well as self-scrutiny, personal insight, and consultation at all levels of training and professional practice are mandatory.

To the arsenal of ethical knowledge and decision-making strategies must be added consumer education and informed consent (APA, 1992). Clients must be alerted to the discomforts and issues that they will face when entering a mental health relationship, and be apprised of their right to services without exploitation or coercion. Clients themselves may propose contacts (invitations, free goods, or for-fee services), which, if accepted, could jeopardize the primary professional relationship. The practitioner should openly discuss the ethical standards that affect the situation, his or her responsibility to protect the client and the profession, and the problems that could occur if the ethical code were disregarded. Pertinent training in addressing these topics with clients should be offered.

But what is pertinent training? Aside from reviewing the content of ethical principles, lists of area resources, and consumer caveats for clients, what are really needed are strategies for developing judgment, the full assessment of which is impossible until a critical situation presents itself. Consistent presentation of hypothetical and real problems will illustrate the steps in the decision-making process and offer both conceptual and role models for addressing and resolving issues. These experiences will serve as templates when new practitioners confront their initial professional dilemmas.

Finally, ethical codes, from Hippocrates to the present, are emphatic about the damage done when therapy, supervision, or pedagogy mix with sexual intimacy (Koocher & Keith-Spiegel, 1985). No research on the incidence of sexual misconduct among service providers to the Deaf community has been found in reviewing the published literature. The fact that nonsexual dual relations are unavoidable, however, is a cause for concern. Several studies confirm that nonsexual relationships may evolve into sexual indiscretions (Borys & Pope, 1989; Gutheil & Gabbard, 1993; Pope, Sonne, & Holroyd, 1993; Strasburger, Jorgenson, & Sutherland, 1992). Ominously, Borys and Pope (1989) showed that nonsexual dual relationships predicted therapist–client sexual misconduct in 78.3% of studied instances.

It would follow that the mental health provider in the Deaf community could be especially vulnerable to the slippery slope of sexual intimacy with clients due to the plethora of possible dual relationships with which he or she will necessary come into contact. (Gutheil & Gabbard, 1993). The need for rigorous training to inculcate ethical guidelines and judgment models, promote the exploration of personal vulnerabilities and values, and to value consultation with mentors and colleagues must be again stressed. Male trainees and professionals should recognize that they are at greater risk (Holroyd & Brodsky, 1977; Pope, Keith-Spiegel, & Tabachnick, 1986; Gibson & Pope, 1993). (See also this chapter's section on the education of therapists.) The training and consultation culture in the Deafness mental health fields should recognize the possibility of sexual attraction to clients, and provide open ways for practitioners to obtain guidance and support.

There are other dangers that present singular challenges in this area for the practitioner in the Deaf community. Nonverbal behaviors in Deaf culture (hugging, touching to get attention, etc.), which could be claimed as cultural norms, nevertheless will not be perceived as such by some clients, and leave the provider open to charges of undue familiarity. Moreover, there are indications that the incidence of child sexual abuse is higher for deaf children than for the general population (Sullivan, Vernon, & Scanlan, 1987). Sobsey's literature survey (1994) shows that those with disabilities frequently experience child sexual abuse, and that the risk is higher for some groups, including those with hearing loss. While physical touch is a common coin of communication among deaf persons, deaf clients who have a history of violated personal boundaries may be more sensitive to physical and psychological boundaries than others, and quite sensitized to even nonsexual touching.

The therapist, teacher, or supervisor in the field of Deafness who conscientiously works to set appropriate, ethical boundaries in therapy and collegial relationships will meet those who jeer at these efforts. They may claim familiarity with Deaf culture, and with the constant dual relationships in the Deaf community, and therefore declare their immunity from any difficulties that the vigilant may foresee. They may assert that membership in the Deaf community has conditioned them to deal easily with any dual relationship hazards that exist. Clients or students may explain away the need for appropriate boundaries because other ways seem more "natural" or "culturally comfortable." Supervisors and teachers must demonstrate their commitment to the effort to maintain appropriate boundaries. They can furnish examples of seemingly harmless exceptions and point out the unsuspected consequences or damage incurred. A review of recent APA ethical dilemmas and actual cases where licenses were suspended or lawsuits brought should be a regular feature of study in each program year, first in coursework, then in trainee groups at training sites.

Any situational exceptions should be undertaken advisedly (Hargrove, 1986), for the responsibility to do no harm, and to avoid and extricate oneself from inappropriate relationships lies emphatically with the practitioner and not with the client or supervisee. At the same time, cultural differences should not be ignored. Not only does Deaf culture have specific character-istics that can affect therapeutic intervention, but also, Herlihy and Corey (1997) and Sue, Ivey, and Pedersen (1996) point out that the mental health field itself can be thought of as having its own inherent cultural expecta-tions. Training should provide guidelines for practice and lead inquiry into those aspects of the cultures of mental health and Deafness, which must be accommodated for truly ethical practice.

In summary, some characteristics of the Deaf community present chal-lenges for the mental health provider in the area of dual relationships. Prac-titioners can protect the rewarding aspects of their work through familiar-ity with ethical guidelines, ethical decision-making models, vigilance, and common sense.

VARIOUS COMPETENCE CHALLENGES

The mental health professions have instituted numerous methods for cer-tifying the professional competence of their members. Diplomas, licenses, ethical codes, credentialing organizations, continuing education require-ments, and review committees are some of the ways that the consumer and society is encouraged to determine professional skill. Koocher and Keith-Spiegel (1985) remind us that, in spite of these measures, there exists no valid definition of competence that accurately detects incompetence, nor are there agreed-upon distinctions within the category of competent. Neverthe-less, practitioners are committed to perform according to some concept of proficiency or efficacy endorsed by their profession. This section will not address all possible issues related to professional competence, but will re-mark on those matters that may be affected by practice within the Deaf com-munity, with consequent implications for the content of training programs. The key issues are "gatekeeping," practice outside areas of competence, and supervision and supervisory relationships.

Gatekeeping

The academic program director or clinical supervisor has the ethical respon-sibility to be a gatekeeper for the profession (APA Committee on Accredi-tation, 1986). In the process of teaching, advising, providing applied train-ing, and giving feedback on performance, supervisors cannot fail to notice that there are those in training who would not be an asset to the profession. Supervisees vary widely in their skills, personal qualities, and in their ability to make contributions to the field. Observation may show that one student signs very well, and sails with ease through the requisite course work. Yet, she may not possess the personal insight or social comprehension to be therapeutically useful to others. Another may be interpersonally congenial, with a certain native ability to be soothing. But it can be seen that he does not have the academic talent to meet minimum program requirements. Still more problematic may be the academically gifted and therapeutically adequate supervisee whose patronizing, self-aggrandizing motives (e.g., "Deaf people need me") for mental health work nullify his potential usefulness.

Supervisors regularly confront decisions about such trainees. The American Association for Counseling and Development's *Ethical Standards* (1988) advise, "Educators . . . through continual student evaluation and appraisal, must be aware of personal limitations of the learner that might impede future performance. The instructor must not only assist the learner in securing remedial assistance but also screen from the program those individuals who are unable to provide competent services." Woodyard and Canada (1992), in citing this guideline, remind the supervisor of the dual responsibility to guard the profession and guarantee due process for the benefit of students. They suggest that closely screening applicants for mental health programs could be an important safeguard for entering students.

Once applicants have entered the program, practica and internships are usually the next critical period when attentive evaluation can provide predictions of future professional performance. Thus, honest appraisal of a student's potential, timely suggestions for remediating skill deficits or impairments, and consultation about the student among both academic and clinical faculty serve to protect the student; the mental health profession he or she is preparing to join; and ultimately, the consumer.

The foregoing responsibilities are no different for the mental health provider who serves deaf clients. But here again, the small community within which the professional in Deafness works presents elements that intensify screening difficulties. The reluctance of supervisors to give "specific articulation of the students' weaknesses" is documented in many settings (Woodward & Canada, 1992). This general discomfort with giving direct feedback is exacerbated in the Deaf community because giving negative feedback may have significant ramifications. The loss of a student from a small program could damage accreditation or funding; academic dismissal or a poor evaluation delaying the graduation of a prominent deaf family member could be felt to have serious repercussions on the personal comfort of the screener or on future job security.

The difficulties that community size present to the screener in the Deaf community are equaled by the community's fluidity. Clients empowered by effective treatment may be inspired to become school psychologists and enroll in the therapist's program. Sign language interpreters who have worked in a mental health agency may decide to take a mental health class taught by an agency therapist. Hard of hearing colleagues who become deaf, or deaf persons who develop vision problems (Usher's syndrome) may reenter the educational system for retraining. Established deaf or hearing mental health practitioners may apply for admission for an advanced degree, thus becoming subject to evaluation by former peers or previous supervisees. Students may be the children of colleagues or may be relatives. A colleague for whom the supervisor has little respect may ask for a letter of reference or endorsement for licensure. Thus, the practitioner with supervisory, faculty, or peer roles may be placed in a variety of difficult dual relationship or gatekeeping positions, which affect his or her social and professional standing in a way that rarely applies to supervisors in larger, less-enmeshed professional communities. The responsibility for the ethical management of these concerns is by no means reduced. Rather, the practitioner and those who enter the field should be made familiar with the extra burden that applies here. It should be added here that, regardless of program or community size, supervisors who are unfamiliar with Deafness may have difficulty differentiating competency issues from communication issues, may patronizingly demand less of a deaf trainee, or may be overly skeptical of a deaf trainee's competencies.

Understanding their vulnerability to these predicaments, supervisors, colleagues, and faculty members must be prepared to address these issues directly. They must take time to define carefully each of their possible roles and clarify these to the trainee and to others (ACA, 1995). As evaluators, they must specify performance guidelines at the outset, and provide regular, specific feedback on progress (Koocher & Keith-Spiegel, 1985). In providing clinical supervision, they must not allow exploration of personal issues with the trainee, which is so important for the development of counseling skills, to transition into a therapeutic relationship. Student disclosures should be handled judiciously, and the supervisor should warn the supervised student that he or she also has a responsibility to insure the integrity of the profession. If the supervision arrangement is superimposed on any existing relationship, this should be treated with extra care (see models in the "The Challenge of Dual or Multiple Relationships" section). If the supervisee cannot be assigned to another supervisor, a cosupervisor or monitor should be identified since friendships and supervision do not mix well, as conflicting expectations and power differentials are still active.

The screening responsibilities of supervisors (those with experience) do not stop at the level of training. The mental health professional community in a given area has guardianship of the public good, and should seek to meet and associate with new providers who enter that area. Such contact can provide resources, information, and support to the new arrival, while adding his or her expertise to the professional pool. This networking also permits some view of his or her practice so that less-than-competent and impaired providers can be discovered.

Mental health practitioners are not immune to stress, fatigue, or crises of physical or mental health, which will negatively affect their professional skills. The ethical provider should regularly examine the particulars of her practice as well as her own performance to assess and maintain her fitness to serve. There are instruments available for this self-assessment (Pettifor, Bultz, Samuels, Griffin, & Lucki, 1994). Further, the APA ethical guidelines charge psychologists to police the conduct of their fellow professionals, and if problems are evident, to decide on possible actions. The psychologist could elect to approach the offending practitioner on an informal basis, lodge a formal complaint with a professional ethics board or state licensing entity, or consider other entities. Or the matter might be referred to someone more equipped to effect a change.

Studies show, however, that the "monitor" mantle rests uneasily on the shoulders of practitioners. Rusch (1981) and Bok (1989) reveal that professionals often do not report colleagues who practice illegally or incompetently. Motives for reporting and not reporting vary greatly, depending on a variety of factors (e.g., personal biases, beliefs, and personality traits), which may have no bearing on the ethical codes themselves (Koocher & Keith-Spiegel, 1985). Motives may include fear of retaliation, insecurity about one's own immunity from charges, or loyalty to the profession and associates. In hypothetical exercises, students in training admit their reluctance to report ethical breaches (Bernard & Jara, 1986).

Given the small and complex community of Deafness professionals, these studies indicate that the monitoring aspects of professional responsibility must be stressed rigorously in mental health and Deafness programs. Now that the field is "hatched" and developing into a full-fledged sphere of study, all participants must be accountable for its future. The personal and professional costs of addressing incompetence or malpractice may well be great, but they must be braved. This value must be incorporated into all phases of practitioner education because the consequences of lax standards or inaction are intolerable.

Supervision and Supervisory Relationships

The Association of State and Provincial Psychology Boards (ASPPB) guidelines (1991) require that

> supervising psychologists shall be licensed or certified for the practice of psychology and have adequate training, knowledge, and skill to render competently any psychological service which their supervisee undertakes. They shall not supervise or permit their supervisee to engage in any psychological practice which they cannot perform competently themselves.

Other codes and standards detail core competencies, desirable personal traits, and roles of supervisors, preferably including conceptual knowledge of the supervision process and the developmental processes of therapists (ACA, 1995; Association for Counselor Education & Supervision, 1993; APA, 1992).

The guidelines for a general supervisor and those for a supervisor training students to work with deaf clients are the same. He or she must be an experienced professional, duly certified in a mental health field, with relevant professional and clinical expertise. However, for the Deafness professional, this expertise is also defined as *possessing linguistic and cultural competence with deaf persons*. Too often, this proviso has been minimized or ignored to the detriment of clients, trainees, and the discipline. Far too frequently, supervisors without any competence in the field of Deafness are assigned trainees who have an interest and competence with Deaf culture issues or who have been assigned deaf clients. They comfort themselves and others by suggesting that the trainee can concern his or herself with as well as educate the supervisor on Deafness, while the supervisor concentrates on handling specifically clinical issues. The assumption that the language and culture of Deafness would not suffuse the clinical picture is naive, and such arrangements cheat the student, and blur appropriate supervisor–supervisee roles and functions. Training and certification for work with other minority population subsets is already advocated as part of graduate mental health training (APA, 1992). Thus, a certification in Deafness could be added to a list of specialties. The author sees this as an area to be pursued as part of assuring quality of services throughout the profession.

Given that the supervisor has adequate training and experience, the primary challenges to ethical clinical supervision in Deafness and mental health are posed by the small number of deaf people relative to the general population, their often necessarily close-knit communities, and the still more limited number of professionals who are qualified to work and communicate with them.

The supervisory relationship, a standard feature of mental health training, is by no means free of ethical problems. "Because supervision is characterized by goals of behavior change, has many qualities similar to therapy, and by definition requires multiple roles of its participants, it should be considered a psychological intervention particularly vulnerable to ethical misconduct" (Sherry, 1991). Several investigators point to the ways in which supervision represents a significant power differential between supervisor and supervisee, which implies vulnerability for the supervisee if their welfare is not esteemed (Harrar, VandeCreek, & Knapp, 1990; Sherry, 1991; Knapp & VandeCreek, 1997). There is also risk for the supervisor if the trainee is not ethical or candid (Ladany & Melincoff, 1998).

Other sources point to the difficulties in maintaining the boundaries of the supervisory relationship. Many models of supervision invite supervisees to explore personal histories, beliefs, values, and concerns, which might influence interventions with clients. Further, supervisees are asked to discuss their feelings about the clients themselves. The supervisor uses this information to help the student modify his technique, understand blind spots, and develop his "therapeutic" personality (Hess, 1997). Interventions to shape the therapeutic personality, will, by definition, have some bearing on the supervisee's personal issues. However, Hess (1997) and others point out that when a supervisor conducts psychotherapy with a supervisee, malpractice may be occurring, and ethical principles may be violated (Sherry, 1991; Miller & Larrabee, 1995). Students should be referred to outside sources for personal treatment.

The clinical supervisor in the field of Deafness deals with additional exigencies. She may observe that a trainee is under great stress from the rigors of his program, either because of emerging personal issues, or because of personal qualities that will hamper his professional effectiveness. It is within the purview of the supervisory relationship to address these sensitive issues (i.e., she may recommend therapy to the supervisee). The supply of therapeutic avenues for the general population in a large city makes it easy for a supervisor to refer the student for support or treatment geared to increase their potential.

But in a small residential or academic community, recommending therapy as a remedy for ineffective coping or therapeutic ineptness during clinical training may put the supervisor in the awkward position of recommending something for which there are only undesirable alternatives. It is not acceptable for supervisors themselves to provide therapy to supervisees. Referral to a therapist who must rely on an interpreter is less than satisfactory. If sign-proficient, experienced practitioners are available for referral, they are more than likely affiliated with the training agency, academic program, or local Deaf community in a way that creates an unacceptable relationship duality at the outset, or will present one as the trainee goes on to other program components. For example, a student who may have sought therapy during predoctoral studies may find that his or her former therapist is in the role of evaluator in graduate class or at an internship site.

Training programs for Deafness practitioners must anticipate these eventualities. Equal attention should be given to developing area resources through grants, cooperative staff agreements, and lobbying for hiring from outside agencies to develop training components and faculty. Trainers should make every effort to discover and evaluate the suitability of available referrals for trainees. Suitability criteria include therapist competence and appropriate professional and institutional distance from the referred trainee. There was an instance in this author's experience where a training program had one referral practitioner who was always flagged to receive ethnic minority clients. Unfortunately, this person was selected for her ethnic identity instead of her therapeutic ability. Always referring all minority (or deaf) clients to one practitioner also creates the certainty of the therapist treating several individuals who know each other and may be in close relationships. This can undermine the effectiveness of and compromise the confidentiality of the therapy. Such habitual referral sources should be carefully evaluated.

Strategies should be devised to chart alternate routes for students to maximize the possibility that they can receive both therapy and training in settings where professional resources are limited. Clearly articulated policies and guidelines should stipulate the options available and how training or therapy services received in one setting will impact access to services or internship opportunities down the line. For example, a trainee might elect to receive therapy services from one provider or agency in order to preserve the option of receiving applied training or supervision from another agency or provider.

Another issue connected to the relatively small number of mental health professionals qualified to work with deaf persons is that supervisees who are interested in this field are often repeatedly assigned to the same supervisor. This limits the supervisee's professional growth, can impose barriers to training if there is not a good personal match between supervisor and supervisee since alternatives may be nonexistent, and can create a discipleship mentality.

The supervisor in programs that serve the Deaf community faces other novel dilemmas. He could find himself in the position of hearing a supervisee describe a new case and realize it is someone whom he knows. The client may be one of the supervisor's former cases, a current student in one of the supervisor's courses, the child of a personal acquaintance, or a direct friend or relative. If it is a case where the supervisor cannot be objective, he will, of course, remove himself from the case. But what is to be done when the supervised case is a former client? Supervisors who have been in this situation recommend encouraging the student to secure an information release from the therapists who saw the client in the past. The release allows them to share information about the case without breaching the confidentiality of the former treatment. Clarity on these issues is essential, since disclosure of the existence of supervision and the name of the supervisor is guaranteed to clients.

Moreover, amazingly tangled situations arise when supervisors in the field of Deafness have administrative and clinical responsibilities for a staff of practitioners. The staff may have deaf members who become aware of the mental health needs of their family members or friends. The community's only resources for direct sign communication and knowledgeable treatment may lie within that same staff. The supervisor then will have the administrative and clinical role of supervising one staff member who is working with the spouse or sibling of another staff member. Similarly, an agency staff supervisor, S, who also maintains a private practice may find that, in his agency affiliation, he is assigned to supervise the case of the spouse or child of one of his private practice clients. This private client may reasonably request at some point to speak with S, in his role as supervisor for his child's case.

In the face of such intricate puzzles, it is tempting to abandon ethical dictates, rationalize that there is no solution, and resolve to "get by." Defeatism of this sort is unwarranted, as the careful application of the ethical decision-making models, informed consent, and common sense will usually supply an answer. The answer may require extra effort (as when the supervisor waits for a release to share information with a trainee about a prior case), but the ethical spirit has been satisfied.

There are less complex supervisory concerns that also require attention. To respect the power of their office and preserve the value of the training experience, supervisors should maintain appropriate boundaries with supervisees. Yet Usher and Borders (1993) report that the collegial and relationship-oriented supervisor is preferred to the simply task-oriented one. And in any training program, and especially in Deafness-related situations, it is unrealistic to suppose that supervisors and supervisees will never interact on a social basis (Harrar et al., 1990). Furthermore, supervision is, for most supervisors and supervisees, an enjoyable interaction.

The temptations to relax boundaries, therefore, are many and subtle. As supervisees are encouraged to assume more professional and responsible roles, it is easy to become lax about the difference between superior and subordinate, staff person and trainee. Slimp and Burian (1994) list ways that the relationship can be compromised, from the introduction of business arrangements (e.g., being hired as lab assistants) to the conflicting expectations that would be raised in more social contacts with supervisees. Although this equal treatment may be flattering and desirable for the trainee, it can also cause him painful anxiety, if he cannot bring himself to admit a lack of knowledge in a certain area or if his assigned work is not within the scope of his traineeship. If the supervisor allows it to be seen that he prefers the company of particular trainees, this will create ill feeling and the view that all may not be fairly evaluated.

These boundary issues exist in all areas of mental health training. Professionals in Deafness, as in other specialties, must maintain these boundaries as an ethical responsibility, but can use these situations as teaching opportunities. Supervisor–supervisee separation concerns can be used as examples of the many dual relationships that trainees will confront in their careers. Supervisors can model friendly, respectful handling of the power and status differential, and role-appropriate handling of all personnel levels within a department, agency, school, or hospital. Observing proper boundaries during this period will also ensure harmony in the future, as the supervisees of today become the coworkers and colleagues of tomorrow.

If there have been times when the supervisor felt that their evaluating role was belittled or dismissed, or situations where the supervisee felt taken advantage of but could not protest, this mistrust will remain. Fruitful collaboration and support cannot be built on this flawed foundation.

Practice Outside Areas of Competence

In a specialty so small, the burden for services usually rests, out of necessity, on the shoulders of a few. Deaf and signing persons with mental health training of any kind are often called upon to provide all manner of interventions. These varied demands for services confront the practitioner with ethical dilemmas. The therapist trained to treat adults is asked to see a child. The American Sign Language-proficient school psychologist is asked to provide grief counseling. The one psychologist at the town hospital who can sign is asked to provide consultation on the education of deaf students who are mainstreamed in the local public school. APA's ethical guidelines (1992) specify that a practitioner does not provide services for which he is not qualified. However, when the pool of available service providers is small and the needs are great, the professional finds him or herself in a quandary, comparing the ethical weights of "giving it a try" or doing nothing. Often the professional finds that, despite a paucity of experience in testing or with a given client type, he is nevertheless the only sign-proficient person in the vicinity who has any experience at all. Such a person becomes a de facto expert. In other words, "In the kingdom of the blind, the one-eyed man is king." A practitioner who, after deliberation, acquiesces to perform such a service just once, may then find himself in the ironic position of being solicited for his expertise again at a later time or called upon to supervise others in this meager skill!

APA ethical guidelines stipulate that when in a new supervisory or practicing role for which one is unqualified, the practitioner is advised to obtain the requisite education, acquire consultation for the problem, and invest time to increase their applied skills in handling the problem (APA, 1992). It is incumbent upon the professional to use whatever resources may be available, and to seek support through professional organizations and consultation. E-mail, relay, and other technologies now permit professional consultation at a distance, which makes the isolation of the past unnecessary, as long as confidentiality principles are observed. The provider must determine to use all available resources and make plans for additional training, while maintaining the awareness that he has only one "eye."

In a small community of professionals, however, a burdened provider may, over time, neglect this self-monitoring, and evolve from a sympathetic character to an unsympathetic one. He gradually becomes oblivious to the fact that he has turned into a Cyclops (i.e., a "one-eyed" practitioner). Having established a bailiwick for which he may have few tangible qualifications, this Cyclops grants himself a personal "grandfather" clause. He forgets his duty to obtain continuing education, assumes that his scanty experience gives him authority, and may refuse to give ground or confer when a "fully sighted" (accredited and trained in a specific field of intervention) professional appears on the scene.

Maintaining expertise is an ethical imperative (APA, 1996; ASPPB, 1991), yet this maintenance is essentially undefined (Koocher & Keith-Spiegel, 1985). With the rapid and divergent growth of content and research areas in psychology, it is unclear to what degree a practitioner should and can remain abreast of these developments. Within the domain of mental health and Deafness, there is a similar pattern of rapid growth, especially as professionals in the field become more organized, and as isolated practitioners and communities connect with each other to compare experiences and generate research. Moreover, this rapid growth is superimposed on a field where early paternalistic attitudes abounded, properly trained mental health providers for deaf clients were scarce, and where research was scanty. Consequently, insistence on definitive competence is essential for corrective growth in the field of Deafness.

A tripartite training effort is required:

1. Prospective Deafness professionals must be prepared to face environments where Cyclopes are frequently bred (i.e., where there is a multitude of needs and few resources). Training would include discussions of practitioner self-evaluation and the mechanisms for detecting stress, burnout, and entrenched attitudes.
2. Trainees must be imbued with a commitment to competence that spurs them to explore all avenues for becoming effective if they choose to provide service, or that permits them assertively to refuse.
3. Finally, they must be steeled to confront the Cyclops in themselves and in their colleagues. Concern for the vulnerabilities of the consumer must be emphasized, and a commitment to the mental health field and Deafness must be inculcated.

THE CHALLENGE OF CONFIDENTIALITY

The mental health provider's preservation of the client's right to confidentiality is axiomatic for ethical practice. Information about a client is divulged to others only with the client's express permission. The right to confidentiality is abridged only in those situations that show imminent probability of harm to the client or others (*Tarasoff v. Board of Regents of the University of California*, 1976). In accordance with statutes that require reporting child or dependent adult abuse, the client is always to be informed of these limitations (Koocher & Keith-Spiegel, 1985). The topic of confidentiality is broad, but our focus here will be confidentiality issues specific to mental health service providers in the Deaf community.

The significance of confidentiality in the Deaf community is immense. The community's small size and multiple relationship potential, which make keeping secrets a formidable task, have been addressed in earlier chapters. These factors are complicated by the premium placed on information in a population to which mass media sources have been historically inaccessible. Added to this is the within-group perception that secrets are impossible to keep.

Consumer education is indispensable for practicing in this environment. Clients in the Deaf community should be educated about their right to confidentiality and the limits to confidentiality in the therapeutic situation. The steps can be explained in simple terms that will allow the therapist and client to lead their lives in privacy when outside of the therapy relationship. Therapists should discuss how and if the client wants to be greeted if both therapist and client are present at a large social gathering or pass each other on the street. Clients should be made aware that because of the size of the community, they should discuss their own treatment with acquaintances judiciously, as it may impact others to hear details of their relationship with the therapist. Walden (in Herlihy & Corey, 1997) posits that including the client in ethical deliberations will be empowering and provide the therapist with valuable community and cultural insight.

Trainees, in addition to learning to educate their clients, should be encouraged in supervision and in the classroom to visualize the ramifications of living without the basic guidelines of restraint, professional boundaries, and relationships. In one case, an ambitious and zealously compassionate trainee explained that it would be no intrusion to be called at home at any time by a troubled client. The supervisor asked her to imagine the call. What would happen if the client were suicidal or needed medical attention and called the clinician instead of an emergency service? Who would call the police or other auxiliary services? Suppose the clinician was sick when she received the call, or talking with a distraught relative, or having a dinner party? Clearly imagining a situation in which the therapist was unavailable, and the effect on a client who had been told and encouraged to call "any time," made it clear that offering unconditional availability can prove harmful and confusing.

The therapist should also educate her own family members, friends, and business associates by helping them to understand her responsibilities to preserve confidentiality and her role in the community. Her relatives and acquaintances might learn, for example, that they cannot expect to be introduced to everyone with whom they may see the therapist speaking. They should be told that they should not tell personal anecdotes about their vacation, visit, or argue with the therapist in public places or certain social gatherings, since this may evoke discomfort in someone who happens to be a client.

Furthermore, mental health providers should be prepared to take logistical measures that will protect the identity of their clients. This could mean avoiding back-to-back scheduling procedures and renting office space configured so that clients do not meet each other as they come and go. Professionals should carefully consider the ramifications of offering treatment to clients who may know each other, or who may know individuals that are personally acquainted with the therapist.

Trainees and practitioners must remain sensitive to confidentiality concerns when presenting or handling case materials. They will excuse themselves when it seems apparent that they know the client being discussed. They will refrain from presenting cases if they know that the details will serve to identify the client. They will be circumspect in settings where clients may gather (e.g., waiting rooms, etc.), as someone they know may be there to receive services from another practitioner. Therefore, although collegial sharing is to be encouraged, it is counterbalanced by the need to preserve boundaries for the protection of clients and other community members.

EDUCATIONAL CHALLENGES

In this section we turn our attention to academic and professional development issues in the field of mental health and Deafness. To be considered will be (1) academic preparation, (2) professional development, and (3) ethics education.

Academic Preparation

First and foremost, ethical education in the field of Deafness presupposes a thorough grounding in a mental health discipline. The appropriate steps for applicable certifications, licensure, and continuing education must follow. The historical paucity and unreliability of Deafness research; the norms for therapy, intelligence, and language development that were established without information on deaf subjects or with faulty information; and the hearing orientation (both physical and cultural) of the field are frequently cited as reasons to neglect the core theories and methods of the mental health disciplines. These past inadequacies do not excuse the Deafness professional from his obligation to master the field. An isolationist view does not ipso facto engender expertise, and one is ill advised to rely upon it as a foundation for practice. Intellectual mastery of the subject matter will impart the tools and credibility to correct past blunders and contribute research and concepts that will enrich the study of Deafness and mental health, and thereby, the mental health fields in general.

To this basic preparation must be added a comprehensive education in Deafness. Competent practice with deaf individuals is impossible without a Deafness knowledge base, which the acquisition of sign language, exposure to deaf people, or even membership in the Deaf community due to deafness does not confer. In addition to the history and culture of deaf persons, a firm foundation will include information about audiological, genetic, and language categories. Further, the professional working with deaf clients must be familiar with issues of cultural differences in the deaf world. A sensitivity to social class, race, gender, and other disability subsets in the Deaf community must be added to an understanding of how the hearing status differences—pre- and postlingually deaf, hard of hearing, deaf child of deaf parents, mainstreamed, late-deafened, and those with cochlear implants—affect the deaf individual's adjustment in the setting. The political, linguistic, and social characteristics of these groups all have implications for accurate empathy, assessment, treatment planning, and responsible research.

Professional Activities

Professionals in mental health and Deafness have the obligation to become active participants in local, regional, and national organizations that focus on Deafness specifically (e.g., ADARA, the National Association of the Deaf), and on mental health generally (APA, 1996; ACA, 1995; National Association of Social Workers, 1996). Participation with Deafness-related entities will increase support for practitioners who may be isolated, foster knowledge exchange and networking, and expand research opportunities. Our presence at more generally focused mental health forums will alert other professionals to the expertise, concerns, and needs within the Deafness field. Creditable representation of the field can encourage others to consider the accessibility of their own services, and may convince some to join the ranks. Moreover, Deafness professionals should take the opportunity, when possible, to obtain training in other areas of concentration. Continuing education will enhance their standing in the larger mental health community, and allow them to provide more comprehensive services. Thus, they will become exemplars within and outside the Deaf community.

Professional activities should be pursued, however, with the recognition that such endeavors are not without special ethical concerns. Due to the small number of Deafness researchers and applied practitioners, and the relatively small deaf population, data sets and case materials may be all too readily identified. The presenter of data about deaf persons in any forum must take particular care to disguise recognizable details, and judge her audience in preparing for any local or national forum. This precaution also applies to case presentations in training programs, agencies, or collegial consultations. The advantages of adding desperately needed tangible data to the field or of career advancement must be balanced by our fiduciary responsibility to clients and their rights to confidentiality and freedom from exploitation.

Trainees in the field should be encouraged to value their potential contributions to service and research. They should understand that their pursuit of expertise, scrupulous attention to ethics, and commitment to the field will have personal and community benefits. Within the tightly knit Deaf community, their professional reputation should be built with care, because their integrity will be rewarded with respect. But conversely, personal turpitude or professional carelessness will be arduous to live down. Educators should encourage those in training to safeguard their personal reputations to benefit their careers and the profession, and to win and preserve the confidence of deaf consumers.

Ethics Education

As this discourse concludes, we consider the ethical challenge of education in ethics for those entering the mental health and Deafness professions. The foregoing sections have all pointed to ethical issues that apply peculiarly to this field, which should unquestionably be reflected in specific training content. The ubiquitous dual relationships, the scant number of deaf and hearing persons so far trained in the profession, the challenges presented by the fluidity and the social/linguistic isolation of the deaf population all combine to create an imperative for ethics training, among other educational issues.

The effective ethical education of professionals in the fields of mental health, and specifically mental health and Deafness, will of course, demand supervised, applied experience in clinical situations. But the foundation of any training effort is course work. To ensure that those entering the field comprehend and comply with ethical mandates, the APA (1996) *Guidelines and Principles for Accreditation* stipulate, "The values of professional and scientific responsibility and integrity should be conveyed to all students, with appropriate policies brought to their attention." Hall (1987) notes that this exposure is suggested, but is not a firm requirement. She presents APA Accreditation Office data (1992–1993) that shows that the approaches taken by academic departments of psychology vary greatly, from those who required both basic and advanced ethics/professional standards course work and internship experiences, to those who offer one course, to those who offer no specific course but embed the discussion of ethics throughout the curriculum. Wilson and Ranft (1993) surveyed students in professional psychology programs who reported that 94% of their programs require ethics training in some form. Currently, documented evidence of ethics training is mandated for APA-accredited programs.

The efficacy of ethics education has been examined from a variety of angles. Six hundred APA members endorsed "discussions with colleagues" and "graduate course work" as most useful (Haas, Malouf, & Mayerson, 1986). Graduate courses that present not only rules but also discussions that focus on problem solving and making choices are seen as more effective (Eberlein, 1987; Tymchuk, 1985; Wilson & Ranft, 1993) than those that merely teach the content of codes and guidelines. Borders & Leddick (1988) note that ethics courses are often taught in isolation from clinical practice, and explain that classroom exposure is insufficient to prevent confusion about ethical actions. Students may be stymied when confronted with dilemmas that demand a choice between actions when both alternatives might be considered correct, as opposed to gross "good" and "bad" options (Haas et al., 1986).

The presentation of correct/incorrect dichotomies in standard ethics course work may promote rigid role concepts that quickly break down when there are "gray" or ambiguous situations. Clarkson (in McGrath, 1994) insists that navigating the choppy waters of dual relationships calls for considerations from the position of role fluency instead of a strictly rule-based role rigidity. Rodolfa, Kitzrow, Vohra, and Wilson (1990) recommend a variety of training formats when teaching the ethical management of sexual attraction to clients, remarking that didactic information on sexual dilemmas was especially helpful to new trainees, with small group discussions more valuable to advanced trainees. Sharkin and Birky (1992) buttress this point, noting that by teaching only the "don'ts" of sexually intimate dual relationships, students are poorly prepared to deal with nonsexual dual relationship issues, and may restrict simple courtesies, or conversely, enter into relations that pose harm but are not the clear sexual crises for which they have been prepared.

Another difficulty with ethics training is identified by Bernard and Jara (1986). They found that, although the students in their study correctly discerned ethical dilemmas and correctly identified the ethical principle in question, they reported that they would fail to take the prescribed action. The students declared themselves loath to report either peers or supervisors, even if they clearly recognized a violation and knew the appropriate corrective measures. Even established professionals in the field may differ greatly about what steps to take to resolve an ethical problem (Haas et al., 1986), and the motivation to report colleagues for even clearly prohibited misconduct (i.e., sexual contact with a client) was quite low. Thus, if the peer monitoring, informal and formal reporting, and censure, which guarantee a desirable standard of practice, are to be observed, ethics training must accomplish much more than conveying a memorized set of principles and their related actions or inactions. Bernard and Jara (1986) stress that such training must also instill the motivation to apply these rules personally and supply the impetus to action. It might be useful to think of making the training environment an "ethical culture," which inculcates a dedication to the well-being of the profession and the consumers it serves.

Additionally, since the accessibility of mental health services for deaf individuals has been limited in many areas, those who would prepare professionals to work in Deafness must also inspire in them an ethical commitment for educating the consumer, so that he or she can knowledgeably seek mental health services and evaluate them appropriately. This education would include not only training in community outreach, but also would explain any direct services provided, their purpose, and likely course. The informed consent advocated by APA and other guidelines may not be sufficient for some consumers who may require more accessible language and explanations that fit their conceptual frame.

In summary, those who are responsible for planning or executing training for professionals in mental health and Deafness can leave no stone unturned in ethics education. Rigorous examination of the principles and boundaries of therapeutic, referring, and supervisory situations should be combined with role plays and practice in ethical decision making at all training stages. The optimal result is a trainee with an informed, flexible approach, who can capably apply ethical principles, assess the environment, and implement appropriate solutions. The ideal product of training is the ability to document departures from usual practice, so that these differences can be available for reevaluation, increased scrutiny from the practitioner him- or herself, and peer review if questions arise (Haas et al., 1986). The final product of successful training is a professional who is linguistically, academically, and culturally competent to serve deaf mental health consumers, motivated to provide high-quality, ethically informed services, and to make sure that others do the same.

REFERENCES

American Association for Counseling and Development. (1988). *Ethical standards*. Alexandria, VA: Author.

American Counseling Association. (1995). *ACA code of ethics and standards of practice*. [Brochure]. Alexandria, VA: Author.

American Psychological Association, Committee on Accreditation. (1986). *American Psychological Association committee on accreditation handbook*. Washington, DC: Author.

American Psychological Association. (1992). Ethical principles of psychologists and code of conduct. *American Psychologist, 47*, 1597–1611.

American Psychological Association. (1996). *Guidelines and principles for accreditation of programs in psychology.* Washington, DC: Author.

Anderson, R. M., Needles, T. L., & Hall, H. V. (1998). *Avoiding ethical misconduct in psychology specialty areas.* Springfield, IL: Charles C. Thomas.

Association for Counselor Education and Supervision. (1993, March). *Ethical guidelines for counseling supervisors.* Retrieved on November 11, 2001, from http://www.siu.edu/~epse1/aces/documents/ethicsnoframe.htm

Association of State and Provincial Psychology Boards. (1991, May). *Code of conduct.* Montgomery, AL: Author.

Bass, L. J. (1996). Future trends. In L. J. Bass, S. T. DeMers, J. R. P. Ogloff, C. Peterson, J. L. Pettifor, R. P. Reaves, T. Retfalvi, N. P. Simon, C. Sinclair, and R. M. Tipton (Eds.), *Professional conduct and discipline in psychology* (pp. 143–155). Washington, DC: American Psychological Association.

Bass, L. J., DeMers, S. T., Ogloff, J. R. P., Peterson, C., Pettifor, J. L., Reaves, R. P., Retfalvi, T. Simon, N. P., Sinclair, C. and Tipton, R. M. (Eds.). (1996). *Professional conduct and discipline in psychology.* Washington, DC: American Psychological Association.

Bennett, B. E., Bryant, B. R., VandenBos, G. R., & Greenwood, A. (1990). *Professional liability and risk management.* Washington, DC: American Psychological Association.

Bernard, J. L., & Jara, C. (1986). Failure of clinical psychology graduate students to apply understood ethical principles. *Professional Psychology: Research and Practice, 17,* 10–14.

Bograd, M. (1993, January/February). The duel over dual relationships. *The California Therapist, 5*(1), 7–16.

Bok, S. (1989). *Lying: Moral choice in public and private life.* New York: Vintage Books.

Borders, L. D., & Leddick, G. R. (1988, March). A nationwide survey of supervision training. *Counselor Education and Supervision, 27*(3), 271–283.

Borys, D. S., & Pope, K. S. (1989). Dual relationships between therapist and client: A national study of psychologists, psychiatrists, and social workers. *Professional Psychology: Research and Practice, 20*(5), 283–293.

Claiborn, C. D., Berberoglu, L. S., Nerison, R. M., & Somberg, D. R. (1994). The client's perspective: Ethical judgments and perceptions of therapist practices. *Professional Psychology: Research and Practice, 25*(3), 268–274.

Eberlein, L. (1987). Introducing ethics to beginning psychologists: A problem-solving approach. *Professional Psychology: Research and Practice, 18,* 353–359.

Gibson, W. T., & Pope, K. S. (1993). The ethics of counseling: A national survey of certified counselors. *Journal of Counseling and Development, 71,* 330–336.

Gottlieb, M. C. (1993). Avoiding explorative dual relationships: A decision-making model. *Psychotherapy, 30*(1), 41–48.

Gutheil, T. G., & Gabbard, G. O. (1993). The concept of boundaries in clinical practice: Theoretical and risk management dimensions. *American Journal of Psychiatry, 150*(2), 188–196.

Haas, L. J., Malouf, J. L., & Mayerson, N. H. (1986). Ethical dilemmas in psychological practice: Results of a national survey. *Professional Psychology: Research and Practice, 17,* 316–321.

Hall, J. (1987). Gender-related ethical dilemmas and ethics education. *Professional Psychology: Research and Practice, 18,* 573–579.

Hargrove, D. C. (1986). Ethical issues in rural mental health practice. *Professional Psychology: Research and Practice, 17,* 20–23.

Harrar, W., VandeCreek, L., & Knapp, S. (1990). Ethical and legal aspects of clinical supervision. *Professional Psychology: Research and Practice, 21,* 37–41.

Herlihy, B., & Corey, G. (1997). *Boundary issues in counseling: Multiple roles and responsibilities.* Alexandria, VA: American Association for Counseling and Development.

Hess, A. K. (1997). The interpersonal approach to supervision of psychotherapy. In Watkins, C. E. (Ed.), *Handbook of psychotherapy supervision.* New York: John Wiley & Sons.

Holroyd, J. C., & Brodsky, A. M. (1977). Psychologists' attitudes and practices regarding erotic and non-erotic physical contact with patients. *American Psychologist 32,* 843–849.

Kitchener, K. S., & Harding, S. S. (1990). Dual role relationships. In B. Herlihy and L. Golden (Eds.), *Ethical standards casebook* (4th ed., pp. 146–154). Alexandria, VA: American Association for Counseling and Development.

Knapp, S., & VandeCreek, L. (1997). Ethical and legal aspects of clinical supervision. In C. E. Watkins (Ed.), *Handbook of psychotherapy supervision.* New York: John Wiley & Sons.

Koocher, G., & Keith-Spiegel, P. (1985). *Ethics in psychology: Professional standards and cases.* New York: Random House.

Ladany, N., & Melincoff, D. C. (1998). Secrets in supervision. Paper presented at *Hot Topics in Supervision.* Roundtable conducted at the American Psychological Association annual meeting, San Francisco, CA.

Lamb, D. (1992). Relationships with former clients: Ethical, legal, and clinical considerations. *Register Report, 18,* 13–14.

McGrath, G. (1994). Ethics boundaries and contracts: Applying moral principles. *Transactional Analysis Journal, 24*(1), 6–14.

Miller, G. M., & Larrabee, M. J. (1995). Sexual intimacy in counselor education and supervision: A national survey. *Counselor Education and Supervision, 34,* 332–343.

National Association of Social Workers (1996). *Code of ethics.* Washington, DC: Author.

Peterson, C. (1996). Common problem areas and their causes resulting in disciplinary actions. In L. J. Bass, S. T. DeMers, J. R. P. Ogloff, C. Peterson, J. L. Pettifor, R. P. Reaves, T. Retfalvi, N. P. Simon, C. Sinclair, and R. M. Tipton (Eds.), *Professional conduct and discipline in psychology* (pp. 71–89). Washington, DC: American Psychological Association.

Pettifor, J., Bultz, B., Samuels, M., Griffin, R., & Lucki, G. (1994). *The professional practice of psychology: Self evaluation.* Edmonton, Canada: Psychologists Association of Alberta.

Pope, K. S., Keith-Spiegel, P., & Tabachnick, B. G. (1986). Sexual attraction to clients: The human therapist and (sometimes) inhuman training system. *American Psychologist, 34,* 682–689.

Pope, K. S., Sonne, J., & Holroyd, J. (1993). *Sexual feelings in psychotherapy: Explorations for therapist and therapists in training.* Washington, DC: American Psychological Association.

Pope, K. S., & Vasquez, M. J. T. (1998). *Ethics in psychotherapy and counseling.* San Francisco: Jossey-Bass.

Pope, K. S., & Vetter, V. (1991). Prior therapist–patient sexual involvement among patients seen by psychologists. *Psychotherapy, 28,* 429–438.

Reaves, R. (1993, February). *Disciplinary data bank.* Paper presented at the Eighth Mid-Winter Meeting of the Association of State and Provincial Psychology Boards, Montgomery, AL.

Rodolfa, E. R., Kitzrow, M., Vohra, S., & Wilson, B. (1990). Training interns to respond to sexual dilemmas. *Professional Psychology: Research and Practice, 21,* 313–315.

Rusch, P. C. (1981). *An empirical study of the willingness of psychologists to report ethical violations.* Unpublished doctoral dissertation, University of Southern California, Los Angeles.

Sharkin, B. S. & Birky, I. (1992). Incidental encounters between therapists and their clients. *Professional Psychology: Research and Practice, 23*(4), 326–328.

Sherry, P. (1991). Ethics in the conduct of supervision. *The Counseling Psychologist, 19*(4), 566–584.

Slimp, P. A., & Burian, B. K. (1994). Multiple role relationships during internship: Consequences and recommendations. *Professional Psychology: Research and Practice, 25*(1), 39–45.

Sobsey, D. (1994). *Violence and abuse in the lives of people with disabilities: The end of silent acceptance?* Baltimore: Paul H. Brookes.

Sonne, J. L. (1994). Multiple relationships: Does the new ethics code answer the right questions? *Professional Psychology: Research and Practice, 25,* 336–343.

Strasburger, L. H., Jorgenson, L., & Sutherland, P. (1992). The prevention of psychotherapy misconduct: Avoiding the slippery slope. *American Journal of Psychiatry, 45,* 544–555.

Sue, D. W., Ivey, A. E., & Pedersen, P. B. (1996). *A theory of multi-cultural counseling and psychotherapy.* Pacific Grove, CA: Brooks/Cole.

Sullivan, P. M., Vernon, M., & Scanlon, J. H. (1987). Sexual abuse of deaf youth. *American Annals of the Deaf, 132,* 256–262.

Tarasoff v. Board of Regents of the University of California, 551 P. 2d 334 (Cal. Sup. Ct. 1976).

Tipton, R. M. (1996). Education and training. In L. J. Bass, S. T. DeMers, J. R. P. Ogloff, C. Peterson, J. L. Pettifor, R. P. Reaves, T. Retfalvi, N. P. Simon, C. Sinclair, and R. M. Tipton (Eds.), *Professional conduct and discipline in psychology* (pp. 17–37). Washington, DC: American Psychological Association.

Tymchuk, A. J. (1985). Ethical decision-making and psychology students' attitudes toward training in ethics. *Professional Practice of Psychology, 6*(2), 219–232.

Usher, C. H., & Borders, L. D. (1993). Practicing counselor's preference for supervisory style and supervisory emphasis. *Counselor Education and Supervision, 33,* 66–79.

Wilson, L., & Ranft, F. (1993). The state of ethical training for counseling psychology doctoral students. *The Counseling Psychologist, 21,* 445–456.

Woodyard, C., & Canada, R. (1992). Guidelines for screening counselors in training. *TACD Journal* (Spring), 11–19.

Zitter, S. (1996). Report from the front lines: Balancing multiple roles of a deafness therapist. In N. Glickman and M. Harvey (Eds.), *Culturally affirmative psychotherapy with deaf persons* (pp. 169–246). Mahwah, NJ: Erlbaum.

8

Defining the Shadow

RECOGNIZING THE IMPRINT OF THE INTERPRETER IN THE MENTAL HEALTH SETTING

Lynnette Taylor

Interpreters in the mental health setting often witness the very intimate and personal journey of an individual towards transformation and healing (Duffy & Veltri, 1997). While they are not the journey's navigator, they form a very intimate bond with client and therapist as all three work toward making and finding meaning. Yet the interpreters' role is one of veiled intimacy—they are not the *makers* of meaning, but the *messengers* of meaning. If we do not unveil the presence of the interpreter, we cannot engage in the journey of making meaning together, and it will be unclear who is navigating the terrain. Kafka's description of the "realities" that lie imbedded in the written work may be illuminating.

The easy possibility of letter-writing must . . . have brought into the world a terrible dislocation [*Zerruttung*] of souls. It is, in fact, an intercourse with ghosts, and not only with the ghost of the recipient but also one's own ghost which develops between the lines of the letter one is writing and even more so in a series of letters where one letter corroborates the other and can refer to it as

I am blessed to have worked with a team of sophisticated clinicians who are willing to look into the complexities of working with an interpreter in the mental health setting. Their work and insights have been invaluable to me and their clients. I would like to thank Wendy Manko, Paige Polisner, Pam Potishman, and Asher Rosenberg for their work and support.

a witness. How on earth did anyone get the idea that people can communicate with one another by letter! (Kafka, 1954, p. 229)

Kafka's metaphors are akin to therapy, in which participants build a relationship shaped between and during the sessions. Each session brings with it the context and history built from the preceding sessions, as well as the unknown content of what each participant has infused in the story during their time apart. If you extend the metaphor, the interpreter not only "witnesses" the letters written, but by interpreting the message, he or she also becomes a kind of "author," bringing to the correspondence additional layers of meaning.

All the inherent therapy anxieties (e.g., "will I be understood?") are amplified with the presence of an interpreter. Although each participant will share common goals regarding the interpreter's role, what may be unique for the deaf person is the hope that with the interpreter present, understanding will occur.[1] Without a conscious collaborative effort to look at what personal filters may be at play in the therapeutic configuration of therapist, client, and interpreter, it is impossible to assess the accuracy of the translation or even to ensure the meaning has been delivered.[2]

Interpreters in therapy may play a variety of roles. Most often, they are present to aid in communication between therapist and client, but sometimes this may include others. Further, since 90% of deaf people are born to hearing parents, it is safe to predict that an interpreter will frequently be necessary if family members are to be included at some point in the therapeutic process. The wish of both therapist and client is often that the presence of this "outside" party will simply be that of a neutral signifier who will not alter the dynamics of the familiar dyadic, or family formation. The reality is that interpreters are anything but neutral signifiers. Their presence simultaneously signifies both the deaf person's historical lack of direct communication access to the hearing world, and the promise of finally being understood. The moment the interpreter begins to sign, his or her presence also makes visible the "invisible disability" of deafness.[3] The interpreter comes as a loaded signifier, and can evoke a full range of feelings depending on the participants' respective and collective life experiences.

---

1. In this chapter, the lowercase form of *deaf* refers to deaf people in general and to those individuals who do not identify themselves as culturally Deaf.

2. This chapter only addresses the therapeutic configuration that includes a hearing therapist. While there are similarities that apply to a deaf therapist, there are also profound distinctions that go beyond the scope of this chapter.

3. While most people (myself included) who are familiar with the Deaf community define it as a cultural group, mainstream culture (and even others who are deaf) often views its members as disabled.

SHIFTING FROM A DYADIC TO A
TRIADIC CLINICAL RELATIONSHIP

If we proceed with the assumption that the interpreter is simply a conduit for information, we are puzzled when we notice that the messages are often indecipherable and sometimes not even sent. The process of interpreting in therapy becomes more intelligible if we move away from viewing interpreters as an "obstacle" (Stansfield, 1981, pp. 18–32); necessary nuisance; conduit for information transmission; "tabula rasa," on which a client's projected feelings can be encouraged and explored (Harvey, 1984, p. 209); or a "symbolic deaf person" (Harvey, 1984, p. 211), and move toward viewing interpreters as simply a third person in the therapeutic formation. Yet this shift is not quite so simple; it requires rethinking the traditional dyad as a clinical triadic relationship. In practical terms, the triadic approach requires externalizing the internal interpreting process and creating a dialogic process of interpreting in which the therapist, along with the interpreter, is guiding translation decisions.

CLARITY OF MEANING VERSUS CLARITY
OF INTERPRETATION

In describing the interpreting process, Seleskovitch says,

> The uniqueness of interpretation lies only in the fact that, before formulating "his" thought, the interpreter appropriates the thought of another person. We might say that interpreting is a process of speech-thought-speech, in which the words of the speaker become the thought of the interpreter and are then reconverted into speech by him. . . . The interpreter understands much better when he has an affinity with the speaker's mental functioning. The line of reasoning seems logical to him. (1978, pp. 38–39)

This "appropriation" of the other person's thoughts, particularly if there are thought disorders, uncomfortable delusional content, or any range of possibilities along the diagnostic continuum, can create very complex issues for both the clinician and interpreter.

One of my first mental health interpreting assignments was with a schizophrenic deaf client. I had not met with the psychiatrist or client before the session, so I was walking in cold. Also, I had recently moved to the area and was not familiar with regional sign language vocabulary or local cultural references.

We were well into the session and everything was going fine when the psychiatrist asked the deaf client how things were at home. The client casually answered, "Fine. I had a nice dinner with my family last night. But during dinner, a ghost started bothering me [and] wanted to have sex." The client was quite graphic, so I had no doubt he was talking about sex. What I did doubt was whether he literally meant ghosts. Because the line of reasoning seemed illogical and the way of thinking foreign to my own, I was not sure I understood the client's intended message. In trying to make the meaning clear, my mind went to more logical meanings—perhaps the sign GHOST had a different local meaning or perhaps it was his friend's nickname.

I was uncomfortable asking the client for clarification. I was concerned the client may feel the material shocked me and close down. I was also concerned that if I asked for clarification, the client may doubt my interpreting abilities, and this could undermine the therapeutic relationship. But the other operative feeling was my own fear of making a mistake and being judged by both the client and the psychiatrist. After what seemed an eternity, I turned to the psychiatrist and asked, "Are ghosts in his repertoire?" When he said yes, I felt relieved. Instead of doubting my interpretation, I could go about my job with more confidence.

For the interpreter to turn to the mental health professional for content clarification, as I did in the above example, may seem like an innocuous intervention to an outsider, but it raises many complex issues for an interpreter. Have I overstepped my boundaries by directly engaging with the deaf person's service provider? Am I intruding on the deaf person's right to confidentiality and privacy? Have I shifted the balance of power by speaking directly to the hearing service provider, thereby aligning with the other hearing person in the room? Will the therapist and client doubt my skill as an interpreter? Will my difficulty in understanding the client influence the clinician's diagnostic assessment? If the deaf person sees me asking questions of the hearing provider, will he mistrust me and consequently mistrust the therapeutic relationship? In order to understand some of our ethical considerations, we need to return to the origins of the interpreting field, which will be explored in the following section.

HISTORY OF AMERICAN SIGN LANGUAGE (ASL) INTERPRETING

The early interpreters were often children of deaf parents, neighbors, or members of the community who knew sign language and helped out by interpreting in certain situations. As Fant (1990, pp. 9–10) describes in his biography of the Registry of Interpreters for the Deaf (RID), "We did not work as interpreters, but rather volunteered our services as our schedules permitted. If we received any compensation it was freely given and happily accepted but not expected." Yet by 1964, there was a growing need for interpreting services, and the Deaf and interpreting communities felt a need to make our field more professional. In response to this need, RID was established. RID, the first national certifying body for sign language interpreters, began administering professional licensing tests that defined the minimum skills necessary for interpreting.[4] In order to attain and maintain RID certification, one must pass both a written and skills examination and continue professional development. RID also established a code of ethics. This chapter will explore aspects of three tenets of the code that are the most likely to create conflict in the mental health interpreting setting.

- Interpreters/transliterators shall keep all assignment-related information strictly confidential.
- Interpreters/transliterators shall render the message faithfully, always conveying the content and spirit of the speaker using language most readily understood by the person(s) whom they serve.
- Interpreters/transliterators shall not counsel, advise or interject personal opinions (Registry of Interpreters for the Deaf, 1997).

In the old days, interpreters had to pass the skills examination before a live board of representatives from their community. This panel usually included respected deaf leaders and interpreters as well as other active members from the local Deaf community. Their criteria, aside from language skill, were in large part, based on their comfort level with the potential candidates. Did the interpreting candidates have the right attitude? Was there potential for growth? Did they fill a particular niche in the community? There was also a tacit understanding that the representatives would teach whomever they brought in by inviting them into the life and activities of the local Deaf community.

Many interpreters who, like myself, went through the old kind of evaluation, saw the shift from local board governance to psychometrically measured tests by remote bodies as a shift away from the Deaf community. While the revised test measured skill and content knowledge, it could not measure "good attitude," an attribute held most dear to the Deaf community. As Anna Mindess (1999) points out in her book *Between the Signs,* good attitude typically means the interpreter has a good heart, cherishes ASL, and respects Deaf culture.

Several factors converged to shift the interpreter's role in the Deaf community. Since 1970, there has been a cultural revolution of sorts in the Deaf community. With the recognition of Deaf culture and ASL, Deaf pride blossomed throughout America. On the heels of these discoveries came civil

---

4. RID was the only nationally recognized sign language interpreter certifying body until 1991, when the National Association of the Deaf (NAD) developed an independent test and certification system that was recognized by RID.

rights protections in the form of Section 504 of the Rehabilitation Act and the Americans With Disabilities Act (ADA); these federal laws require the provision of qualified sign language interpreters in more arenas than had heretofore been accessible to the Deaf community. With this new expansion of service delivery in college classrooms, courts, hospitals, etc., there was a greater need for sign language interpreters. Interpreter training programs began taking hold across the country and, for the first time in deaf history, people from the outside knew more about ASL and Deaf culture than did many deaf people. So whereas in the past, deaf people had been the experts and gatekeepers; the role was now reversed. It was an ironic shift, because now interpreters could enter the profession without ever having met a deaf person as someone other than the consumer of their services.

With the introduction of interpreter training programs and then remote certification boards, the locus of power shifted. Hearing people who had no Deaf cultural heritage or understanding of deaf people's minority status and their distinct forms of historical oppression could now act as cultural gatekeepers. The recent venture between RID and the National Association of the Deaf to form the National Council on Interpreting is one visible symbol of a field that is searching to meet the needs for professional development while maintaining true to community needs.

The Helper Model Versus the Conduit Model

In recent years, many interpreters have been taught that the "only function of an interpreter is to facilitate communication . . . and remain neutral" (Harvey, 1984, p. 207; RID, 1976). This pedagogy of neutrality became enacted as invisibility (e.g., "To be truly neutral, I will pretend absence, and thereby the two parties can relate as if I am not here"). What is also insinuated is that the acknowledgment of self (interpreter) will negate the presence of the other (client), and conversely, if the interpreters' presence is not acknowledged, then the difference between the deaf individuals and their hearing counterparts will likewise disappear. This *conduit model* is at one extreme of the continuum, and developed in part as a reaction to the older *helper model* at the other.[5]

In an era before TTYs, faxes, e-mail, and other technological advances that would open the borders of the Deaf community, signing communities were often insular, and often, there were thin, if any, boundaries between the interpreter and the deaf client. Far from being a neutral facilitator of information, these family members, church members, or friends were involved on every personal and emotional level. The helper model, which entailed

---

5. There are several other interpreting models. I address these two because they reflect the extremes in our profession.

doing *for* the deaf person, often reflected a historical pathological perspective, which viewed deaf people as disabled instead of culturally and linguistically different. Often, these interpreters interacted with the deaf individual from a patronizing stance.

My friend (a PhD candidate) told me of one experience with an interpreter during a doctor's visit. "Imagine! I went to sign in and the interpreter had already collected the intake form for me. When I asked her for it, she said, 'No. I know how difficult these terms are. I will interpret the questions and then fill it out for you.'"

During the exam, the interpreter kept talking to the doctor and asking a lot of personal questions of my friend, which made her uncomfortable. She wanted to attend to the doctor, not to the interpreter. To make a bad experience worse, the day before her scheduled follow-up visit, the interpreter called to remind her of the appointment.

Another example, told to me by a deaf mother, was her experience during a parent–teacher meeting with an interpreter who operated more from an advocate model (often the distinctions between helper and advocate models are hard to distinguish). The teacher had no previous exposure to deaf people, sign language interpreters, or the ADA, so understandably, communication was a bit tentative. The mother's son was hearing. During the meeting, the teacher turned to the interpreter and said, "Tell her that her son is doing well." The interpreter corrected her, saying, "You speak to her directly; don't say, 'Tell her.'"

When the teacher suggested that one of the teachers who knew some sign language interpret her son's school play, things began to go downhill. The interpreter became incensed (understandably) and angrily told the teacher that the school had a legal obligation to provide certified interpreters under the ADA. The teacher couldn't understand why she was being chastised for performing a positive act. She had included an interpreter. This experience did not make her look forward to another meeting with the mother. It took a while for the deaf mother to rebuild her relationship with her son's teacher.

The deaf mother and interpreter had two different objectives for the communication event. The interpreter's foremost concern was to advocate for the rights of deaf people, and the mother's foremost concern was to establish positive communication with the teacher so her son would be well treated.

In reaction to the helper model, the conduit model emerged. While the helper model is overly engaged, often blurring personal boundaries, the conduit model, with its sense of neutrality, is overly disengaged.[6] A deaf

---

6. There are also positive aspects to the helper model. Those early interpreters often had no training, yet through their caring, personal relationships with the Deaf community, they attained a natural membership.

colleague shared the following example: "I had one interpreter in college who would wait outside the classroom until the professor began his lecture. She never once said hello or acknowledged me in any way. It made me feel terrible, like I was invisible." Ironically, the interpreter's intent was not to make the deaf client feel badly, but conversely to show respect by acting "ultraprofessional."

This model's goal of an utterly neutral and invisible interpreter resulted in a dehumanized or robotized interpreter who was expected to do both more and less than ever before. No longer permitted to intervene on a personal level, the interpreter was nonetheless supposed to counterbalance the historical imbalance of power by signing every word, every sound (i.e., airplanes overhead, toilets flushing) in order to create a simulacrum of the hearing person's experience. The interpreter, in this way, became the human equivalent of an amplification device.

The following story illustrates the neutrality of the professional interpreter taken to the extreme. One of my colleagues was on stage interpreting the opening of a conference when the emcee turned to him and asked his name in order to introduce him. The interpreter, instead of answering, interpreted the emcee's question—"What is your name?"—to the deaf audience. The interpreter's insistence on his own absence made his presence all the more intrusive. Unfortunately, this is not an uncommon story, but it demonstrates many of the ideological beliefs and theories (sometimes tacit, sometimes overt) in the interpreting profession that can infiltrate the mental health setting.

Deaf Consumer Perceptions

The changes in demographics and professional orientation (helper versus conduit) models can have a strong impact on the therapeutic interaction, especially if the deaf person's prior experience has been with interpreters who work more from the helper model. The shift towards professionalism has incited various reactions from both the interpreting and Deaf communities. This neutrality can be a relief for some deaf consumers, but it may make some deaf people feel too distant, as if interpreters are aloof and uncaring because they are not conforming to deaf social norms.

From the interpreter's perspective, the term *professional* has been hard-earned and makes it clear they are not like the patronizing helpers of the past. But in looking for a model of professional behavior, many turned to the norms established in the hearing American culture, which posits the individual over the collective. This runs counter to the cultural values of many in the Deaf community. Because of these differences, the interpreter's position of neutrality is viewed by many deaf people as foreign and almost the antithesis of having a good heart.

One elderly deaf woman told me that after a meeting with her medical doctor, she asked the interpreter to join her for a cup of tea. The interpreter declined, saying that she was done with her appointment and was too busy. The deaf woman said, "The interpreter looked terrified. As if I were going to bite her or something." From the deaf woman's perspective, the refusal of tea did not allow her to reciprocate the "favor" of interpreting. Also, it did not allow for a social bond to occur; after all, the interpreter had just witnessed a very private moment in this woman's life. This social bond is critical to establish yet can be difficult to navigate as a metal health interpreter.

Because the Deaf community and the people who know sign language are relatively small, it is not unusual for interpreters and clients to know each other from other social or professional contexts. Interpreters working in the mental health setting for a deaf client may find themselves attending the same church on Sunday or hanging out at the local bar on "Deaf Night." This blurring of boundaries can create unusual complexities for the interpreter and deaf client.

Such concerns do not arise because interpreters are seen as outsiders, but because they have a floating or migratory membership in the Deaf community. By *migratory*, I mean that interpreters' insider/outsider status depends on circumstances. If an interpreter is the only other person in the room who knows sign language, she is going to be viewed by the deaf person more as an insider; however, if everyone else in the room is deaf, then the same interpreter may be seen as more of an outsider. So because interpreters hold a double position, it can sometimes create confusion for both the interpreter and the deaf person as to which rules they are going to abide by.

In part, because of the interpreter's insider status, it can sometimes be hard for the deaf person to believe that the interpreter won't also feel compelled to "share the news" with the community. In the Deaf community, "to have great change in one's life and keep it to oneself would be perceived as an insult . . . although some Deaf people complain about the lack of privacy, others feel comforted knowing that news of their troubles will be disseminated to their acquaintances without much effort on their part" (Mindess, 1999, p. 94). For this reason, a deaf person may reasonably be doubtful that the interpreter can keep their interpreted session confidential.

SPECIFIC CONCERNS

As mentioned earlier, three pertinent ethical tenets that seem to be problematic in relation to interpreting in the mental health field are (1) maintaining interpreter confidentiality; (2) refraining from counseling, advising, or interjecting personal opinions; and (3) rendering the message faithfully. While these issues are discussed in more depth later in this chapter, it is important to take time to note how these concerns may be addressed among the interpreter, therapist, and client. Because all the participants in the therapy configuration have different experiences, orientations, and knowledge about therapy and interpreting, it is important to make sure to begin with a common understanding. For example, the parameters of confidentiality must be specified early in treatment. Does the therapist consider waiting room conversations between the deaf client and interpreter as part of the therapeutic material? If so, the interpreter and client will need to know this. Also, the interpreter will need to know if this conversational information is expected to be shared during the post-consultation time with the therapist. The interpreter and client need to know that any revealed information that indicates that the client is a threat to himself or others must be reported to the therapist. However, it is not appropriate for the interpreter to share history obtained from past knowledge of the client or any other information obtained outside of therapy. A previous or ongoing personal relationship (whether positive or negative) between the client and interpreter present an exception to this prohibition and must be mentioned, but delicately and with respect for both parties' privacy. The therapist must reassure the client and the interpreter that all information will remain among the three, with any legal exceptions to confidentiality made clear.

The remaining two tenets, interjecting personal opinion and rendering the message faithfully, will be addressed in the case studies later in this chapter.

Before the Session

In most jobs, the interpreter and deaf client meet beforehand to spend some time getting to know each other and discuss the nature of the assignment. This social time is important because it allows a mutual language assessment to occur and a comfort level to be established. For mental health interpreting, this social time between the interpreter and client can be tricky. The mental health provider needs to consider the interpreter's influence on the communication dynamics as part of the overall clinical approach.

For example, it might be advantageous for the interpreter and the deaf client to socialize beforehand so the client will not be surprised when a familiar interpreter walks into the room. Another positive development might be if the client learns that the interpreter has a deaf family member, which may make the client feel more confident in the interpreter's ability. In this case, however, the client may have increased concerns about confidentiality. Another concern is that if they form a close relationship, the client may worry about the interpreter's feelings during therapy. Another possible concern is that while socializing, the interpreter may innocently trigger some unexpectedly strong responses. An interpreter does not have the skills to deal with such situations, and it may be detrimental to the formation of a bond with the therapist.

Sometimes, because interpreters are seen as insiders, the deaf client may disclose very personal information while sitting in the waiting room, such as, "My lover just left me. He is HIV positive. I am sure I am. I wish I could die." Yet during therapy, none of this is revealed.

The interpreter must then determine whether it is a breach of confidentiality to tell the therapist of the prior conversation. Because of all of these pros and cons, it is best for interpreter and therapist to discuss whether it is better and more comfortable for the interpreter to wait with the client or in a different area before the first visit. Thereafter, it should be a decision jointly made with the interpreter, therapist, and if appropriate, the client.

During the Session

Once the clinician, interpreter, and client are all in the office and ready to begin, the clinician should make the introductions with the interpreter translating. The initial introductions may go something like the following:

Clinician: Are you Mr. Doe?

Client: Yes. And you are?

Clinician: I am Dr. Jess. And this is our interpreter, Ms. Lune.

Client: Yes. I know her. I have seen her around.

Clinician: I asked her to come because, unfortunately, I don't sign and I want to make sure we understand each other. (If the therapist is learning to sign, it is polite to sign HELLO and offer to fingerspell his or her name.) I value our communication, and the interpreter will help us communicate clearly. You said you know the interpreter, Ms. Lune. Do you know her well?

Client: I don't know her well. I have seen her interpret at some events. She is very good.

Interpreter: Thank you.

Clinician: Do you feel comfortable with the three of us working together? If at any time you don't, please tell me.

Client: I am fine right now.

Of course, the deaf client might have said, "I can't work with this interpreter," at which point the clinician could go ahead with the scheduled meeting but try to find another interpreter for the next appointment. If getting another interpreter on a long-term basis is not an option, the client's discomfort with the interpreter may become one of the issues addressed as part of the clinical work together. Some options for handling this situation would be to bring in another interpreter for one or two sessions to discuss the issues. Another option would be to address these issues with the "contested" interpreter present. It is important that the therapist speak with the interpreter before the session about any plan to address these sensitive issues in order to help make the interpreter feel safe in the therapeutic setting. Of course, the interpreter must also agree to proceed as part of the team. If at any time the interpreter feels unsafe or ineffective, this agreement needs to be revisited.

Interpreters as Cultural Mediators

Because interpreters are often in the role of mediating two cultures, they are used to creating an initial bond with a deaf client by virtue of their shared language and contextual knowledge. The interpreter also knows from experience that it is partly his or her task to make sure the alignment occurs between the client and the hearing provider, by allowing natural stages of attachment to occur. As the deaf person becomes more comfortable with the interpreted setting, a natural transformation will follow, and all participants will hold different and equally valuable positions in the triad.

Mediating Cultural Differences

A frequent quandary for the mental health interpreter is whether the deaf client's presentation will be seen as a diagnostic feature or a cultural feature. Because there are cultural differences in the way hearing and deaf people present information, this determination can be sticky for the interpreter. Interpreters may feel an uneasy weight placed upon them if they believe their interpretation will cause the deaf person to be perceived as ill or pathological, when the interpreter may see it as cultural. Differences in the way information is presented—in particular, attention to chronological detail—may seem to the service provider to indicate a perseverance, obsessiveness, or thought disorder. The interpreter may see it as part of his or her function to mediate these cultural differences by culturally rendering the details and giving an appropriate equivalent.

For example, the therapist asks the client, "How did you get here this morning?" The client might answer, "I got up this morning and brushed my teeth. I ran and caught the bus on the corner near my house. It was cold on the corner. The bus was crowded. Wow! Lots of Christmas shoppers; there were so many bags. It was terrible. I couldn't move." This discourse may get translated as "I took the bus. It's such an experience traveling around town during the height of the holiday season." To the interpreter, the equivalent meaning is important and expected as a cultural adjustment. Yet, without prior knowledge of the client's history, the interpreter can't make informed interpreting decisions about such events. In this case, if the interpreter had known the client was agoraphobic, the content would have an entirely different meaning and, in all likelihood, a different interpretation. Such cultural adjustments are the kinds of issues clinician, interpreter, and, at times, client will have to discuss and work out as they form a working relationship.

Accuracy

A clinician needs specific linguistic accuracy in order to help make a diagnosis, and the interpreter needs a way to gauge the accuracy of the interpretation. Yet accuracy is often difficult to gauge if the client's thought pattern is unfamiliar and the interpreter does not have guidance as to what information is relevant. Sometimes simply checking in with the therapist can go a long way. The check-in can allow the clinician to explain what features he or she is looking for, so the interpreter can see that deletions or atypical use of language may be relevant content to be conveyed. With interpreters who are not familiar with mental health interpreting, clinicians may just ask them to provide information about where, when, and why they have difficulty understanding the client.

I once worked with a psychiatrist treating a deaf schizophrenic patient who had been repeatedly hospitalized for attempted suicide. In her previous attempt, she had used a knife. The psychiatrist, who was probing to see if there was anything that triggered the client's impulse asked, "Are there certain days that are harder than others?" The client answered, "Yes. Thursday. Knife. Thursday. Knife" Her choice of signs—a SWITCHBLADE and the sign for THURSDAY—have the same handshape, so when combined, they make what would be the equivalent of a poor rhyme in spoken English. This choice of signs seemed to trigger a connection for her. Her language delivery was also unusual in that she intently stared at her signs rather than keeping eye contact with either the clinician or me. When I later mentioned this to the psychiatrist, he smiled and said it went along with the diagnostic features of a schizophrenic client. In this case, my observation regarding linguistic accuracy and delivery did not determine a diagnosis or provide a radical new insight. It was just more evidence that confirmed an already made diagnosis.

THE INTERPRETER'S FILTERS

If interpreters don't know how to select relevant information, they may see their function as making the client's meaning coherent. To do so, they may fill in deletions without the knowledge that deletions can be reflective of the client's mental status. Sometimes, it is difficult for the interpreter to see that he or she is looking for a "bundle of confusion." This can be a tricky challenge for an interpreter. Interpreters may have difficulty accepting or recognizing that they don't understand a client. Not only will feelings of inadequacy or guilt lead to denial, but it also takes a certain amount of skill and sophistication to recognize that you don't understand a client. That is why it is critical to have a highly qualified and experienced mental health interpreter in your sessions. The more experienced and fluent the interpreter is, the less likely he or she will feel threatened by these "bundles of confusion." Meaning does not always surface on the lexical level; sometimes the interpreter's personal filters become a part of the therapeutic dynamic, as in the following example.

A 15-year-old deaf female and her mother have no shared common language and are unable to have complex conversations. The mother's language is spoken Spanish, and the daughter uses ASL and English. At home, they communicate by gestures and by writing simple English or Spanish words. Because communication is so sparse at home, the daughter has many questions about her history that have never been adequately answered. For example, her parents divorced when she was young. Her father never kept in contact, and the girl always wondered why he left.

In therapy, part of the daughter's clinical work has been to address questions of her past. When the daughter requested the meeting with her mother, the therapist (who is hearing and signs fluently) appropriately brought in a Spanish interpreter and an ASL interpreter so she could focus on the therapeutic issues rather than the interpreting issues.

Early in the session, the mother revealed that the reason the father left the family was because he couldn't handle his daughter being deaf. The daughter, clearly upset, broke eye contact, and looked to the floor for a long time. The mother, from across the room, told the daughter through the interpreter, "I am so sorry I never learned to sign. You are a good daughter. I love you." The interpreter tapped the young girl to get her attention and interpreted what the mother had said. The daughter responded by asking if she could go out on a date with a boy that weekend. The mother said, "No, not until I can meet his family." The young girl looked to the sign language interpreter and said, " I don't understand." After many attempts at interpreting and getting the same response, the sign language interpreter said, "Well. I'm not much help here. She doesn't seem to understand me." She got up and walked out of the session.

Perhaps the material was too provocative for the interpreter, raising ghosts for which she wasn't prepared. But even on a more basic level, the client repeating "I don't understand" was likely perceived by the interpreter as a reflection of her own failure to successfully interpret. What the interpreter did not know was that this client's typical defense was to shut down by saying, " I don't understand." Without the larger context, the interpreter had no way to situate the girl's response, other than to see it as a direct reflection of her job skills.

An interpreter's primary function is to convey meaning from one language to another. If interpreters are not understood, their very reason for being is challenged. Even if this interpreter had stayed through the session, her feelings were so strong that they would have influenced the session's dynamics. If therapists are unaware of interpreters' need to be understood, then they may not be able to understand the source of the shadows hanging over the session.

Addressing the Interpreter's Filters

In a pre-consult, the therapist and interpreter can get to know each other and their working styles. If provocative material is expected or presented, the interpreter and therapist can discuss strategies for dealing with the situation. At this time, the therapist can share some of the client's prior history, and perhaps the interpreter could identify his or her own vulnerable areas, such as doubts about his or her interpreting ability or previous experience or lack of experience with mental health settings, and alert the therapist to any emotional issues the material may trigger.

Useful information to discuss during pre-consult is the client's mental status (e.g., violent, delusional, paranoid, or depressed). What are the features of the client's delusions? Does the client have a typical defense pattern? Other helpful information might include

- Who does the client frequently talk about in therapy?
- What is the presenting problem?
- What is the client's country of origin; what languages does the client sign or speak?
- Are there other cultural factors (regarding the gender of the interpreter, for example) to consider?
- What are the norms for eye contact, facial expressions, and signing space?
- What are the therapist's objectives for the session?
- What does the therapist expect from the interpreter?

During the pre-consult, clinician and interpreter can agree to meet after the session for a post-consult.

POST-CONSULTS

We cannot predict all the things that may come up in a therapy session, nor can we prepare to meet all of an interpreter's emotional responses. What interpreters can prepare for, however, are feelings that might be provoked. Post-consult is a place to take these feelings after the session. It should not become a therapy session for the interpreter; rather, the issues should be addressed in terms of how they affected the communication. This time is usually spent debriefing and discussing any unusual features the interpreter noticed, or answering any questions the clinician may have had during the session.

Ethical Considerations for Pre- and Post-Consults

For many interpreters, a pre-consult can be seen as a conflict with the interpreter's code of ethics. Because interpreters are sensitive to the historical oppression of deaf people, they may feel that a pre- or post-consult is outside the realm of interpreting (because they may be asked to reveal what they consider to be "insider" information or to provide an opinion) or is a breach of confidentiality. Interpreters have experienced a form of vicarious oppression in dealing with hearing providers who are very anti-deaf, and who see all deaf people from a pathological perspective. Many of us have spent years shielding deaf people in subtle ways from the majority culture's rudeness or ignorance. To ask an interpreter to reveal what they consider to be insider information can be a major challenge. It will be difficult for them to trust that the mental health professional will do "the right thing" with the shared information.

A useful approach for a clinician to address and respect interpreters' concerns is to convey that he or she is not relying on them for a diagnosis but rather for their professional experience and expertise. For example, a therapist may not know the norm for speed of signing, but would regard rapid speech (or sign) as a possible indicator of a manic state, so he or she requests the interpreter's help in placing the client's signing speed on a continuum from unusually slow to unusually fast. This approach helps the interpreters to see that they are informing, not guiding, the mental health professional's decision to make roles in the relationship more clear.

UNDERSTANDING THE CLINICAL TRIAD

Although the feelings, issues, and questions described in this chapter may arise in other interpreting situations, they become critical in a mental health setting. There are infinite combinations of feelings, issues, and questions that surface for each participant in the clinical formation (Manko & Taylor,

1996). It is necessary for the mental health interpreter to recognize what issues may be operating in each participant's experience and to understand their impact on communication within the triad. This awareness can be used as a tool to inform the session's dynamics and interpreting techniques in an effort to respect the integrity of the communication so that a client's clinical needs can be addressed.

Issues for the Interpreter

Interpreters may have an infinite number of responses to provocative material. Interpreters may feel a lack of confidence in the treatment provider. They may feel like intruders. They may feel judged by the client and clinician. They may feel anxious sitting through moments of silence and ambiguity. They may feel burdened because they bear the weight of communication, and have a desire to fix it. They may experience uncertainty about distinguishing between cultural and clinical material, and they may feel left out.

If we ignore the interpreter's presence, sooner or later their presence is sure to rupture. Rupture is not always a negative experience; it can also be a moment of uncontained glee that nevertheless has the potential for therapeutic repercussions. For example, I had been interpreting for years with a clinically depressed deaf woman. The psychiatrist had been trying to get her to be more social and encouraged her to join a group. The client had been reluctant for years, but as she was leaving on this particular day, she turned and asked for the group's contact person. I let out a little squeal of delight! During our post-consult, the psychiatrist and I discussed how my outburst of excitement called attention to the difference between the client's and my experience. These moments of reality are not always predictable, so we must be ready to deal with them when they arise in the therapeutic setting. Ignoring or erasing them does not alter their presence.

Issues for the Clinician

Clinicians also respond to the dynamics within the triad. Some of the clinician's responses may include feeling naive about deafness, ASL, and Deaf cultural issues; intruded upon by the interpreter; distrust of the interpreter's skill; fear of being judged by the interpreter and client; discomfort with the change in pace of dialogue; ambiguity about who is responsible for the communication flow; and concern about sustaining a therapeutic alliance despite constant shifts in client eye contact. The more informed clinicians are about their own reactions and filters, the more likely they will be in control of interpretation, and the safer they will feel.

Issues for the Client

Some of the responses that may surface for the clients include feelings of vulnerability, exposure, and concern around confidentiality. These responses might result in distrust of the interpreter's skills, distrust of the clinician's skills and his or her ability to understand and help them, anxiety about being misunderstood, transference reactions to both the interpreter and clinician, confusion about whose message is being transmitted, ambivalence about their need for an interpreter, mixed feelings about the interpreter, feelings of incompetence, and feeling left out.

Professional Filters

Aside from the personal, individual, and social filters that have been discussed throughout this chapter, professional filters also come into play. Such filters may include how the interpreter and therapist define or perceive their professional function and theoretical positioning (e.g., Is the clinician a Freudian psychoanalyst or a behaviorist? Is the interpreter a conduit, a helper, or an advocate?). These respective positions will factor into how both the clinician and interpreter evaluate their own success in executing their jobs.

Seeing the influence of my own personal filters impact a therapeutic setting made me rethink my approach to mental health interpreting. A gifted colleague of mine, Wendy Manko, a clinical social worker at the Lexington Center for the Deaf's mental health clinic, asked me to interpret in sessions with her client Luis. Although Wendy had a very strong command of sign language, she felt they had come to an impasse and wondered whether it was due to her sign language limitations.

———

Luis was a male from the Dominican Republic, about 35 years old. Deaf since the age of 5, he had sporadically attended a deaf school in his region. He was an adult when he and his family moved to America. When therapy began, he was working part-time in a grocery store and living with his mother, who knew no sign language and with whom he had a difficult relationship. Luis mostly used ASL, although initially he showed a limited range of language, which could either be because his primary language was another signed language or because he had limited language or cognitive issues. Luis presented as one of his main concerns a need for privacy. He also constantly worried about how expensive everything was.

Our greeting ritual was the same every week. Wendy would greet Luis in the waiting room and escort him to her office, where I would be waiting. The walk alone in the hall gave them time to reestablish their primary bond. Luis would enter the office, hang up his coat and hat, and turn to say "hello." He would smile very politely, turn first to Wendy and then to me (using both the sign and his voice). This act was significant because it expressed his need to acknowledge my presence in the room.

In the initial work together, my interpreting served as a confirmation of Wendy's "read" of Luis. Many months were spent with him describing in detail his day at work, from the polishing and stacking of apples, to the way he cut and wrapped a watermelon. He often complained that his mother went through his things, read his mail, and took his Supplemental Security Income money. Wendy suggested renting a mailbox. Months were spent discussing the various prices of mailbox rentals, most of which cost about $12 a month, which he said was too expensive. Luis was compulsive about saving his money, yet never expressed any desires, plans, or fantasies about how he wished to spend it. After each session, both Wendy and I would be exhausted. We were experiencing, in a very small way, the tedium of Luis's daily routine. But for Wendy, the sensory experience of both seeing and hearing the monotonous detail of stacking and polishing apples was almost overwhelming. Since she could sign, she asked that I no longer interpret the elements that she easily understood into spoken English. Because I was now sitting for long periods of time not interpreting, my role changed from being an interpreter to a silent listening partner. Though I did not always interpret Luis's dialogue into English, I continued to interpret Wendy's English into ASL.

One day in therapy, Luis mentioned seeing a coat he liked in a store. It was the first time he had exhibited a desire with even a touch of enthusiasm. Then he quickly reverted back to talking about work with little or no affect. Later in the session, Wendy tried to go back and explore his desires. She asked him, "Are there things you wish for?" The structure of the question required me to make some decisions, particularly regarding the term *things*. Because I was still unsure of the client's linguistic range, I had to make a translation choice between concrete things and states of existence. I translated two questions into ASL: (1) "Do you in the future want (or wish for) a new car, house, coat, etc.?" and (2) "Do you (in looking to the future) imagine yourself married, happy, with children, traveling, etc.?"

I decided to translate Wendy's question with a specific example (a common way of translating in ASL). I chose what I thought was safe material. Because he had mentioned the coat earlier in the session, I decided to integrate that example into my translation, so that it would be more "emotionally safe." However, I also added a hypothetical element to the translation. What I ended up signing was, "If you had $100, would you like to buy that coat or a . . .?" I never completed the question because the client became so agitated that I was stopped in my tracks. Luis interjected that he would *never* spend $100 on a coat—that was way too much money! The whole course of therapy was detoured for that day because of my translation choice. Even though Wendy used the mistake as part of her therapeutic material, it was not the initial course she had been trying to set.

———

In thinking about it later, I realized my translation choice was driven by my own personal filters. Several things were operative. My desire to "get in" was so strong that my interpretation was almost steering the client to an opening. Also, I was driven by my need to be understood. That need was so strong that I overcompensated by building in too many examples and adding a specific hypothetical. I needed a response, and indeed I got one! The other filter that reared its head was related to class. The class difference between the client and myself was made acutely apparent by my perception that $100 for a coat is reasonable, which clearly the client did not share. I did not take into consideration the client's very real and present anxiety about money when thinking about my translation choice.

It was a fortuitous mistake, for, at that point, I realized I didn't want to be responsible for driving the session in the wrong direction. After that session, Wendy and I began to formulate our working strategy, and we decided to bring the internal part of the interpreting process to the surface. If I needed specific examples for translation, I would ask her to supply them, or I would verbalize my sentence construct first to see if this was the direction she wanted to go. This allowed her to monitor, edit, and shift the material and allowed me to monitor my own filters.

Another intervention choice Wendy made was to have me acknowledge the client's responses by being an *active listener*, which meant giving the appropriate head nods to signal that I understood him. Since I was now interpreting less, it felt culturally inappropriate not to be visibly acknowledging the conversation. We agreed to change my role to a *natural listener*— not an overactive one, but one who is clearly present and listening to the conversation. Also in our post-consultations, Wendy and I began to look at and discuss our respective filters in terms of how they affected our communication process.

It was amazing how much freer I felt in the following sessions. I could now fully attend to the construction of meaning knowing it was (at least more closely) matching her intent. Likewise, I would inform the deaf client, "I don't understand her yet. I will interpret in a second." Then I would ask Wendy to clarify, or, if I understood, nod my head and proceed. (As a byproduct, this also had therapeutic value because the client saw that hearing people don't always understand each other as well.)

As time went on, the client became part of the process, saying, "Oh you need more information," and then actively waiting. Reciprocally, I repeated the process with the client. If there were areas of content or linguistic uncertainties or deletions, I informed Wendy of my confusion. For example, I might tell her, "Someone stole his money. I am not sure whom. I think he just said, but I couldn't understand it. Do you want me to clarify?"

My work with Luis and Wendy helped me realize that we can get lost in the detail and lose the big picture. A particular piece of unclear information may not be important to the therapist at a given moment. By determining when and where to go in for clarification, interpreters may be preventing the therapist from making more natural observations. In short, the internal part of the interpreting process was brought to the surface, with me using the therapist as my interlocutor to determine when and how to go in for clarification. From our work together, we began to look very closely at the shifting dynamics when an interpreter is in session. It was from our many hours of conversation that we began to reformulate how we worked together.

Luis, Wendy, and I went from being a dyadic model with the semi-present interpreter trying to facilitate and form the dyad between therapist and client, to a triadic model with the interpreter being present and actively interpreting. In practical terms, this approach means the communication questions and choices are relayed back to the therapist, so that they are always the ones mapping the sessions while the interpreter lays the roadwork. We took on the search for meaning together.

The resulting dynamic was very interesting. As it became clear that the three of us were building meaning, the client's linguistic expression began to expand. Somehow the reassurance that Luis was understood by both of us made him more relaxed. He stopped going over every detail at work and started talking about his internal life more—his childhood, his loneliness, and his relationships with people at work. Both Wendy and I noticed that when he felt unsure about whether he was understood, he would go back to the more repetitive mimetic depictions of his day at work (e.g., the stacking of apples) and the more gestural communication that could be understood by someone who did not know sign language.

Luis was eventually able to get a better job, make plans to get married, and even considered renting an "expensive" tuxedo. With his new work schedule, we could not work out a time when all three of us were available, which brought up the discussion of bringing in another interpreter or proceeding without one. Additionally, unlike in typical mental health situations, termination with the interpreter was also addressed. (Wendy and Luis ultimately agreed to continue without an interpreter.)

It may seem that the client's dependence on the interpreter is counter to the formation of a dyadic relationship, but this example illustrates that the client's initial alliance with the interpreter actually led him to give full trust and power to the therapist. Remarkably, the dyad was much stronger after the interpreter's presence was acknowledged and some of the interpreting process was brought to the surface.

Bandler and Grinder (1975, p. 41) provide a useful explanation of surface structure versus deep structure: "The Surface Structure itself is a representation of the full linguistic representation from which it is derived—the Deep Structure. In the case wherein the linguistic process of deletion has occurred, the resulting verbal description—the Surface Structure—is necessarily missing for the therapist." I see the distinction as the interpreter provides the surface structure, but the therapist guides the deep structure. This must be a reciprocal process. If the interpreter makes too many adjustments without the therapist's knowledge, the therapist will not have access to the client's deep structure, and change in the client's deep structure will be difficult to achieve. Therefore, a dialogue must take place between therapist and interpreter for the client to obtain the full meaning from the session (Manko & Taylor, 1996).

THE TRIADIC MODEL IN ACTION

According to Bandler and Grinder (1975 p. 41), linguistic information "may also be missing from the client's conscious model of the world. If the model of the client's experience has pieces missing, it is impoverished. Impoverished models imply limited options for behavior. As the missing pieces are recovered, the process of change in that person begins."

Let me share another case with you in which the triadic model was applied. Pam is a hearing therapist who knows ASL. One of her clients was Rose, a Deaf woman of Puetro Rican descent in her early 30s. Rose lives in Brooklyn and is very tough and street savvy. She is fluent in ASL, and her language is peppered with "street" signs. Because Rose signs very rapidly with great intensity, she can sometimes be difficult to understand, and her affect can sometimes be misleading.

Rose was referred to Pam because the state Agency for Children Services (ACS) removed her 3-year-old son from the home as a result of alleged child abuse and placed him in a series of foster homes. Because her family was responsible for reporting her to ACS, Rose felt betrayed and had a hard time trusting anyone. She was also extremely wary of social workers because they represented the professionals who took her son away. Pam and Rose had worked together for a while, and at a certain point, they reached an impasse. At the time I began interpreting the therapy sessions, Rose's son was 8 years old, and they had just recently been reunited.

Rose presented as anxious, paranoid, and angry, saying things like, "They think I'm a sucker. I'm not! I can see through them! I know they're trying to play me. I know they're trying to take my son away again." By "them" she was referring to the people who work for social service agencies, anyone who suspected her of the abuse, doctors, or anyone in authority.

Rose's son had been having difficulty in school. He was suspended several times for fighting. Rose was very worried about her son fighting because any bruises that appeared would make the authorities suspicious of her. Pam asked how Rose felt when her son got into fights. Rose said, "Angry." Pam asked, "Do you worry or feel scared that he will get hurt?"

I interpreted, " Do you worry . . .?" when Rose vehemently interrupted, saying, "No. I'm angry!" I told Pam that I didn't have a chance to interpret the complete question.

The session continued, and each time the terms *fear* or *worry* appeared, the client said, "No, angry." Later in the session, on a totally different topic, I interpreted Pam's question "Are you concerned about his grades?" as "Are you worried he may not pass?" Rose responded, "No, I'm angry." As the session moved on, Pam gently explored the other feelings attached to anger, such as fear and worry. Rose began to incorporate the sign for WORRY into her responses. She combined the ANGER and WORRY signs, making them almost a compound sign: ANGER/WORRY.

Later in the session, Pam tried to convince Rose to let her son start counseling on his own with a separate therapist. The following conversation took place.

> *Rose*: I can trust you [i.e., Pam]. You have been good to me. I have been coming here for many years now. But someone new? They are hearing? I don't know.

> *Pam*: Yes, we've been working together a long time. A lot has changed. You remember it used to be just the two of us. Then we talked about adding an interpreter to help us communicate.

> *Rose*: Yes. But it is better with the interpreter, faster. I did a quick study of her. I can see through her. She is ok, like you. I can trust her. She is a good signer. You are too. You have improved a lot. I helped you improve your signing. I've taught you more signs.

> *Pam*: Yes, you have. But see, before you only trusted me. You trusted my choice to bring in an interpreter and that was ok. So maybe it would be ok to let Edwin [Rose's son] see another therapist. His own, like you have me to talk about problems with; he can have his own.

> *Rose*: But I can't see through the wall [Edwin's counselor's office is in the next room] to see what they are talking about. I don't trust her. She will take my son away.

Pam kept on working in the session to get to a place where she could make Rose feel comfortable with the idea of letting her son see his own therapist. Pam suggested that she set up a meeting with the new therapist so Rose could meet her, and they continued their dialogue.

> *Rose*: Does the other therapist know sign language?
>
> *Pam*: Yes, she does. She is the woman down the hall. You have seen her before.
>
> *Rose*: Oh yes, her. I don't want to meet her. She doesn't sign well. I can't understand her.
>
> *Pam*: Would you feel better if we all met together? Me, you, the interpreter, and the new therapist?
>
> *Rose*: Yes. That would be better.
>
> *Pam*: I know this is a scary thing to let him go with someone you don't know.
>
> *Rose*: Yes, I feel angry/worried.

Rose had an initial meeting with me, Pam, and the new therapist, and then she met with Edwin's therapist on her own. She later told Pam that she sometimes had a hard time understanding the new therapist, but most of the time they did just fine.

———

This case was particularly interesting in terms of the triadic model because the interpreter served several functions. In addition to serving as the interpreter, I also provided language modeling for the therapist. A signing therapist whose first language is English may need to see other ways of conveying her thoughts into ASL. Also, accepting another person in the therapeutic alliance was a big step for Rose. Since trust was such a big issue for Rose, allowing me to become a part of her relationship with Pam was significant.

MAKING THE MENTAL HEALTH TRIAD WORK

There are many variables to consider in a clinical triad. Time and consistency are both crucial. In the cases presented in this chapter, I had the luxury of working together continuously with therapist and client, because the therapists and I work in a mental health clinic that provides administrative support for these constellations to work. The setting allows therapists, interpreters, and colleagues to discuss issues raised in therapy when using an interpreter. The clinic provides time for post-consults. It also provides clinical supervision with a staff psychiatrist for consultation to help interpreters sort through the issues that may be at play in certain therapy configurations. An additional support is that there is more than one interpreter on staff, which allows for the best possible match between interpreter, client, and therapist. If therapists are working with freelance interpreters, extra time must be built into the contract for pre- and post-consults. It is very advantageous to find an interpreter who can commit to regular sessions. These resources are important ways in which the triadic construct can be supported.

CONCLUSION

As a mental health interpreter, I believe that it is also valuable to have personal experience in therapy. Over the past 20 years, I have experienced therapy with different kinds of therapists at different stages in my life. From my own journey, I have seen that there is a time and place for working with a variety of therapists. Without this personal knowledge, I doubt I would have believed effective therapy could take place between a hearing therapist and deaf client. It takes a lot of courage to place trust in a stranger who is perceived as an *other* in order to reach the self. During my initial stages of bicultural/bilingual discovery (I am a child of deaf parents), I assumed that the only effective therapy configuration would be a deaf client working with a deaf therapist, or at the very least that the therapist would have to be a native signer. I have changed my views over the years. There is a time and place for all configurations and constellations to work. In my professional and personal experience, I have seen each configuration bring forth different results and raise different issues. And, just as the hearing therapist can offer an opportunity for a reparative therapeutic experience to occur for the deaf client, so too can the interpreter—but not without the guidance of the therapist.

REFERENCES

Bandler, R., & Grinder, J. (1975). *The structure of magic: A book about language and therapy.* Palo Alto: Science and Behavior Books.

Duffy, K., & Veltri D. (1997). *Interpreting in mental health settings* [Video]. San Francisco: Treehouse Video.

Fant, L. (1990). *Silver threads*. Silver Spring, MD: RID Publications.

Harvey M. (1984, June). Family therapy with deaf persons: The systematic utilization of an interpreter. *Family Process* 23(2), 205–221.

Kafka, F. (1954). In W. Haas (Ed.), *Letters to Milena.* New York: Schocken Books.

Manko, W., & Taylor, L. (1996). *Interpreting in the mental health setting: A triadic model.* Paper presented at the Beth Israel Medical Center, Mental Health Seminar, New York City.

Mindess, A. (1999). *Between the signs.* Yarmouth, ME: Intercultural Press.

Registry of Interpreters for the Deaf. (1997). *Code of ethics.* Silver Spring, MD: RID Publications.

Seleskovitch, D. (1978). *Interpreting for international conferences: problems of language and communication.* Washington, DC: Pen and Booth.

Stansfield, M. (1981). Psychological issues in mental health interpreting. *Registry of Interpreters for the Deaf, 1,* 18–32.

9

Ethical Issues in Genetic Counseling and Testing for Deafness

Kathleen S. Arnos

Genetic counseling is a recognized medical specialty designed to assist families with obtaining information and support regarding the diagnosis of a genetic condition in the family. Modern genetic counseling is characterized by respect and caring for families, with attention to their religious and cultural beliefs and family experiences, which can often determine their reaction to the presence of a genetic condition in themselves or their child. Most genetic counselors place great emphasis on the importance of the nondirective provision of information and patient autonomy. Recent advances in biotechnology have allowed the identification and characterization of genes for many conditions, including hereditary forms of deafness. This has made genetic testing for some of these conditions available on a research or clinical basis. The availability of genetic testing presents many ethical challenges to the practice of genetic counseling. With the recent availability of genetic testing for specific forms of hearing loss, we are now faced with many of the same ethical issues for hereditary deafness. The existence of cultural and linguistic differences among deaf individuals lends uniqueness to the discussion of the ethical implications of genetic testing (Jordan, 1991).

GENETIC EVALUATION AND COUNSELING

Genetic counseling has been defined by the American Society of Human Genetics as "a communication process which deals with the human problems associated with the occurrence, or the risk of occurrence, of a genetic disorder in a family" (Ad Hoc Committee on Genetic Counseling, 1975). Genetic evaluation and counseling is often performed by a team of individuals that includes MDs, PhDs, and MS/MGC genetic counselors who are certified by the American Board of Genetic Counseling and/or the American Board of Medical Genetics. Other healthcare professionals such as nurses, social workers, and audiologists are often part of the evaluation team. The goals of genetic counseling include the provision of accurate information about the cause of a particular condition; the medical, educational, and psychosocial implications of that condition; the chance of recurrence in future children or other family members; and options for reproduction, testing, or treatment. A genetic counselor is trained to present this information in an understandable way and then to assist the family in understanding their options when making choices, as appropriate. Other psychosocial goals of genetic counseling include reducing guilt and restoring self-esteem, and helping the family cope with the risk and impact of the genetic condition (Peters, Djurjinovic, & Baker, 1999). Genetic counseling is tailored to the needs of the family, their educational level, and the specific condition. Genetic counseling can be appropriate during several different stages of life: prenatal, newborn, childhood, adolescent, and adult.

The ethical responsibilities of genetic counselors are detailed in the National Society of Human Genetics' *Code of Ethics* (n.d.). The code of ethics includes standards for the personal conduct of genetic counselors, the counselor–client relationship, genetic counselors' relationships with their peers and other health professionals, and the role of genetic counselors in promoting the well being of society. It specifies, "The counselor–client relationship is based on values of care and respect for the client's autonomy, individuality, welfare, and freedom." Rather than giving advice, genetic counselors value the nondirective provision of information, which allows clients to make their own choices. Genetic counselors are deeply committed to this embodiment of respect for patient autonomy and value neutrality (Green, 1999). Nondirectiveness has its roots in the desire of genetic counselors to distinguish modern genetics practice from the abuses resulting from the eugenics movement of the late 1800s and early 1900s, maintaining neutrality regarding abortion, recognizing the impact that genetic decisions can have on the entire family, and recognizing the difficulty of reproductive decisions in some situations (Sorensen, 1993; Bartels, 1993; Davis, 1997). Through genetic counseling, families are assisted in coping with genetic diagnoses; with a psychosocial perspective, genetic counselors are able to assist families with dealing with upsetting news and difficult choices. Peters, Djurjinovic, and Baker (1999) provide an informative discussion of the biopsychosocial concept of the "genetic self" and the similarities and differences between genetic counseling and family psychotherapy.

Genetic counseling training programs provide an interdisciplinary curriculum that emphasizes biological content, but also provides training in psychological counseling and ethical and societal issues (Marks, 1993). Most genetic counselors are trained to deal with a wide variety of families, including those from varying ethnic or religious backgrounds, or varying cultural beliefs, such as members of the Deaf community. A model for adapting genetic counseling services to meet the special medical, linguistic, and cultural needs of deaf and hard of hearing people has been developed (Arnos, Cunningham, Israel, & Marazita, 1992).

THE HUMAN GENOME PROJECT

Genetics first became recognized as a medical subspecialty in the 1950s, when the clinical impact of chromosome abnormalities was first recognized. Numerical and structural changes in the chromosomes were found to be associated with developmental delay and malformations in newborns, as well as infertility and miscarriages. The advent of molecular genetic technologies in the 1970s and 1980s increased the ability of scientists to identify genetic conditions, leading to more clinical applications. The Human Genome Project (HGP), which is jointly supported by the National Human Genome Research Institute of the National Institutes of Health and the Department of Energy, was established in 1990 by the U.S. Congress, with the goals of developing genetic and physical maps of the human chromosomes as well as determining the coding sequence of the entire genome. In addition, the HGP examines the ethical, social, and legal implications of genetic research. The Ethical, Legal and Social Implications (ELSI) branch of the HGP was also established in 1990 and continues to actively support studies regarding the impact of these technologies. ELSI projects are also aimed toward educating healthcare professionals about advances in genetics and developing recommendations about how, when, and if it is appropriate to integrate these new technologies into healthcare practice.

The technologies developed as a result of the HGP have had a tremendous impact in accelerating the pace of discoveries related to all types of hereditary traits, including deafness. The draft sequence of the human genome was completed in 2000, with one important finding being that rather than the 80,000–100,000 protein-coding genes that were originally thought to be contained in human cells, there appear to be only 30,000–40,000—only about twice as many as a fly or a worm (International Human Genome Sequencing Consortium, 2001). In the coming years, emphasis will be placed on determining the human genome sequence more precisely, sequencing the genomes of other organisms, identifying how the genetic sequences are arranged into specific genes, determining for which proteins these genes code, and developing pharmacological tools that target specific disease-causing gene mutations. An understanding of the effects of variations in genetic sequences on human disease in combination with the environment and other factors will also be examined. All of these efforts will lead to an increased understanding of strictly hereditary diseases, most of which affect few people, as well as common diseases such as cancer, heart disease, and Alzheimer's disease, which affect many people.

GENETIC TESTING

Using modern biotechnology such as that made possible through the HGP, it is increasingly common to identify and characterize genes, understand their protein products, and develop tests to identify the changes in them that lead to disease. Types of genetic testing include prenatal, preimplantation, and presymptomatic, as well as carrier screening. Prenatal testing can detect the presence of a genetic condition in an embryo or fetus. DNA techniques, biochemical testing, and testing for numerical or structural changes of the chromosomes can be done using samples obtained from amniocentesis or chorionic villus sampling. Preimplantation testing is a new method that involves the genetic testing of fertilized human eggs in vitro (Lewis, 2000). The DNA in a single cell is removed and analyzed for the presence of the genetic disorder in the embryo. Embryos that do not have the gene change can then be implanted in the mother. This technique has been used successfully for only a few genetic disorders, and because of its expense, is out of the reach of most couples. Presymptomatic testing involves testing for genetic conditions that occur later in life, such as Huntington's disease, polycystic kidney disease, or cancer. Genetic screening involves the use of various types of genetic testing to identify individuals who carry certain genes. Examples include reproductive screening and prenatal testing; newborn screening for disorders such as phenylketonuria (PKU); screening of children and adults to identify carriers of Tay-Sachs disease, sickle cell disease, or cystic fibrosis; and occupational screening to identify workers who may be genetically susceptible to environmental agents to which they may be exposed in the workplace.

The availability of such tests does not necessarily mean that their routine clinical use for diagnostic testing or screening is appropriate (Wilfond & Nolan, 1993). However, tests for conditions such as hereditary breast cancer, cystic fibrosis, Huntington's disease, some forms of hereditary cancers, and a common form of hereditary deafness are now being used clinically. Development of policy for the clinical use of such tests is often driven by professional practice, consumer demand, and legal forces rather than a rational analysis of data concerning accuracy, reliability, quality control, acceptable costs and provisions for consumer and professional education, as well as public participation in evaluation issues related to the testing (Wilfond & Nolan, 1993).

ETHICAL CONCERNS RELATED TO GENETIC TESTING

Concerns regarding the ethics of genetic testing in general revolve around issues of consent, privacy/confidentiality, discrimination, and access (Cunningham, 2000). Genetic information provided through genetic testing can be either empowering or disabling (Peters et al., 1999). The benefits, as well as the risks, of a genetic test must be fully disclosed to individuals who are considering such testing. This includes the possible psychological burden of the information, and the potential implications for employment, insurance coverage, and family relationships. Genes transcend individuals (Green, 1999) because other family members share them. Genetic testing undertaken by one family member can reveal information about relatives that these individuals may not want to know or may wish to keep private. This can be particularly true when testing for susceptibility to late-onset genetic disorders. Genetic testing and information can strain even the strongest family bonds. Privacy of genetic test results is also important, including confidentiality of medical records containing information about family history and genetic status. Many states, as well as the federal government, have enacted or encouraged legislation to ensure privacy and prohibit discrimination by insurance companies or employers on the basis of results of a genetic test. Intertwined with these issues is the question of access—for example, whether insurance companies that pay for genetic tests have a right to access the results of that testing, as well as an individual's right to equal access to genetic testing, insurance, and medical care, regardless of socioeconomic status. The ethical considerations of genetic testing in general continue to be a topic that is much discussed in the genetics literature (Hamel, 2001; Tauer, 2001; Epstein, 2000; Wilfond, Rothenberg, Thomson, & Lerman, 1997; Wilfond & Nolan, 1993).

GENETICS AND DEAFNESS

Genetic factors are known to cause 50–60% of moderate to profound deafness that occurs at birth or in the first few years of life (Marazita, Ploughman, Rawlings, Remington, Arnos, & Nance, 1993). At least 400 types of hereditary deafness have been described (Gorlin, Toriello, & Cohen, 1995). Approximately two-thirds of these types involve isolated hearing loss; there are no other associated physical or medical features. This is referred to as nonsyndromic deafness. The other one-third of hereditary types of deafness occurs as part of a genetic syndrome. A syndrome is a group of medical or physical characteristics that have the same cause. Common examples include Waardenburg syndrome (pigmentary changes of the eyes, hair, and skin associated with deafness) and Usher syndrome (retinitis pigmentosa and deafness).

Most types of hereditary deafness (approximately 80%) are inherited as autosomal recessive traits. The most common family pattern associated with this type of inheritance is the birth of one or more deaf children to hearing parents. Both parents, by chance, are carriers of the same recessive gene for deafness; children are deaf only when they inherit a gene for deafness from both parents. Most often, there is no other history of deafness having occurred in the family. It is quite common for hearing individuals to be carriers of deafness; it is estimated that 1 in 8 hearing individuals carries a gene that would cause deafness if present in a double dose. Autosomal dominant genes for deafness are less common, accounting for about 15–20% of hereditary deafness. A small proportion of hereditary deafness is inherited in an x-linked recessive mode. Mitochondrial genes also account for a small proportion of hereditary deafness overall.

Over the past few years, remarkable strides have been made in identifying genes that cause deafness. As of May 2001, 20 genes that cause nonsyndromic forms of deafness have been characterized, meaning that the coding sequence and protein product have been identified (VanCamp & Smith, 2001). In 1997, a gene for nonsyndromic deafness, called connexin 26, was discovered (Kelsell et al., 1997; Denoyelle et al., 1997). This gene codes for a protein that forms tiny pores between the cells, which support the cochlear hair cells, through which small molecules and chemicals (potassium ions) that are important to the functioning of the inner ear are exchanged. To date, researchers have identified more than 40 changes in the connexin 26 gene, which can alter the protein that is made (VanCamp & Smith, 2001). One mutation, called 30delG or 35delG, is the most common variant and accounts for about 70% of the connexin 26 changes that can cause deafness (Denoyelle et al., 1997). In most situations, changes in the connexin 26 gene that cause deafness are inherited in an autosomal recessive fashion. It has been estimated that about 1 in 31 Americans is a carrier of a change of this gene (Cohn et al., 1999). Recent research studies around the world have estimated that mutations in the connexin 26 gene are the cause of deafness in 50–80% of people who have deaf brothers and sisters and hearing parents (Denoyelle et al., 1997). This family situation is consistent with recessive inheritance. In addition, it has been estimated that changes in the connexin 26 gene account for up to 37% of people with "unknown" causes of deafness (Estivill et al., 1998). These are individuals who are usually the only deaf person in their family. As research progresses, it has become apparent that connexin 26 may account for one-third or more of all early-onset deafness. Given that there are known to be more than 400 types of hereditary deafness, it is astonishing that one type may account for such a large proportion.

Testing for Genes for Deafness

Clinical geneticists, genetic counselors, and family members alike have eagerly embraced the increasing availability of genetic tests for specific forms of hereditary deafness. Currently, testing for the connexin 26 gene is available in a small number of research and clinical laboratories. Due to the molecular characteristics of this gene, testing for connexin 26 mutations is relatively easy in comparison to other, more complex genes for deafness. There are tests for a handful of other genes, most of which are not widely available and are done only in research laboratories. In many situations, genetic testing has allowed geneticists to provide much more accurate information about the cause of the hearing loss and the expected clinical course, and has opened up new options to families to make choices that may have a profound effect on their lives and the lives of their children.

The use of genetic tests to allow early identification of the exact cause of hearing loss through genetic testing has many advantages for deaf or hard of hearing individuals of all ages. For infants and young children newly identified with hearing loss, genetic testing may help confirm a diagnosis of the exact cause. As a result, it may be possible to avoid other forms of medical testing (e.g., thyroid function studies, cardiac evaluation, imaging studies of the inner ear structures) that would normally be a part of a diagnostic work-up for a child identified as having a hearing loss. In the future, as more is understood about the mechanics of hearing itself through the understanding of the effects of molecular variations, it may also be possible to more accurately address parents' questions about progression of the hearing loss or the effectiveness of treatment modalities, such as cochlear implants. There are also potentially many emotional and psychological benefits for the parents, the individual with hearing loss, and other family members. When the deafness is identified as having a genetic cause, genetic counselors can work with the family to assist them with emotional issues and psychological adjustment to the diagnosis of deafness. Parents may feel guilty about having "bad" genes, may feel overwhelmed with the choices to be made, and may feel a sense of hopelessness about their current child and future children. There is much a skilled genetic counselor can do to help them deal with these feelings. In many situations, referral to a family counselor and support groups is appropriate to help the family continue to deal with the diagnosis of deafness in a child.

Parents of older deaf and hard of hearing children, as well as deaf and hard of hearing adults, have also found genetic testing to be beneficial in some situations. Many deaf or hard of hearing teens and adults seek genetic evaluation and testing to satisfy their curiosity about the cause of their hearing loss, to assist them with family planning issues, or to learn more about the possible relationship of other medical or physical characteristics with their deafness. The results of genetic testing and the information it can provide can be quite empowering to deaf and hard of hearing adults. Information from genetic tests can give these individuals options that would allow them to avoid or ensure the birth of deaf or hard of hearing children simply by means of selection of a marriage partner (Nance, Liu, & Pandya, 2000).

Similar risks related to consent, privacy/confidentiality, discrimination, and access described in the previous section also exist related to testing for genes for deafness. Families should be informed about these risks as well as psychological risks prior to participating in genetic testing. For example, there is a risk that they may inadvertently learn information about their genetic makeup, perhaps unrelated to the deafness in the family, which they did not wish to know or may find upsetting. If their reasons for wanting genetic testing are not carefully thought out, they may find themselves having to make choices that they would have preferred not to make or are not ready to make. If they are undertaking genetic testing for the purposes of prenatal diagnosis, the choices they may have to make after receiving the results of such testing should be carefully explained. For some forms of genetic testing, such as presymptomatic testing for cancer, heart disease, or Huntington disease, for example, risks related to privacy/confidentiality, discrimination regarding employment and health insurance, or access to test results are of great concern. These risks would not be expected to be as great for children and adults who already know they have a specific condition such as deafness, but may apply to some forms of prenatal testing. Discrimination may be less likely if genetic testing were performed for the purpose of identifying the cause of an existing condition rather than the potential for developing a condition such as cancer or heart disease. It is important that appropriate genetic counseling regarding both the benefits and risks, including psychological risks, be provided to all individuals by a qualified geneticist before genetic testing is undertaken.

Consumer Attitudes Toward Genetic Testing for Deafness

Until very recently, little was known about how members of the Deaf community, hard of hearing people, and parents of deaf children viewed the availability and implications of genetic testing. Middleton, Hewison, and Mueller (1998) were the first to demonstrate the variation in opinions about genetic technology. These researchers distributed a questionnaire that assessed preferences for having deaf or hearing children, the use of genetics technology, and whether genetic testing devalued deaf people. The results of this small study in a group of 87 deaf adults from the United Kingdom indicated predominantly negative attitudes toward genetics and genetic testing. Most participants said they were not interested in prenatal diagnosis for deafness and felt that the use of genetic testing devalued deaf people. A much larger survey of over 1,300 deaf, hard of hearing, deafened, and hearing individuals with either a deaf parent or a deaf child (Middleton, Hewison, and Mueller, 2001) showed that self-identified culturally Deaf participants were significantly more likely than hearing or hard of hearing/ deafened participants to say that they would *not* be interested in prenatal testing for deafness. Of those hearing, hard of hearing/deafened and deaf participants who would consider prenatal diagnosis, the vast majority said they would use such information for preparing personally or preparing for the language needs of that child. Only a small number in each group said that they would have prenatal diagnoses to terminate a deaf fetus, and only 3 out of 132 (2%) of deaf respondents said that they would have prenatal diagnosis to terminate a hearing fetus in preference of a deaf one.

Stern et al. (2000) used an adaptation of the Middleton questionnaire to examine the attitudes of deaf and hard of hearing individuals in the United States regarding genetic testing for deafness. The sample consisted of 337 individuals from the National Association of the Deaf, Self Help for the Hard of Hearing, Inc., students at Gallaudet University, and a small number of parents of deaf children. This survey's results were similar to those of Middleton et al. (2001); overall, the deaf and hard of hearing participants had a positive attitude toward genetics, had no preference about the hearing status of their children, did not express an interest in prenatal diagnoses for hearing status, and thought pregnancy termination for hearing status should be illegal.

Middleton et al. (2001) discuss the results of these attitude surveys and point out important issues to be discussed among genetic counselors and other professionals, specifically those related to the appropriateness of genetic testing for prenatal diagnosis for the purpose of termination of pregnancy based on hearing status. While attitude surveys have revealed that a small number of individuals would be interested in genetic testing and prenatal diagnosis for the purpose of pregnancy termination for a child of the "wrong" hearing status, further studies are needed to examine the effect that genetic testing for deafness has on actual behaviors and choices made by families.

It is understandable that some deaf people would want to have children who are also deaf, since they view their deafness as a cultural difference, rather than a medical condition. Being deaf and passing deafness on to one's children is a very positive experience within the Deaf community. Based on their code of ethics and the value placed on nondirectiveness, genetic counselors would support the right of families to make reproductive decisions that are fully informed and right for them. It remains to be seen if the availability of information from genetic testing will change marriage patterns in the Deaf community, since knowledge regarding the specific cause of one's deafness would sometimes allow the choice of a partner to either ensure or avoid the birth of deaf children. The technique of preimplantation diagnosis could also conceivably allow deaf or hearing couples to choose embryos that were either deaf or hearing while avoiding the need for abortion; however, it remains to be seen if this expensive technique will become widely available and to what use it will be put. As pointed out by Middleton et al. (2001), the role of prenatal diagnosis in this process needs to be made clear, because if the procedures become available, then they should be available to all individuals, regardless of whether they are deaf or hearing.

With the advent of genetic testing and its increasing use in the healthcare setting, conflicts will increasingly arise regarding the appropriateness of the nondirective, patient-centered autonomy model so valued by genetic counselors. This is especially true in situations where a parent with a "disability" requests assistance from a genetic counselor with producing a child with the same "disability." There may be many people, both deaf and hearing, who may feel that it is inappropriate for hearing parents to use prenatal diagnosis for the purpose of selective termination of a deaf child. The data of Middleton et al. (2001) and Stern et al. (2000) indicate that many hearing parents of deaf children, as well as deaf and hard of hearing people themselves, feel that prenatal diagnosis for the purpose of selective termination based on hearing status is inappropriate and should not be allowed. As prenatal diagnosis for deafness becomes more widely available, a better idea of the demand for this procedure can be obtained. There may be instances in the future when deaf parents ask for assistance in ensuring a deaf child through genetic testing and prenatal diagnosis. Although the data of Middleton et al. (2001) show that three deaf individuals would be interested in prenatal diagnosis for the purposes of ensuring the birth of a deaf child or the abortion of a hearing child, the authors point out that survey responses may not be an indicator of true behaviors. However, such a request would be troubling to most genetic counselors. A hearing genetic counselor may find his or her role in this situation to be troubling because it may involve the abortion of a healthy baby only because it is hearing. This discomfort may occur, even though genetic counselors value patient autonomy and nondirective counseling. In fact, Nance (1993) refers to this situation as the "ultimate test of nondirective counseling." Rather than seeing this as a conflict between patient autonomy and the obligation to the society at large (Green, 1999), Davis (1997) argues that this should be recast as a conflict between parental autonomy and "the child's right to an open future." As stated by Davis, "A decision, made before a child is even born, that confines her forever to a narrow group of people and a limited choice of careers, so violates the child's right to an open future that no genetic counseling team should acquiesce in it. The very value of autonomy that grounds the ethics of genetic counseling should preclude assisting parents in a project that so dramatically narrows the autonomy of the child to be." Clearly, genetic counselors, ethicists, and parent representatives who are deaf and hearing need to openly discuss these issues.

FUTURE IMPLICATIONS

Ethical dilemmas are expected to occur more frequently in the future as clinical applications of genetics technologies occur at a more rapid pace. New technologies will be made available by the HGP and other research efforts. As demonstrated in the previous discussion, there is a need for geneticists and other healthcare professionals, including mental health professionals, to develop a more clear idea of the ethical boundaries that should be adhered to when offering genetic testing. This emerging discussion should also include representation from the population of consumers who may undertake such testing, so that the variation in opinion regarding this topic can be fully considered.

REFERENCES

Ad Hoc Committee on Genetic Counseling. (1975). Genetic counseling. *American Journal of Human Genetics, 27,* 240–242.

Arnos, K. S., Cunningham, M., Israel, J., & Marazita, M. (1992). Innovative approach to genetic counseling services for the deaf population. *American Journal of Medical Genetics, 44,* 345–351.

Bartels, D. M. (1993). Preface. In D. M. Bartels, B. S. Leroy, & A. L. Caplan (Eds.), *Prescribing our future: Ethical challenges in genetic counseling* (pp. ix–xiii). New York: Aldine de Gruyter.

Cohn, E. S., Kelley, P. M., Fowler, T. W., Gorga, M. P., Lefkowitz, D. M., Kuehn, H. J., Schaefer, G. B., Gobar, L. S., Hanh, F. J., Harris, D. J., & Kimberling, W. J. (1999). Clinical studies of families with hearing loss attributable to mutations in the connexin 26 gene (GJB2/DFNB1). *Pediatrics, 103,* 546–550.

Cunningham, G. C. (2000). The genetics revolution: Ethical, legal, and insurance concerns. *Postgraduate Medicine, 108*(1), 193–202.

Davis, D. S. (1997). Genetic dilemmas and the child's right to an open future. *Hastings Center Report, 27*(2), 7–15.

Denoyelle, F., Weil, D., Maw, M. A., Wilcox, S. A., Lench, N. J., Allen-Powell, D. R., Osborn, A. H., Dahl, H.-H. M., Middleton, A., Houseman, M. J., Dode, C., Marlin, S., Boulila-ElGaied, A., Grati, M., Ayadi, H., BenArab, S., Bitoun, P., Lina-Granade, G., Godet, J., Mustapha, M., Loiselet, J., El-Zir, E., Aubois, A., Joannard, A., Levilliers, J., Garabedian, E.-N., Mueller, R. F., MacKinlay-Gardner, R. J., & Petit, C. (1997). Prelingual deafness: High prevalence of a 30delG mutation in the connexin 26 gene. *Human Molecular Genetics, 6,* 2173–2177.

Epstein, C. J. (2000). Some ethical implications of the Human Genome Project. *Genetics in Medicine, 2*(3), 193–197.

Estivill, X., Fortina, P., Surrey, S., Rabionet, R., Melchionda, S., D'Agruma, L., Mansfield, E., Rappaport, E., Govea, N., Mila, M., Zelante, L., & Gasparini, P. (1998). Connexin-26 mutations in sporadic and inherited sensorineural deafness. *Lancet, 351,* 394–398.

Gorlin, R. J., Toriello, H. V., & Cohen, M. M. (Eds.). (1995). *Hereditary hearing loss and its syndromes* (Oxford Monographs on Medical Genetics No. 28). New York: Oxford University Press.

Green, R. M. (1999). Genetic medicine and the conflict of moral principles. *Families, Systems & Health, 17*(1), 63–74.

Hamel, R. (2001). Genetics and ethics: Issues and implications of the Human Genome Project. *Health Progress, 82*(2), 22–23.

International Human Genome Sequencing Consortium. (2001). Initial sequencing and analysis of the human genome. *Nature, 409,* 860–921.

Jordan, I. K. (1991). Ethical issues in the genetic study of deafness. *Annals of the New York Academy of Sciences, 630,* 236–239.

Kelsell, D. P., Dunlop, J., Stevens, H. P., Lench, N. J., Liang, J. N., Parry, G., Mueller, R. F., & Leigh, I. M. (1997). Connexin 26 mutations in hereditary non-syndromic sensorineural deafness. *Nature, 387,* 80–83.

Lewis, R. (2000). Preimplantation genetic diagnosis: The next big thing? *The Scientist, 14*(22), 16–20.

Marazita, M. L., Ploughman, L. M., Rawlings, B., Remington, E., Arnos, K. S., & Nance, W. E. (1993). Genetic epidemiological studies of early-onset deafness in the U.S. school-age population. *American Journal of Medical Genetics, 46,* 486–491.

Marks, J. H. (1993). The training of genetic counselors: Origins of a psychosocial model. In D. M. Bartels, B. S. Leroy, & A. L. Caplan (Eds.), *Prescribing our future: Ethical challenges in genetic counseling* (pp. 15–24). New York: Aldine de Gruyter.

Middleton, A., Hewison, J., & Mueller, R. F. (1998). Attitudes of deaf adults toward genetic testing for hereditary deafness. *American Journal of Human Genetics, 63,* 1175–1180.

Middleton, A. M., Hewison, J., & Mueller, R. (2001). Prenatal diagnosis for inherited deafness—What is the potential demand? *Journal of Genetic Counseling, 10*(2), 121–131.

Nance, W. E. (1993). Parables. In D. M. Bartels, B. S. Leroy, & A. L. Caplan (Eds.), *Prescribing our future: Ethical challenges in genetic counseling* (pp. 89–94). New York: Aldine de Gruyter.

Nance, W. E., Liu, X. Z., & Pandya, A. (2000). Relation between choice of partner and high frequency of connexin-26 deafness. *Lancet, 356,* 500–501.

National Society of Genetic Counselors. (n.d.). *Code of ethics.* Retrieved May 8, 2001, from http://www.nsgc.org/about_code.asp

Peters, J. A., Djurdjinovic, L., & Baker, D. (1999). The genetic self: The Human Genome Project, genetic counseling, and family therapy. *Families, Systems & Health, 17*(1), 5–25.

Sorenson, J. R. (1993). Genetic counseling: Values that have mattered. In D. M. Bartels, B. S. Leroy, & A. L. Caplan (Eds.), *Prescribing our future: Ethical challenges in genetic counseling* (pp. 3–14). New York: Aldine de Gruyter.

Stern, S. J., Oelrich, K., Arnos, K. S., Murrelle, L., Nance, W. E., & Pandya, A. (2000). The attitudes of deaf and hard of hearing individuals toward genetic testing of hearing loss. *American Journal of Human Genetics, 67*(4)(Suppl. 2), 32.

Tauer, C. A. (2001). Personal privacy and the common good: Genetic testing raises ethical considerations for both patients and clinicians. *Health Progress, 82* (2), 36–42.

Van Camp, G., & Smith, R. J. H. (2001, May). *Hereditary hearing loss homepage.* Retrieved May 8, 2001, from http://www.uia.ac.be/dnalab/hhh

Wilfond, B. S., & Nolan, K. (1993). National policy development for the clinical application of genetic diagnostic technologies: Lessons from cystic fibrosis. *Journal of the American Medical Association, 270* (24), 2948–2954.

Wilfond, B. S., Rothenberg, K. H., Thomson, E. J., Lerman, C. (1997). Cancer genetic susceptibility testing: Ethical and policy implications for future research and clinical practice. *Journal of Law, Medicine & Ethics, 25,* 243–251.

10

—

Ethical Conduct in Research Involving Deaf People

Robert Q Pollard, Jr.

The American Psychological Association (APA) is perhaps the leading international organization promoting ethical conduct in mental health and behavioral research. The APA continually updates its policies and publications regarding ethical research practices. The association's most recent (ninth) revision of its code of ethics (APA, 1992) contains over a dozen specific standards pertaining to research, as well as many more that relate to certain types of research activity. The APA has published several texts on research ethics, including Sales and Folkman's (2000) *Ethics in Research With Human Participants* and *Ethical Principles in the Conduct of Research With Human Participants* (APA, 1982). Understanding the APA's ethical guidelines for human subject research is only the starting point for a discussion of research ethics pertaining to mental health and the deaf population. One also requires an understanding of ethical principles that pertain to cross-cultural research. I have previously reviewed the literature on this subject and presented arguments regarding why and how ethical principles in cross-cultural research apply to most research involving deaf people and some research on hearing loss (Pollard, 1992). In the sections that follow, I first will discuss the application of some of the APA's general ethical guidelines to research involving deaf or hard of hearing people. Then, I will discuss the application of some cross-cultural research ethics guidelines to this field.

GENERAL PSYCHOLOGY RESEARCH ETHICS
AND DEAF SUBJECTS

To establish a basic foundation of knowledge in the area of human subject research ethics, Sales and Folkman's (2000) book, the APA's older publication on the topic (APA, 1982), and the article "Ethical Principles of Psychologists and Code of Conduct" (APA, 1992) should be studied. The 1982 APA text is an expansion on Principle 9 ("Research With Human Participants") of a prior iteration of the APA's code of ethics (APA, 1979). The Sales and Folkman book is an update of this document with a more narrative style, including illustrations of ethical reasoning and challenges in human subject research. The 1982 APA text explicates 10 ethical principles designed to guide the conduct of human subject research in the behavioral sciences. The first three principles pertain to how to decide whether or not to conduct a given study. (This issue will be discussed below in the section "Cross-Cultural Research Ethics and Deaf Subjects," as it is a more complex matter in that context.) The remaining principles in the 1982 text address avoiding coercion and exploitation in research relationships, confidentiality, informed consent, prevention of and response to harmful effects that may befall research participants, and communication and other responsibilities to participants following their engagement in research. The 1992 APA code of ethics addresses these issues and others, such as cooperation with institutional research review boards (IRBs), inducements (e.g., payments) for research participants, care and use of animals in research, and guidelines for determining publication credit.

A comprehensive review of all these general principles and their application to research with deaf and hard of hearing participants is beyond the scope of this chapter. Instead, I will discuss three ethical issues that commonly arise in behavioral research: the use of deception, preserving the anonymity of research participants, and obtaining informed consent. Each of these three topics raises special concerns in research involving individuals who are deaf or hard of hearing.

Deception

Certain behavioral science investigations could hypothetically be made more feasible or powerful if participants were not informed, or were actually misinformed, about certain aspects of the study. Withholding or disguising information about the purpose of a study in order to prevent participants from yielding biased data is a commonly cited situation where deception may be desired by a researcher. The need to surprise research participants with certain stimuli or the use of "confederates" (assistants who are playing a predetermined role in the experiment, unbeknownst to the research participants) are other examples of how deception is sometimes used. Current APA ethical guidelines require that deception be used only when no acceptable alternative is available, and when the benefits of employing deception in a study clearly outweigh the risks to participants. Furthermore, participants must be alerted to the use of deception and provided with full, reparative information as soon as possible during or immediately after the experiment.

In considering the participation of deaf and hard of hearing individuals in behavioral research, there are several unique factors that pertain to deception. The first is ambient auditory information that is not accessible to participants with hearing loss but otherwise available to hearing participants. If sound information might be significant to hearing individuals' participation or performance in a study, and if that information is less available to deaf or hard of hearing participants, then this may lead to an unintended form of deception. Researchers should consider the auditory experiences of hearing versus deaf participants (even if the study only involves deaf people) and rectify any informational differences if they are significant to participation in the study. Sign language interpreters commonly inform deaf individuals of ambient sounds in the environment—a knock on the door, a telephone ringing, the laughter of others, an airplane flying overhead, etc., for similar reasons.

A second factor that has bearing on deception is the adequacy of communication arrangements between the researchers and participants who are deaf or hard of hearing. When instructional or other information regarding a study is inadequately conveyed due to poor communication arrangements, information gaps or misinformation could result, leading to a preventable form of deception. Researchers must ensure that communication arrangements for deaf and hard of hearing participants are adequate to yield an equivalent degree of information conveyance that hearing participants would experience. Of course, conveying information through oral modalities (e.g., relying on speechreading) and/or writing are methods that frequently are inadequate for deaf individuals, especially those who communicate more effectively through sign language.

Third, *fund of information* may play a role in what assumptions can or cannot be made regarding the information participants have at their disposal when engaging in behavioral research. Fund of information is the accumulated pool of facts one knows and is a rather separate matter from intelligence. Fund of information differences between deaf and hearing people are common, and arise from differing degrees of access to overheard conversation, radios, and other auditory information sources, as well as differences in literacy (Brauer, Braden, Pollard, & Hardy-Braz, 1998; Harmer, 1999; Pollard, 1998). When fund of information may be significant to participation in a study, researchers must take extra precautions to ensure that sufficient information is conveyed so that an unintended form of deception will not occur. For example, in a study involving the administration of a general anesthetic, a physician-researcher warned a deaf woman that participating in the study would entail "the usual risks associated with anesthesia." The sign language interpreter on hand correctly judged that this individual might not be aware of the "usual risks" of anesthesia, which include respiratory arrest. The interpreter informed both parties that more specific information was needed in order to adequately convey what was meant by "usual risks." When the researcher provided further details, the deaf participant expressed dismay that such critical information was almost withheld from her, and she chose to withdraw from the study.

Anonymity

Preserving the anonymity of research participants is another general ethical tenet. In many localities, the Deaf community is rather small and close-knit. Even in sizable Deaf communities, such as those in Washington, DC, and Rochester, NY, many deaf people know one another. Research focused on deaf individuals is quite likely to involve a participant pool with much greater interpersonal familiarity than a comparable pool of hearing participants. Additional precautions may be necessary to preserve the anonymity of deaf research participants in some studies. This is especially the case when deaf individuals are members of the research team—as they should be, in accordance with cross-cultural research ethics guidelines (see below)—or when any members of the research team are active in the Deaf community. Interparticipant breaches of anonymity may be easier to avoid, for example, by scheduling deaf or hard of hearing individuals' research participation on different days. Avoiding unnecessary participant identification by members of the research team, however, may require special measures.[1]

The training of all research team members must emphasize the heightened risk of confidentiality breaches when conducting studies with members of the Deaf community (as would be the case in any small community). In addition to the usual methods of preserving anonymity (e.g., avoiding the documentation of names, phone numbers, and other information that could lead to identity disclosure, or confining such information only to the principal investigator), deaf participants should be informed of the names of

---

1. This is not a comment on deaf (or hearing) researchers' abilities to *maintain* confidentiality. Deaf and hearing researchers alike herein are assumed to have the training and ability to follow such ethical tenets. Rather, this commentary pertains to situations where it is not necessary for a given researcher or research assistant to learn a participant's identity, and the special precautions that then may be needed to avoid accidental breaches of participant anonymity when researchers are active in or familiar with the Deaf community.

researchers and research assistants (including interpreters) who may have access to data yielded in the study. This will afford participants the opportunity to decline participation or discuss anonymity or data security issues if they are concerned about familiarity with members of the research team.

In a study on group psychotherapy being conducted at our facility, deaf participants were interviewed by a hearing researcher who informed them of the identities of the members of the research team. One potential participant indicated that she was a friend of one of the researchers. This prompted a discussion of the arrangements for participant anonymity and data security. The participant took several days to consider whether or not she wished to proceed. She eventually chose to participate and was grateful that this aspect of the study had been revealed to her early enough to put the decision about any anonymity risks in her hands.

The assignment of tasks to various members of the research team should be done with awareness of the possible familiarity researchers or assistants may have with participants. In another study conducted at our facility, one that involved data from the medical records of deaf psychiatric patients, the research team decided that the principal investigator would handle the tasks of obtaining the records (which required that patients' names be known), drawing certain data elements from those records (dates of birth and psychiatric diagnoses), and assigning an anonymous code to each patient. The other members of the research team, which included deaf and hearing individuals who were active in the Deaf community, would then conduct other aspects of the study with this now-anonymous patient data.

Research involving the video documentation of deaf participants using sign language creates greater risks for breaches of confidentiality in contrast to participants who provide data through writing, voice, or other modalities where their faces are not captured on film. Even techniques for disguising facial features will not hide characteristic signing styles that may lead to inadvertent identification of participants. (Plus, obscuring facial features will diminish a considerable degree of the linguistic information conveyed in American Sign Language [ASL].) When videotaping deaf or hard of hearing research participants, beyond the usual precautions of obtaining informed consent regarding the taping itself and who will have access to the tape, rigorous steps should be taken to assure the security of video data and erasure or destruction of the video tapes as soon as possible after the study is concluded.

Informed Consent

The issue of informed consent underlies both of the above topics, and directly or indirectly relates to the majority of ethical responsibilities in research. As noted, deaf and hard of hearing participants' rights to fully informed consent may require greater effort on the part of researchers when communication, literacy, or fund of information issues present barriers to information conveyance or comprehension. This is most likely to arise when researchers assume that acquiring a signature on a consent form is adequate documentation that fully informed consent has been obtained. Rarely is this the case, even with hearing subjects.

The literacy level of consent forms or other written materials should be a first consideration (Harmer, 1999). In research with deaf individuals or anyone for whom English literacy may be compromised, great care should be taken to draft materials that are both informative and of a modest literacy level. This can be a daunting task, especially when IRBs require that certain technical language be included in consent forms. Researchers who face this barrier should strive to educate their institution's IRB. The literacy level of consent forms and any other written materials used in the study (e.g., psychological tests) should be measured and reported in the study write-up.

In most cases, consent forms alone will not be an adequate means of conveying the necessary information to yield informed consent. Informed consent *conversations* with research participants are imperative, which again raises the issue of the adequacy of communication arrangements with deaf and hard of hearing participants. Assistive listening devices and/or *qualified* sign language interpreters or sign-*fluent* researchers will usually be necessary. Yet, the presence of an interpreter or sign-fluent researcher does not ensure that communication has been adequate, since the distribution of sign (and English) fluency in the deaf population is very broad (Pollard, 1998). It is possible that some potential research participants will lack the linguistic ability to comprehend essential elements of informed consent, even when the communication resources and arrangements of the research team are thorough. In such cases, these individuals nevertheless must be excluded from the investigation.

Even when communication is satisfactory, fund of information concerns, ambient sound issues, the composition of the research team, and other factors may extend the length and complexity of the informed consent process. Yet, no other ethical responsibility is as basic and pervasive as the duty to provide *full* information about a research study prior to obtaining consent, which must be free of *any* information gaps, misinformation, or coercion.

Even when fully informed consent has been obtained at the beginning of a participant's research experience, he or she still must be free to withdraw from the study at any time (APA, 1992). A participant might desire to withdraw for any variety of reasons after a study begins, including reasons that the researcher may consider minor or inconvenient, such as boredom or a conflicting engagement. Researchers must not protest, cajole, or otherwise coerce further participation when a study participant conveys, even subtly, discomfort with further involvement. Even when the right to withdraw at any time is adequately conveyed and understood, research participants may not remember or feel completely free to exercise that right once the study has begun. Researchers periodically should remind participants about the right to withdraw at any time and seek a "renewal" of the participant's consent, especially when the nature of the research experience shifts from one element to another.

CROSS-CULTURAL RESEARCH ETHICS AND DEAF SUBJECTS

In the aforementioned review of cross-cultural research ethics and their application to studies involving hearing loss or deaf people (Pollard, 1992), I concluded that the following four guidelines represent scholars' consensus opinions as to the special responsibilities borne by those conducting cross-cultural research with *any* host population. Here, the term *host* refers to a foreign or minority community that is the focus of cross-cultural research.

1. There must be formal channels of communication between the visiting researchers and the host community's political and scientific bodies.
2. Through these communication channels, the perspectives of the researchers and the host community are shared as they relate to all aspects of the research endeavor. Particular attention is focused on: (a) the researchers' interests and the concordance of the research agenda with the host community's interests and needs, (b) the purpose and methodology of specific research projects and their appropriateness in the cross-cultural setting, (c) the risks and benefits of the proposed studies (for the community as well as for individual participants), (d) the implementation of informed consent and other safeguards, and (e) the manner in which the research results will be communicated to the professional and lay public.
3. The research agenda, design, activity, and reports cannot be harmful or inappropriate from the perspective of the host community or the researchers. In fact, the research must benefit the host community in ways that are recognized and valued by that community, not just by the researchers.
4. The research collaboration must foster the skills and self-sufficiency of host community scientists. To the greatest degree possible, they should conduct it, on an equal-status basis with the visiting researchers (p. 90).

Further discussion of each of these guidelines, and their application to research with deaf or hard of hearing people, can be found in the source article (Pollard, 1992; also reprinted as Pollard, 1994). Here, I will limit my remarks to three areas that have broad relevance to the principles noted above—collaborative relationships with the host community, research methods, and host community scientists.

Collaborative Relationships With the Host Community

Each guideline above requires or implies that researchers maintain a collaborative relationship with the host community's own scientific network as investigations are planned, carried out, and reported. How can researchers satisfy these requirements if there are no formal scientific bodies that have been established by deaf Americans to represent their interests, values, and priorities in research, as is presently the case? Even in the absence of formal scientific bodies, there are national political bodies, and some regional and local ones as well, that are active in the scientific arena. The National Association of the Deaf (NAD) has committees and work groups that pursue objectives established at NAD's biennial convention; some of these pertain to scientific matters. For example, the NAD has an ongoing task force on cochlear implants and recently revised its original position paper on the subject (NAD, 1991; 2001). The NAD has other committees dealing with health care and mental health. The national organization Self Help for Hard of Hearing People has issued several position papers on scientific topics and hosts a research symposium at its annual convention.

In the absence of formal scientific organizations, researchers can satisfy the spirit of this ethical responsibility through earnest efforts to learn and incorporate into their research enterprise the scientific values and interests that are expressed or pursued by organizations of deaf and hard of hearing people. Further, researchers should communicate and collaborate with such organizations whenever possible. This responsibility not only is borne by individual researchers but by organizations that promote, conduct, or fund research in the deafness field, such as the Department of Education, the National Institute on Disability and Rehabilitation Research, the Rehabilitation Services Administration, the National Institute on Deafness and Other Communication Disorders, the Deafness Research Foundation, and others. Such organizations should seek out and incorporate the views of national deaf and hard of hearing organizations when setting research funding priorities and invite the participation of such organizations on study panels and other research infrastructure decision-making bodies.

In addition to collaboration with national organizations, researchers should forge relationships with local and regional organizations of deaf and hard of hearing people, especially when studies will involve deaf or hard of hearing participants from that locality or region. Collaboration with these organizations can improve the quality of research, promote informed consent, and even aid in the recruitment of participants, research assistants, and coinvestigators. More on the significance and value of collaboration with deaf organizations can be found in Pollard (1992).

Research Methods

One of the greatest ethical challenges in conducting mental health research with deaf and hard of hearing people is that addressed in guideline 2(b) above, which requires that research methods be appropriate in the cross-cultural setting. The risk of bias in data gathering and evaluation methods is very great. The aforementioned concerns regarding fund of information and literacy in the deaf and hard of hearing population are relevant here, as are sources of bias that may arise from the different sensory, and often, sociocultural experiences of deaf and hard of hearing individuals in contrast to hearing people. Rosen (1967) aptly demonstrated how misleading research data could be when personality tests designed for hearing persons are administered to deaf individuals. Yet, such evidence of bias does not necessarily mean that only psychological tests developed for, or normed with, deaf and hard of hearing individuals are appropriate for research. Judging the fairness and utility of psychological tests or other data-gathering tools for use in cross-cultural research is a complex matter (American Educational Research Association, American Psychological Association, & National Council on Measurement in Education, 1999; Sandoval, Frisby, Geisinger, Ramos-Grenier, & Dowd-Scheuneman, 1998).

If deaf and hearing subject samples yield different but reliable results on a given research tool, this may or may not indicate a problem with the tool or the data-gathering method. If the tool is allowing error to invade the data or is leading to bias suggestive of erroneous conclusions, then alternative methods, test revisions, or deaf or hard of hearing norms may be needed. An example would be the Facial Recognition Test (Butters & Albert, 1982), a neuropsychological tool where respondents are asked to identify pictures of famous people, including Golda Meir, Bob Hope, Fidel Castro, and Farah Fawcett. Fund of information limitations in deaf participant samples (e.g., unfamiliarity with entertainment and political figures due to lower literacy, the minimal captioning of television programs before the 1990s, and the still infrequent captioning of news broadcasts) could lead to lower scores on this test and erroneous conclusions suggestive of neuropathology. On the other hand, the routine development of deaf population test norms could lead to problems if deaf/hearing data differences are real and not attributable to error. In such cases, renorming could obfuscate potentially important research findings. For example, if depressive symptoms are more prevalent in persons who lose their hearing later in life (Pollard, 1998) then developing special norms for late-deafened individuals on a test of depressive symptomatology might lead a researcher to overlook the significance of a (re-defined) "normal" degree of depressive symptoms in a late-deafened participant sample.

To judge the appropriateness of data collection tools in research involving deaf or hard of hearing participants, one must carefully evaluate five elements of the tool being considered. The first to consider is whether its *purpose* is relevant to the question at hand. A measure of reading ability may be needed in a particular study but use of the Wide Range Achievement Test–3 (Wilkinson, 1993) would be ill advised when employing a deaf participant sample. This test gauges "reading" ability through a task involving word pronunciation. While word pronunciation and general reading ability may be sufficiently correlated for hearing participant samples, this assumption would not extend to deaf participant samples.

The second element to consider is the nature of the task *instructions*. Literacy issues, fund of information, and the adequacy of communication arrangements with deaf and hard of hearing participants are all potentially critical to the appropriate conveyance of instructions. Tests or other data-gathering methods with long or complicated English-based instructions are particularly likely to present a challenge to the fair and complete conveyance of information to deaf research participants. Highly skilled interpreters or sign-fluent researchers are imperative in such situations, as well as the opportunity for participants to discuss the instructions at length until they are fully comprehended. Never should instructions be assumed to be self-explanatory, especially if hearing research participants would be provided with verbal instructions. This error is commonly made when deaf individuals are given tasks that appear to be highly "visual," such as the performance subtests of the Wechsler Adult Intelligence Scale–3rd Edition (Wechsler, 1997). Mimed, demonstrated, printed, written, "lipread," or inadequately signed research task instructions seldom will substitute for the degree of task comprehension that hearing participants would experience in their preferred communication modality.

The third element to consider in judging the fairness of data-gathering tools is the *nature of the task* that participants are asked to engage in, including the nature of any test items to which they must respond. Test items and research tasks must be appropriate, not only to the purpose of the study and the participants' communication preferences and proficiencies, but also in relation to their sensory abilities (e.g., hearing loss), fund of information, socialization experiences, and cultural affiliation. Brauer et al. (1998) discuss Messick's (1995) related concepts of *construct underrepresentation* and *construct-irrelevant variance* in the selection of test items or tasks used to assess deaf individuals. The Trail Making Test, Part B (Army Individual Test Battery, 1944; Spreen & Strauss, 1991) is a neuropsychological measure where respondents sequentially connect numbers and letters of the alphabet, but must alternate between numbers and letters (i.e., 1-A-2-B-3-C, etc.).

Errors in the connection order or tardiness lead to speculations regarding neuropathology, but only because the test presumes respondents have an "overlearned" familiarity with the English alphabet. It is not unusual to find deaf individuals who do not have an overlearned degree of familiarity with the order of the English alphabet. Thus, even if the test directions are clearly conveyed, the nature of this task may lead to erroneous conclusions with deaf participant samples. Bias in the sensory or sociocultural content of test items is evident in the Minnesota Multiphasic Personality Inventory–2 (Butcher, Dahlstrom, Graham, Tellegen, & Kaemer, 1989), the most widely used personality test in the world. It contains items such as "I think there's something wrong with my hearing," "I find it hard to make talk when I meet new people," and "I like poetry." The implication of "scored" responses to such items typically is psychopathology or personality deviance, not sensory or sociocultural differences in an otherwise normal individual.

The fourth element to evaluate in a data-gathering tool is the *response modality* involved. Here, it is English-dependent response requirements that are most likely to lead to bias or error. For example, respondents to the Suicide Probability Scale (Cull & Gill, 1988) indicate how frequently they experience certain thoughts, feelings, or behaviors associated with suicide risk. To each item on the test, they must indicate "none or a little of the time," "some of the time," a "*good part of the time*" (emphasis added), or "most or all of the time." Even if the test is appropriate to the purpose of the study and the test instructions and items are clearly understood, comprehension of the response condition, a "good part of the time," is critical to obtaining accurate data. "A good part" is an English idiom (which has nothing to do with the usual meaning of "good") and might not be readily understood by some deaf participants without further elaboration.

The fifth element to consider in evaluating a data-gathering tool is the *scoring* method employed. Scoring methods must be appropriate in relation to each of the issues raised above (e.g., communication modality, sensory and sociocultural experiences) and, if normative-based, must employ appropriate standardization samples. This may or may not imply the need for deaf or hard of hearing test norms, as noted earlier. The Symbol Digit Modalities Test (SDMT) (Smith, 1982), a screening tool for neurological impairment, has no task or scoring bias that should require a special normative sample. The task content (rapidly matching digits and symbols according to a key) and the scoring (counting correct or incorrect symbol-digit matches) should be fair for hearing, deaf, or hard of hearing respondents, regardless of their preferred communication modality (*if* the instructions were adequately conveyed) or sociocultural characteristics, provided they are very familiar with the numerals 0 through 9. Special norms for the SDMT should not be needed and, if developed, could obfuscate evidence of neuropathology that might exist in a deaf or hard of hearing research sample (e.g., if the etiology of hearing loss was associated with neuropathology, as might occur with prematurity, meningitis, anoxia, etc.).

The Rorschach inkblot test looks ideally suited for use with deaf candidates until the matter of scoring is examined. The Rorschach's purpose is to yield data relevant to personality and certain psychological disorders. Its content is visual, and the nature of the task is to describe, in one's preferred language, the images perceived in the blots. Assuming the test's minimal instructions are conveyed appropriately to deaf respondents, and their answers are translated from sign to English by a skilled interpreter or bilingual researcher, it would seem that the Rorschach is an appropriate research tool based on the four criteria addressed above. However, the scoring methods usually employed with this test (Exner, 1993) are deeply embedded in the styles and norms of English speech and could lead to substantial bias when applied to responses translated from ASL. For example, perceived movement is an important Rorschach scoring element. Even movement that is passive, such as a percept involving an animal that is merely hanging from a branch (versus swinging), earns a "movement" score. Consider a deaf subject who perceives the image of an opossum in an inkblot. Assume further that the individual's fund of information is a bit limited, and that he or she has seen opossums, or pictures of them, but has not learned the name of the animal. In responding to the blot, the participant signs ANIMAL, and then uses ASL classifiers to indicate the animal is hanging by its tail over a slim, cylindrical object, perhaps a tree branch. How should this response be translated? "Animal hanging?" "Animal hanging by its tail from a branch?" Or simply, "opossum?" How much movement of the tail classifier is needed to denote "hanging" from "swinging?" Each of these possible translation decisions would yield different Rorschach scores! Despite the considerable body of research on the use of the Rorschach with deaf individuals, scoring challenges with this test raise questions as to its appropriateness with persons who respond in ASL or who are in any way not fluent in English. Hopefully, further research will continue to elucidate this issue.

In summary, when evaluating the fairness of a research tool, the key is to think through the data-gathering method from start to finish, including the purpose of the tool and its appropriateness to the research question, the plans for the conveyance of instructions, the item content or nature of the task, the response modality, and the scoring methods and norms. If, in any of these five areas, English knowledge, hearing loss, fund of information, or sensory or sociocultural aspects of life as a deaf or hard of hearing individual would play an undesirable role, then the test or data-collection tool is suspect.

Host Community Scientists

Cross-cultural research critics have cited numerous examples of host community exploitation by scientists conducting psychological research (Casas, Ponterotto, & Guttierrez, 1986; Howard, 1991; Manson, 1989; Pedersen & Marsella, 1982; Warwick, 1980). Such problems may well have been avoided or curtailed if the host communities were more directly involved in the planning and conduct of the research. As suggested in the cross-cultural ethical guidelines listed earlier, inclusion of host community scientists in the research endeavor procures expertise regarding community priorities for research objectives and appropriate research methodologies and, ideally, strengthens the host community's abilities and resources to conduct its own scientific investigations. Involving deaf and hard of hearing people on research teams and fostering the scientific education and career development of persons with hearing loss are means of addressing this ethical responsibility (Pollard, 1992; 1996). Despite Pintner's (National Research Council, Division of Anthropology and Psychology, 1929) call for the establishment of a mental health research center that employs deaf researchers, such efforts have been rare in the history of the mental health and deafness field, leading to predictable, negative consequences in the outcomes of research investigations and the perceptions of deaf people toward hearing researchers (Lane, 1992; Pollard, 1993).

Allan and Beatrice Gardner conducted many of the well-known studies attempting to demonstrate that chimpanzees could learn sign language. Violations of guidelines 2(b) and especially 4 above are evident in how the Gardners' deaf research assistants were allegedly treated (Pollard, 1993).

> Arden Neisser, writing in *The Other Side of Silence* (1983), reports that there was a high turnover rate among the few deaf persons employed on the Washoe project. They were treated like second-class citizens, he says, and were critical of the lax linguistic criteria being employed in the study. Their resentments grew as hearing members of the project, who were the exclusive recipients of the academic credit and media exposure, continued to misrepresent ASL in interviews and publications. (p. 41)

I have previously described a number of steps for involving and promoting the research careers of deaf and hard of hearing scientists and students (Pollard, 1992). Sartorius (1988) and Tapp, Kelman, Triandis, Wrightsman, and Coelho (1974) provide further insights. While locating deaf or hard of hearing scientists or students with whom to collaborate may appear challenging, there is a considerable lineage of deaf scientists (Lang & Meath-Lang, 1995) and an increasing number of deaf and hard of hearing students receiving advanced education in scientific fields, including the mental health professions, in part due to the impact of the Americans With Disabilities Act (ADA).

Networking with the APA, ADARA (formerly the American Deafness and Rehabilitation Association), Gallaudet University, the National Technical Institute for the Deaf, and other universities' disability services offices can yield information regarding potential deaf and hard of hearing research collaborators. The April issue of the *American Annals of the Deaf* annually lists post-secondary and other academic programs that serve sizable populations of deaf students. A Gallaudet University survey (1988) identified over 25 master's and 9 doctoral-level programs training specialists in the hearing-loss field. Over 400 students were enrolled in these programs, and an estimated 130 graduated annually. Some schools offer graduate programs that particularly attract deaf students, such as doctoral and masters degree programs that have specific emphases on services to deaf and hard of hearing individuals. Such programs exist at Gallaudet University, the National Technical Institute for the Deaf, New York University, Northern Illinois University, San Francisco State University, the University of Arkansas, and Western Oregon State College. In psychology specifically, a survey of 90 clinical, counseling, and school psychology programs (Gutman & Gibbins, 1989) found that over 14% had enrolled deaf or hard of hearing students in the previous five years, and seven of those were clinical psychology programs. Another survey (Woodring, 1987) identified at least 29 deaf or hard of hearing individuals who were enrolled in graduate psychology programs. Over a decade later (and post-ADA), these numbers are certainly much higher.

Not only do individual scientists bear responsibility to seek out, include, and mentor deaf and hard of hearing researchers, funding bodies that support research on deaf and hard of hearing people bear similar responsibilities, perhaps even more so. The National Institutes of Health (1992; 2000) offer scholarships for the doctoral-level education of persons with disabilities as well as funding supplements to scientists who involve persons with disabilities on their research teams. While probably not motivated by cross-cultural ethics per se, these and related efforts to increase diversity in the scientific community are laudable. Researchers and teachers should remain up-to-date on such funding opportunities and diligently pursue and advance them on behalf of their own deaf and hard of hearing students and research colleagues.

CLOSING

Ethical conduct does not mean following personal instincts about right and wrong. A benevolent heart or moral or religious convictions are not substitutes for the formal study of ethics and their application to mental health practice and research. Ethics is a field of knowledge as much as it is a category of behavior. Arising from a combination of philosophical and historical events and scholarship, and continually evolving as world events and progress in the sciences and humanities lead to new questions and challenges, the ethical professional must dedicate a portion of his or her time to continuing education in this most important of topic areas.

REFERENCES

American Educational Research Association, American Psychological Association, National Council on Measurement in Education. (1999). *Standards for educational and psychological testing.* Washington, DC: American Educational Research Association.

American Psychological Association. (1979). *Ethical standards of psychologists.* Washington, DC: Author.

American Psychological Association. (1982). *Ethical principles in the conduct of research with human participants.* Washington, DC: Author.

American Psychological Association. (1992). Ethical principles of psychologists and code of conduct. *American Psychologist, 47*(12), 1597–1611.

Army Individual Test Battery. (1944). *Manual of directions and scoring.* Washington, DC: War Department, Adjutant General's Office.

Brauer, B. A., Braden, J. P., Pollard, R. Q, & Hardy-Braz, S. T. (1998). Hearing impairments and test interpretation. In J. H. Sandoval, C. L. Frisby, K. F. Geisinger, J. Ramos-Grenier, & J. Dowd-Scheuneman (Eds.), *Test interpretation and diversity: Achieving equity in assessment* (pp. 297–315). Washington, DC: American Psychological Association.

Butcher, J. N., Dahlstrom, W. J., Graham, J. R., Tellegen, A., & Kaemer, B. (1989). *The Minnesota Multiphasic Personality Inventory—2: Manual for administration and scoring.* Minneapolis: University of Minnesota Press.

Butters, N., & Albert, M. S. (1982). Processes underlying failures to recall remote events. In B. S. Cermak (Ed.), *Human memory and amnesia.* Hillsdale, NJ: Erlbaum.

Casas, J. M., Ponterotto, J. G., & Gutierrez, J. M. (1986). An ethical indictment of counseling research and training: The cross-cultural perspective. *Journal of Counseling and Development, 64,* 347–349.

Cull, J. G., & Gill, W. S. (1988). *Suicide probability scale manual.* Los Angeles: Western Psychological Services.

Exner, J. E. (1993). *The Rorschach: A comprehensive system. Volume 1: Basic foundations* (3rd ed.). New York: John Wiley & Sons.

Gallaudet University (1988). *Clinical psychology proposal; Graduate degree program proposal.* Unpublished manuscript, Gallaudet University, Washington, DC.

Gutman, V., & Gibbins, S. (1989). *Training in psychology and deafness.* Unpublished manuscript, Gallaudet University, Washington, DC.

Harmer, L. M. (1999). Health care delivery and deaf people: Practice, problems, and recommendations for change. *Journal of Deaf Studies and Deaf Education, 4*(2), 73–110.

Howard, G. S. (1991). Culture tales: A narrative approach to thinking, cross-cultural psychology, and psychotherapy. *American Psychologist. 46*(3), 187–197.

Lane, H. (1992). *The mask of benevolence: Disabling the Deaf community.* New York: Knopf.

Lang, H. G., & Meath-Lang, B. (1995). *Deaf persons in the arts and sciences: A biographical dictionary.* Westport, CT: Greenwood Press.

Manson, S. M. (Ed.). (1989). *American Indian and Alaska Native Mental Health Research: A Journal of the National Center, 2*(3) [Special issue].

Messick, S. (1995). Validity of psychological assessment: Validation of inferences from persons' responses and performances as scientific inquiry into score meaning. *American Psychologist, 50,* 741–749.

National Association of the Deaf. (1991, March). Cochlear implants in children: A position paper of the National Association of the Deaf. *The NAD Broadcaster, 13,* 1.

National Association of the Deaf. (2001, January). NAD position statement on cochlear implants. *The NAD Broadcaster, 23,* 14–15.

National Institutes of Health. (1992). *Research supplements to promote the recruitment of individuals with disabilities into biomedical research careers.* Bethesda, MD: Author.

National Institutes of Health. (2000, February). Predoctoral fellowship awards for students with disabilities (PA-00-068). Retrieved February 24, 2000, from the National Institutes of Health web site: http://grants.nih.gov/grants/guide/pa-files/PA-00-068.html

National Research Council, Division of Anthropology and Psychology. (1929). *Research recommendations of the second conference on problems of the deaf and hard of hearing* (Reprint and Circular Series of the National Research Council No. 88). Washington, DC: National Research Council.

Neisser, A. (1983). *The other side of silence.* New York: Knopf.

Pedersen, P. B., & Marsella, A. J. (1982). The ethical crisis for cross-cultural counseling and therapy. *Professional Psychology, 13,* 492–500.

Pollard, R. Q. (1992). Cross-cultural ethics in the conduct of deafness research. *Rehabilitation Psychology, 37*(2), 87–101.

Pollard, R. Q. (1993). 100 years in psychology and deafness: A centennial retrospective. *Journal of the American Deafness and Rehabilitation Association, 26*(3), 32–46.

Pollard, R. Q. (1994). Cross-cultural ethics in the conduct of deafness research. *Journal of the American Deafness and Rehabilitation Association, 27*(3), 29–41.

Pollard, R. Q. (1996). Professional psychology and deaf people: The emergence of a discipline. *American Psychologist, 51*(4), 389–396.

Pollard, R. Q. (1998). Psychopathology. In M. Marschark and D. Clark (Eds.), *Psychological perspectives on deafness, Vol. 2* (pp. 171–197). Mahwah, NJ: Erlbaum.

Rosen, A. (1967). Limitations of personality inventories for assessment of deaf children and adults as illustrated by research with the Minnesota Multiphasic Personality Inventory. *Journal of Rehabilitation of the Deaf, 1,* 47–52.

Sales, B. D., & Folkman, S. (2000). *Ethics in research with human participants.* Washington, DC: American Psychological Association.

Sandoval, J. H., Frisby, C. L., Geisinger, K. F., Ramos-Grenier, J., & Dowd-Scheuneman, J. (Eds.). (1998). *Test interpretation and diversity: Achieving equity in assessment.* Washington, DC: American Psychological Association.

Sartorius, N. (1988). Experience from the mental health programme of the World Health Organization. *Acta Psychiatrica Scandinavica, 344,* 71–74.

Smith, A. (1982). *Symbol Digit Modalities Test manual.* Los Angeles, CA: Western Psychological Services.

Spreen, O., & Strauss, E. (1991). *A compendium of neuropsychological tests: Administration, norms, and commentary.* New York: Oxford University Press.

Tapp, J. L., Kelman, H. C., Triandis, H. C., Wrightsman, L. S., & Coelho, G. V. (1974). Continuing concerns in cross-cultural ethics: A report. *International Journal of Psychology, 9*(3), 231–249.

Warwick, D. P. (1980). The politics and ethics of cross-cultural research. In H. C. Triandis & W. W. Lambert (Eds.), *Handbook of cross-cultural psychology. Vol. 1: Perspectives* (pp. 319–71). Boston: Allyn and Bacon.

Wechsler, D. (1997). *Wechsler Adult Intelligence Scale* (3rd. ed.). San Antonio, TX: Psychological Corporation.

Wilkinson, G. S. (1993). *WRAT–3: Wide Range Achievement Test administration manual.* Wilmington, DE: Wide Range.

Woodring, J. (1987). *Graduate departments of psychology survey: Students with disabilities.* Washington, DC: American Psychological Association, Office of Educational Affairs.

Contributors

Kathleen S. Arnos is Professor of Biology at Gallaudet University. She also directs the research and clinical activities of the biology department's genetics program. She obtained her PhD in human genetics from the Medical College of Virginia, and specializes in developing and implementing culturally sensitive approaches to genetics counseling with deaf individuals.

Patrick J. Brice is Professor of Psychology at Gallaudet University, and the director of the clinical psychology's doctoral program. He received his PhD in clinical and developmental psychology from the University of Illinois at Chicago, and previously taught in the Department of Counseling at Gallaudet. He specializes in assessment and therapy of deaf children, and has research interest in parent-child attachment, as well as attention and learning problems in children.

Carolyn A. Corbett received her clinical psychology doctorate from Pennsylvania State University and worked at the Gallaudet University Counseling Center as a staff psychologist before coming to the Department of Psychology where she is Associate Professor in the clinical psychology program. Her clinical and research interest include ethnic and racial issues in deafness, multicultural assessment and home-based services with African American families. She recently completed a postdoctoral course of study in neuropsychology.

Virginia Gutman is Chair of the Department of Psychology at Gallaudet University. She established the Gallaudet Clinical Psychology doctoral program, and was its director for 11 years. She received her PhD in clinical psychology from Duke University, and completed a certificate program in the Supervision of Psychotherapy at the Washington School of Psychiatry. A former director of the Counseling Center at Gallaudet, her research and clinical areas of interest include ethical issues in Deafness, gay and lesbian issues, crisis intervention/disaster services, and community services with deaf adults with severe mental illness.

Irene W. Leigh was the third deaf teacher at the Lexington School for the Deaf in New York City before obtaining her master's degree in rehabilitation counseling and her doctorate in clinical psychology, both from New York University. She previously served at the Lexington School for the Deaf/Center for the Deaf as Director of Guidance Services and as Assistant Director of the center's Mental Health Services affiliate. Currently she is Professor of Psychology at Gallaudet University and teaches in the Clinical Psychology Program. She is also the author (with John Christiansen) of *Cochlear Implants in Children: Ethics and Choices*, and editor of *Psychotherapy With Deaf Clients from Diverse Groups*.

William P. McCrone is Professor in the Department of Counseling at Gallaudet University. A certified rehabilitation counselor, a certified mental health counselor, and a lawyer, he is formerly the Dean of the School of Education and Human Services, and in that position, supervised the Mental Health Center at Gallaudet. He received ADARA's Boyce R. Williams Career Achievement Award in 1997, and has worked as a legislative fellow for Senator Tom Harkin.

Kathleen Peoples is Director of Graduate Education in the Graduate School and Professional Programs at Gallaudet University, and is an adjunct faculty member in the Department of Psychology. A clinical psychologist, she formerly held the position of Coordinator of Training at the Gallaudet Mental Health Center, and was Director of the University's Counseling Center. She previously served as Executive Director of Student Development and as Interim Vice President for Academic Support and Student Development. Her doctorate is in clinical psychology from the University of Michigan.

Robert Q Pollard, Jr., is Associate Professor of Psychiatry (Psychology) at the University of Rochester School of Medicine. There he heads the Deaf Wellness Center, home of numerous initiatives pertaining to health care, mental health services, and professional education opportunities for people who are deaf or hard of hearing. His "Program for Deaf Trainees" has received national acclaim. For this and other accomplishments, the American Psychology Association (APA) honored him with their 1994 Early Career Award for Distinguished Contribution to Psychology and the Public Interest. Pollard is a Fellow of the APA Division of Rehabilitation Psychology, where he founded and chairs a Special Interest Section on Deafness, and has served on several disability and public interest-related boards and committees.

Janet L. Pray is Professor in the Department of Social Work at Gallaudet and currently the faculty fellow in the university's Office of Planning, where she is responsible for coordinating implementation of the university's strategic plan. She is formerly Chair of the Gallaudet Social Work Department and Director of the MSW Program. Her clinical experience includes work with deaf and hard of hearing people at the Family Life Center in Columbia, MD, and in the Evening Mental Health Clinic of MetroHealth Center, a teaching hospital at Case Western University in Cleveland. Pray coordinates the psychosocial component and teaches in Gallaudet's Hearing Loss in Later Years Elderhostel.

Lynnette Taylor is Staff Interpreter of both the New York City Board of Education Office of Interpreting Services and the Lexington School/Center for the Deaf in Queens, NY. A trainer of interpreters, she provides workshops on ethics and on mental health interpreting, and is the author or director of a number of publications and videos related to interpreting in mental health settings and in the arts. She is a theatrical interpreter for Broadway and off-Broadway shows, an educational interpreter in New York area universities, and an interpreter of literature and poetry for the Manhattan Theatre Club's Writers in Performance series.

Index

183